Praise for Mark Fergu

"For anyone seriously considering buying their first home, or even their first investment property, this book covers the A to Z of the entire purchasing and selling process. Mark explains it in an easy to understand step-by-step guide to give you confidence to go and make it happen! It's a crackin' little book!"

Reed Goossens - RSN Property Group
www.RSNPropertyGroup.com

"Mark is a savvy investor, knowledgeable broker, and an astute observer of the market. If you are looking to buy a home, getting educated first and foremost is vital, especially in this appreciating market. And there is no better guy to learn from than Mark. I highly recommend this book to anyone that wants to be in the know before pulling the trigger!"

Daniil V. Kleyman - True Vision Analytics, LLC

"This is a great resource for anyone looking to buy or sell a house. Too many people take the home buying process lightly and do not treat it as the biggest financial decision of their lives. This book shows you exactly how to get great deals, get great financing, and build wealth."

Joe Fairless - Host at Best Real Estate Investing Advice Ever Show
www.joefairless.com

"Mark Ferguson is one of the greats who has tackled buying and selling homes. He's not only a top producing Realtor, but has also personally bought and sold more houses than most investors reach in a lifetime. When facing what can be the greatest financial decision in your life, don't go it alone, get Mark's book to learn the step by step process. This book shows you exactly how to get great deals, get great financing, and build your wealth. That's Smart Real Estate Investing.®

Nate Armstrong, President, Home Invest
www.homeinvest.com

"I have worked with Mark and the Ferguson Team for many years. I have a great deal of respect for what Mark has built and for the principles that he and his team exhibit every day. I choose to do business with the Ferguson Team because together we are customer focused and driven to educate our clients to put them in a position to make smart, educated decisions that will meet their family goals. If you're looking for an excellent Realtor for your next home purchase or your next investment purchase Mark and his team will be an excellent choice."

Michael Bowen, The Bowen Team

How to Buy a House

What everyone should know before they buy or sell a home.

From Real Estate Expert

Mark Ferguson

ISBN: 9781521055656

Cover Design: Pixel Studio
Interior Design: Justin Gesso
Editing: Gregory Alan Helmerick
Printed in the USA

The information presented herein represents the view of the author as of the date of the publication. This book is presented for informational purposes only. Due to the rate at which conditions change, the author reserves the right to alter and update his opinions based on new conditions. While every attempt has been made to verify the information in this book, neither the author nor his affiliates/partners assume any responsibility for errors, inaccuracies, or omissions.

Table of Contents

Introduction

There has been a lot of talk about real estate being a bad investment. Many financial and economic advisors suggest buying a home may be worse for your finances than renting. However, I think most people do not take the home buying or selling process seriously. They put all their faith in other people to get the right deal done. If you blindly buy a house based on what your real estate agent or lender tells you, it may not be a good investment! However, if you find great deals, get a good loan, and take care of your home, real estate can be an incredible wealth-building tool. I am a real estate agent and investor, and I've succeeded in buying hundreds of houses. I try to teach what I know to others to help them make smarter and better decisions. If you know the right way to buy a home, it beats renting every time.

Since 2001, my team and I have sold thousands of houses. The real estate transaction has become second nature to me, but for many others, buying a home can be stressful and confusing. Luckily, there are many professional agents and lenders who can help you buy a great house while reducing the stress. There are also some bad agents and lenders who cost buyers a lot of money and time. I wrote this book to help anyone who is looking to buy a house understand the process. I also discuss how to take care of your home and how to sell it for the most money.

There is a lot of information in this book, and depending on your real estate experience, you may know...or be familiar with...some of it. Inside, you'll find four sections with many chapters to make it easy to navigate. The first part of the book focuses on buying and selling basics, while later sections go deeper into each aspect of real estate. I hope you enjoy the book and learn how to make your real estate purchases awesome investments.

If you have any questions along the way, feel free to email me! Mark@investfourmore.com

Part I: Introduction to Buying and Selling Houses

This book has multiple parts to make it easy to navigate and read. The first part of the book is a general overview on buying or selling a house. It goes over the most important things to know before jumping into the biggest investment most people will ever make.

The other parts of the book go into more detail on each subject discussed in the first part. There are some subjects that are repeated to remind you what I'm talking about. If you want to skip to certain parts of the book, I made the chapters short so that topics are easy to find using the table of contents.

This first section on buying and selling will help you avoid being taken advantage of by lenders or real estate agents. It also gives you pointers and tips on how to make money during the purchase. A house can be more than just a place to live. It can also make you money, both during the purchase and after.

CHAPTER 1

What Are the Basics of Buying and Selling Houses?

I have seen silly mistakes kill many real estate deals over the years. Often, the deal could have been saved if the buyer or seller knew the basic concepts involved in the transaction. In some cases, the buyer had no idea a simple purchase could disqualify them from obtaining a loan. In other cases, the buyer or seller let their egos or emotions get in the way. Buyers and sellers can use some simple guidelines to prevent a deal from going south. Real estate agents and lenders *should* tell their clients what and what not to do, but that does not always happen. The more proactive a buyer or seller can be, the better chance they have of selling for the most money or getting the best deal on a purchase.

What are the main components of a real estate deal?

A real estate transaction may seem simple: the buyer pays money and the seller receives money. However, the buyer must get a loan, make sure the house is in the condition they think it is in, and avoid significantly changing their ability to qualify for a loan. The seller must make sure they negotiate in good faith, are not trying to hide anything, and are willing to work through any issues with the inspection or appraisal. Here are the basic steps that occur in most real estate transactions:

- The seller lists with a real estate agent so that they can sell quickly and for the most money
- The seller makes sure their house looks great and is priced well
- The seller discloses any problems they know about

- The buyer finds a real estate agent who searches for houses
- The buyer qualifies with a lender to see how much they can afford
- The buyer looks at houses with their agent until they find one they like
- The buyer makes an offer on the house they want to buy
- The seller reviews the offer and decides if they want to accept it or counter it (via a change in price or terms)
- The seller and buyer come to an agreement and sign the contract (when both parties sign the contract, it is called going "under contract")
- The buyer pays earnest money to secure the contract (usually this is refundable under certain conditions)
- The buyer completes an inspection to determine the condition of the house
- The buyer and seller negotiate any items to be fixed or price changes after the inspection
- The buyer's lender completes an appraisal on the house to determine the value
- The buyer and seller negotiate or try to fix any problems with the appraisal
- The buyer waits for their loan to be approved
- The buyer and seller go to closing where the house deed is transferred from the seller to the buyer

How can the buyer's loan cause a deal to fall apart?

The biggest problems in a real estate deal come from the buyer's loan, the inspection, and the appraisal. Lenders can be very picky about who they lend money to and have strict guidelines for:

- Credit score.
- Debt-to-income ratio.
- Income.
- Time at current job.
- Previous foreclosures or bankruptcies.

The lender should look at these items before qualifying a buyer for a loan. The buyer should also get qualified before they look at any houses. If the lender does not qualify the borrower effectively, or if any of these items change during the transaction, it can kill the deal.

How does the buyer qualify for a loan?

When someone is interested in buying a house, one of the first things they should do is talk to a lender. The lender can pre-qualify a buyer, which means they check the buyer's credit, income, and background for foreclosures or bankruptcies. If you are a buyer, do not lie to your lender! The lender will find out eventually, and if they discover inaccuracies or false information during the transaction, you could lose the house.

The buyer must have a certain credit score, which can be as low as 550 for some loans or as high as 720 for others. The lender can tell you what score you need for the type of loan you apply for. If the buyer needs a credit score of 620 to get a loan, their score must be 620 at the time they buy the house, not just when they qualify. Some of the biggest mistakes I have seen involve a buyer doing something to change their credit score right before the purchase.

- **When you apply for credit, your credit score will be pulled.** If your credit score is pulled too many times in a certain timeframe, it can reduce your score. Even if you just apply for a car loan, it might reduce your credit score low enough to disqualify you.
- **You must work at your current job, or at least be in the same field of work, for at least two**

years. If you were a truck driver for 30 years but quit your job to sell insurance, you may not qualify for a loan until you have been an insurance agent for two years. If you quit one insurance agency to join another, your ability to qualify most likely won't change because you stayed in the same line of work. If you quit your job or get a new job right before closing and the lender learns this, the deal could fail. The same goes for retiring right before you buy.

- **Your income must be a certain amount compared to your debts**. If you take out a loan, causing your debt to go up, or reduce the hours you work, causing your income to go down, you may be disqualified.
- **Sometimes paying off debt can hurt your credit!** Common sense dictates that paying off debt helps you, but that is not always the case. Some loans require a buyer to have a certain amount of cash in the bank, and if they use that cash to pay off debt, it may hurt their ability to get a new loan. Some debt will also help your credit because it shows you can responsibly manage your debt.

When a buyer applies for a loan, they need to tell their lender everything! Do not try to hide a new purchase or pay off debt without first asking your lender if the purchase or debt payoff will hurt your chances. The lender will pull your credit and check everything before the closing.

How can the condition of a house cause a deal to fall apart?

The seller should disclose any material facts known about their house. In Colorado, that means if the seller knows the roof leaks, they must tell any potential buyers. If they know the foundation is bad, they must disclose it, even if the buyer does not ask. A material fact is something that relates to the physical condition of the house. If the seller suspects there are ghosts in the house or they know someone died in it, that is not considered a material fact in Colorado. However, some states do require that known deaths be disclosed.

If the seller fixes something, they may not have to disclose there was ever anything wrong. Along with the seller providing any known information, the buyer usually orders an inspection. The inspection involves the buyer or someone the buyer hires looking at the house to determine its condition. Inspections kill many deals because the buyers find problems and cannot come to an agreement with the seller to fix the items or change the price.

Along with an inspection, almost all lenders will require an appraisal. The appraisal is a report completed by a licensed appraiser which assigns a value to the house and mentions any problems that may cause issues with the buyers qualifying for a loan. The appraiser does not inspect the house as closely as the inspector but does look for obvious problems with the roof, heating system, foundation, electrical system, plumbing, or other major areas.

What is the best way for buyers and sellers to negotiate issues discovered during the inspection?

On most real estate deals, the inspection is usually done before the appraisal. The inspector reviews the entire house and creates a report that lists any problems. The inspector usually does not guarantee anything in the report unless the buyers pay an extra fee. The inspection can cost from $250 to $500 depending on the size of the house. If you want to obtain a guarantee from the inspector, the cost can easily double or triple. Here are some mistakes buyers make with inspections:

- **The buyer asks for everything to be fixed**. The inspection report might include every minor deficiency, including missing outlet covers. The more a buyer asks for, the smaller the chance the seller will agree to fix things. The buyer should try to ask for major repairs and to have safety issues resolved but be willing to fix the minor issues themselves.

- **The buyer does not understand how serious the problems are.** Some inspectors will list all the code violations they fine. Code violations sound serious, but the building code changes over the years, and almost all older houses will have code violations. The trick is knowing if the code violations are serious or dangerous. The best way to handle code violations is ask to a professional in that field. If the house has electrical code violations, ask an electrician how serious they are and if they are dangerous. Fixing all violations can be very expensive and could very easily kill the deal.
- **The buyer freaks out when they see the inspection report**. There are going to be problems with every house, even new ones. I have ordered inspections on new construction that revealed code violations, even though the city inspected the house and cleared it. The number of items in an inspection report can be overwhelming, and some buyers panic and want out, even before they really analyze the report. When you first see the report, don't be scared. Do be willing to go through it to see how serious the issues are. Don't be afraid to ask the seller to fix most of the problems if that is the only way you'll feel comfortable with buying the house.

Some sellers can also kill a deal by refusing to negotiate. Sellers might risk losing thousands of dollars because they don't want to spend $500 to fix a furnace, which any buyer will want done. When a seller must put their house back on the market, they may need to disclose the issues as "material facts," and the house will usually sell for less than if the first deal went through. It can also take months to get a house under contract again, which can also cost the seller a lot of money. It usually makes sense for the seller to fix some inspection items, or even lower the price, to save a deal. Making less money than you wanted isn't fun, but in the end, the seller needs to make the most money they can, not let their ego get in the way of common sense. The seller should also have an idea of what repairs might be called out from the appraisal.

How can the seller and buyer negotiate appraisal issues?

The appraisal is done after the inspection. It is ordered by the lender and is meant to confirm the house is worth as much as the contract price. This protects the bank. The appraisal can also be used to confirm the house is in livable condition. Here is an example of what happens if the appraisal is too low:

- Let's say you are buying a house, and the seller asks for $200,000. You have enough cash for a 5 percent down payment. That means you must pay 5 percent—or $10,000—yourself, and the bank will finance the remaining $190,000 (you will also have to pay closing costs, which could total 2 to 4 percent of the loan amount).
- If the house appraises for $200,000, the lender bases their loan off $200,000 and lends you $190,000.
- If the house appraises for $190,000, the lender bases their loan off $190,000 and only lends you $180,500. Because the seller still wants $200,000 yet the loan is based off the appraisal amount, instead of needing a $10,000 down payment, you now need a $19,500 down payment.

When an appraisal comes in low, many problems can occur since the buyer may not have the extra cash to put down. One option to resolve this is to ask the seller to lower the price to $190,000, which is great for the buyer but not so great for the seller. The seller could choose to keep the price at their original ask, but if they do, the buyer may cancel the contract and the seller would have to put the house back on the market. If the buyer is using an FHA loan, the appraisal must be used for the next 6 months, which means the seller would have to find a different buyer with a different loan to sell for more money. If the buyer can come up with a little more cash and the seller can lower their price, it may be a win-win for both parties.

If the house is not in livable condition, many lenders will not loan anything. Livable condition usually means the heating system, plumbing, electrical system, roof, and foundation are all in working order. There also cannot be holes in the walls or floors, and there cannot be any other major problems. If the appraiser sees any problems, they will call them out on the appraisal. The lender will see those problems and usually require them to be fixed before closing.

If the seller knows there are problems that will affect financing, they should fix those problems or accept an offer either in cash or through a loan that doesn't have livable-condition requirements. Buyers should also be aware they may have problems getting a loan if the house needs a lot of repairs, especially if the seller is not willing to perform them. If the seller wants to make the most money, they should fix any problems. The seller will greatly limit the buyer pool if the house can only be bought with cash.

How can the buyer and seller make sure the deal goes smoothly?

Most people don't take much time to learn about the house-selling process, even though it is the largest transaction most people will ever be involved in. Buying or selling a house can be overwhelming. As you saw in the first part of this chapter, there are a lot of components to the process. If you take the time to learn the most important parts, it will save you a lot of money and headaches. The best thing a buyer or seller can do to make the process go smoothly is hire good people. Hire both a great real estate agent and a great lender.

Great agents and lenders will handle any issues for you, but the trick is finding them. If you don't know anything about buying a house, you could have the worst agent in the world but think they are great because you don't know any better. The more you know about buying houses, the better chance you have of hiring the right people. If you know the main components of buying or selling, you can also tell if your agent or lender is doing a bad job.

How can a great real estate agent help you buy or sell?

A lot of people think they can save money by selling a house themselves, but that is not usually the case. Using a real estate agent will help you value a house, complete the transaction, and ultimately make you more money than if you sold the house yourself. I will talk much more about the selling process later in the book.

Since the seller typically pays for the real estate agents for both the buyer and seller, it makes sense for the buyer to have an agent representing them. One of the most important things a great real estate agent can do is recommend a great lender. The fastest way to cost yourself a lot of money and kill a deal is to use a bad lender. A great agent can also tell you if your lender is any good. Using local lenders is usually better because they have experienced completing loans in your area. I usually have bad luck with out-of-town lenders, especially online national lenders. They don't know local customs, they don't know how long it takes to hire an appraiser, they don't know how local title companies work, etc. Here are some specific problems I've seen:

- There is one bank in our area where almost every appraisal comes in low. We are pretty sure the bank pressures their appraisers to value houses low because we don't have the same problem with other banks. This bank has killed many deals.
- There was another lender who missed a buyer's bankruptcy within the last two years. The worst part was the lender did not catch it until a week before closing, when it should have been caught in the qualification process. This cost the seller and buyer a lot of money.

- Other lenders have waited three weeks to order an appraisal when it takes at least three weeks to get an appraisal done in Colorado thanks to a shortage of appraisers. That delayed the closing by two weeks!

Good real estate agents will have lenders they have used for years in your area. They should also give you a couple of choices so you can pick the lender you are most comfortable with.

How can a good agent help you get a great deal?

Many buyers don't try hard enough to get a good deal. They don't want to pay too much, but they also don't try to learn values or to buy below market value. Most people can get a really good deal by being patient and by being flexible with their purchase criteria. The most important thing a buyer can do is learn market values in their area so they know how to spot a good deal. A solid real estate agent should be able to help a buyer value properties, and they should also be able to act fast enough when a great deal comes on the market.

Buying or selling a house, including the process of writing contracts and the quantity of paperwork involved, is an overwhelming and complicated process, which is why real estate agents still exist. Even though estate agents can help you buy a house, the more a buyer or seller knows about the process, the better deal they can get and the more money they can make. We will cover all these topics in much more detail throughout the book.

CHAPTER 2

Why Have Housing Prices Increased So Much?

I wrote this book in 2017, and in the last five years, housing prices in Colorado have more than doubled. The first thing I want to discuss is whether or not now is a good time to buy, or if timing the market is wise or even possible.

I live in Greeley, Colorado, and here, the median price has increased from $120,000 to over $260,000. Colorado has lead the nation in house appreciation, and many other parts of the country have also seen huge price increases. In the United States, the average house price has increased about 25 percent in the last four years. Despite this increase, prices are still not as high as they were in 2008. The current average price in the U.S. according to Zillow is about $186,000, and in 2008, it was about $195,000. While it seems like housing prices are out of control, especially in some areas like Colorado, the overall market is increasing at a stable rate. When you consider the overall housing price index over the last 30 years, we are right on track for where housing prices should be. We just had a huge bubble and crash, which makes prices seem much more out of whack than they actually are.

How was the original housing bubble created?

Many people ask or speculate if we are in another housing bubble, simply because prices have increased across the country. They figure the housing crisis was caused by unsustainable price increases, and if we're seeing a price increase again, another crash must be coming. However, just because prices are rising does not mean they are going to crash again. You must look at the underlying causes for the increase, and you must ask if the increases make sense or are caused by an unsustainable anomaly.

In the early 2000s, housing prices went crazy in many parts of the country. I was an agent during that time, and I also flipped houses. I was not as experienced and knowledgeable as I am now, but I could still see major fundamental problems with the housing market. I remember asking my dad, who was also an agent, a question about lending guidelines during that time:

"Why are banks lending people 120 percent of the value of their house?"

He speculated that lending on housing was safer than lending on credit cards. Not only were banks lending people 100 percent of the value of their houses, but they were also:

- Lending more than 100 percent to homeowners.
- Lending 100 percent to investors.
- Lending 100 percent to people with credit scores below 600.
- Lending 100 percent to people on stated-income loans.
- Lending 100 percent to people with ARMs (adjustable rate mortgages) that would contain huge increases in payment amounts in a couple of years or less.

The increase in prices in the early- and mid-2000s was due to an increase in demand caused by loose lending guidelines. There were plenty of houses for sale because it was easy for builders to get financing to develop and build. Builders could construct houses so fast because demand was very high. As a result, prices kept rising, which allowed many homeowners to refinance and take money out. They could use that money to buy cars, furniture, or to take vacations, which fueled the economy.

Everything came to a halt when builders could not sell houses as easily since there were not enough people to occupy all the newly constructed houses. This drove builders to lower prices. Additionally, many homeowners had cashed out their equity, and everything started to fall apart. Banks went from lending to anyone to only lending to the most qualified buyers, and demand decreased greatly. Supply finally surpassed demand, and very few buyers could get a loan. The market crashed because it had been built up through an unsustainable demand for housing which was caused by loose lending guidelines. The economy was driven by home equity lines of credit, the housing industry, and refinances.

How is the housing market different this time?

A lot of people assume we will see a housing crash again because prices have been rising (remember this is part of what caused the 2000s crash). However, housing prices have always risen, and we have never seen a housing crisis like we saw 8 to 10 years ago. I think the market is fundamentally different that it was during the last crisis, and in my professional opinion, the market is much more sustainable this time around.

From what I see in my market and many other markets around the country, housing prices are being pushed up by low supply. Yes, there are some loans that allow owner-occupants to buy with a credit score below 600, but lending guidelines are much stricter than they previously were. There are no longer 100 percent investor loans, stated income loans are very rare, and you cannot get a 120 percent line of credit. The U.S. government also cracked down on fraud, which helped fuel the housing price increase during the previous bubble.

There are many reasons supply is low in many parts of the country:

- It is much harder for builders to get financing from banks for large projects.
- Building costs increased 37 percent in the last ten years.
- Water, building-permit, and government costs have increased in the last ten years.
- Many builders are still worried about building too many houses and getting burned by another market downturn.
- Homeowners are scared to sell because they are worried they will not be able to find another house.

In Colorado, builder are constructing fewer houses now than they have in the last few years. It is obvious to almost everyone in the area that there are not enough houses for the population, but they still aren't building. In the United States, there are fewer houses being built now than in the 1970s. This is because banks and the government have made it harder to build. Before the housing crisis, builders could build houses in the $170,000 range, but now, new houses cost at least $270,000. However, builders don't realize $100,000 more in profit because water, land, labor, and building materials are more expensive.

Even though prices are going up at an incredible rate in Colorado and elsewhere, I do not think it is unsustainable like it was during the last housing crisis. Unlike then, low supply, and not "false demand," is now driving the price increase.

How much have housing prices increased?

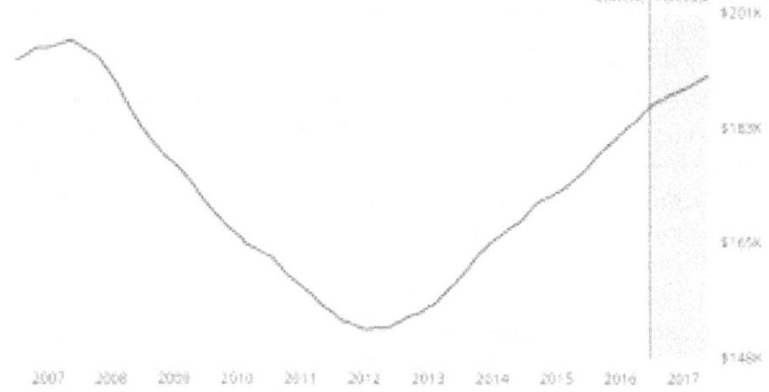

In Colorado, prices have risen more than 100 percent in less than five years. However, prices have not risen at that rate across most of the country. When you look at historic housing prices, U.S. prices are still below what they were in 2008. In fact, the median value in the U.S. has not climbed back to its 2008 peak.

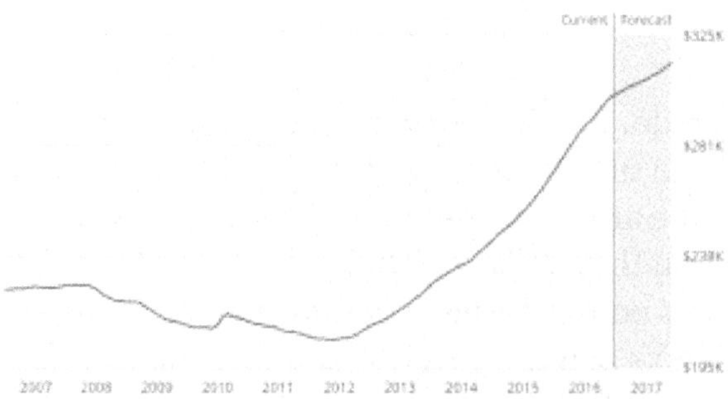

The median value in Colorado tells a completely different story. Prices have far surpassed their 2008 peak, and they didn't drop nearly as much as in the U.S. as a whole.

If you are wondering if housing prices are at an unsustainable level, I think you need to look at the local housing market, not the entire U.S. In Colorado, the population is growing, we have one of the best economies in the country, and house supply is too low for the influx of people. Prices may seem completely out of whack when simply looking at recent appreciation, but when you look at the driving factors, they make sense.

Though house prices have not reached their 2008 U.S. peak, there is a very healthy appreciation curve if you remove the housing bubble and housing crash.

http://www.economist.com/blogs/graphicdetail/2015/11/daily-chart-0

How will interest rates affect housing prices?

Interest rates could have a huge effect on housing prices. I agree that low rates are helping to push housing prices higher because lower rates mean people can afford a more expensive house. The big question is if and when rates will increase. I cannot answer that, and I do not believe the experts can answer that either. Experts have been predicting rates will rise for years, yet they have not, at least not by much. I think the government has backed themselves into a corner by lowering rates to boost the economy. They don't want to raise them now because it may hurt the economy and we could lose all the momentum we have gained. I think there is a chance rates could go up, but I do not think they will rise significantly unless inflation starts to rise. If inflation goes up, it's possible wages will rise, which would make housing prices more affordable and balance out the higher interest rates. That is my theory; however, I am not an economist or an expert on interest rates or inflation.

Conclusion

Local and national factors affect real estate markets. While it may appear the housing market is growing too fast in some markets, it may actually be sustainable based on the economy and supply. Just because prices go up does not mean they must come down. Historically, prices have always risen given enough time.

I know many real estate investors are waiting for another crash so they can get great deals again. As an agent myself, the housing market upturn has been awesome for the rental properties I currently own in Colorado, but it has made it difficult to buy new rentals that provide cash flow. I am neither expecting a crash nor am I expecting to ever be able to buy houses as cheaply as I could a few years ago.

If you are thinking of buying a house and are worried about the housing market crashing again, try to study your local market as much as you can. Don't rely on national stories to tell you what your market will do. Don't assume that just because housing prices are rising they must fall. They could drop, but they could also continue to rise.

CHAPTER 3

Can You Predict Real Estate Markets?

House prices have historically risen, but that doesn't mean you can predict when and how much prices will rise. In the last decade, house prices in the United States have gone through a huge upturn, a huge downturn, and another huge upturn. I like when appreciation causes my houses to go up in value, but I also like to make money by buying houses below market value. When I buy below market value, I make money as soon as I close the deal. I like appreciation, but I do not rely on it because there are so many factors that are beyond our control. While it may appear that certain areas are sure to see continued appreciation, there are no guarantees in real estate.

Why do some housing markets appreciate more than others?

Real estate market values constantly fluctuate, with some markets fluctuating much more than others. California has seen huge increases in real estate prices along with huge decreases. Check out this graph from aboutinflation.com, which shows historical prices in Southern California.

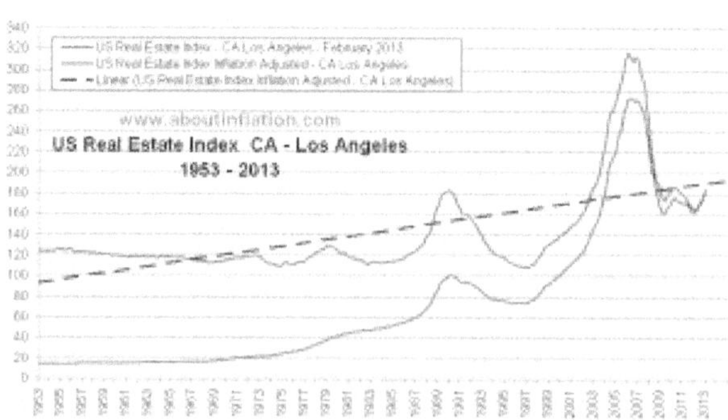

Notice there have been ups and downs over the last 60 years. This graph does not show the large price increases in the last few years, but prices have shot up again. Many investors feel California has many things going for it, including great weather, a solid economy, and rising population. These factors will continue to push prices up. But California had those same things going for it when the market crashed. Markets with the highest population growth and the best economies usually see the highest appreciation. However, areas with the highest appreciation also see the biggest decline in values when the market turns.

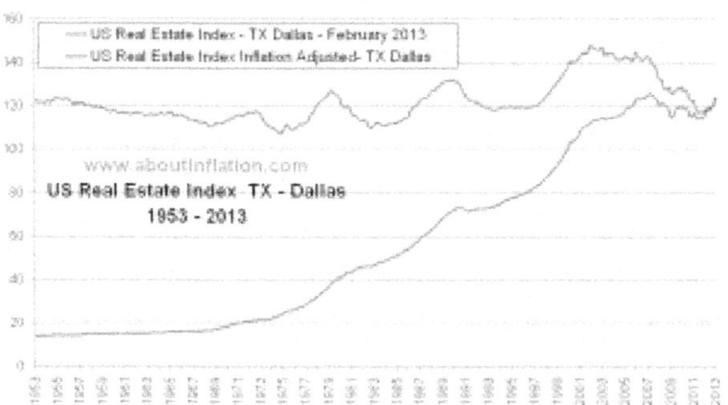

In this graph, you'll notice Dallas has a much more stable real estate market. Companies like Toyota are relocating to the area, which is leading to new house inventory as builders try to keep up with demand. Prices in Dallas did not appreciate as much as in California, but they also did not decrease as much. Even with decades of steadily rising prices, Dallas saw a sharp decrease in prices during the housing crisis. If you buy and hold properties in stable or declining markets long enough, the house will most likely appreciate given enough time. You must be prepared to weather the storm when the price drops.

What are the risks of buying for appreciation?

The Dallas and California markets show the difference between highly volatile markets and stable markets. Buyers get into trouble when they assume their house value will immediately rise. Maybe they get an adjustable rate loan or stretch their finances extremely thin thinking they can sell or refinance when prices increase. This is how many people got into trouble in the housing crisis. I do not think we will go through another huge drop in values like we did in the mid-2000s, but prices do go down. I think buying in a hot market is fine, but make sure you are not depending on that market to continue to be hot. Have a contingency plan in the event values fall. Maybe that plan simply involves living in the house a few years longer than you first planned.

Is it possible to predict which housing markets will appreciate and when?

Many buyers look at every economic indicator they can to predict which markets will appreciate. Are there jobs, local colleges, emerging technologies, etc.? Buyers believe good economic indicators and a strong housing market will lead to even higher housing prices. I do not believe this to be the case because there are so many variables to consider. Many people went bankrupt in the last housing crisis because they bet on appreciation since economic indicators looked strong. In reality, all the following factors will affect housing prices:

- **Interest rates:** If interest rates rise, it could dramatically affect how much house people can afford while negatively affecting housing prices.
- **National economy:** The national economy was a huge part of the last housing crisis—unemployment skyrocketed, and people could not afford their houses anymore.
- **World economy:** It doesn't seem like China's economy should hurt the U.S. housing market, but it can. The Chinese economy can affect the U.S. stock market, and a decline in the U.S. stock market could cause broader economic concerns and affect the housing market.
- **Building supplies:** If the cost of building supplies continues to rise, new-construction prices will continue to rise. If there is a shortage of completed houses, people turn to new construction. The cost of

new houses can greatly affect the cost of completed houses. A surplus of new houses can cause local markets to greatly decline.

- **Lending guidelines:** The housing crisis was caused in part by loose lending guidelines. People could finance more than 100 percent of the value of their homes, but when values stopped rising, people went underwater. After the crisis, lending guidelines changed, making it harder to get a loan. Now, lending guidelines are loosening up again, and we may see an increase in foreclosures.
- **Foreclosures:** The more foreclosures there are, the lower prices will be due to higher supply. I doubt we will see the huge price decreases we saw during the housing crisis, but a large increase in foreclosures could easily cause prices to stop appreciating and fall again.

Given all the national and local factors that affect housing prices, I think it is difficult for an individual investor to predict what prices will do. If any of these variables change, prices could continue to rise, or they could fall sharply.

Are you the only one betting on appreciation?

Some will argue that their local economy is so strong that they can withstand the national variables that may cause prices to fall. While this may be true, it is very hard to predict what will truly happen. Good schools, good economies, and good climates can all push prices up. However, that does not mean prices cannot also drop due to other factors. You also do not know if these factors have already pushed prices up. Prices may be at their peak because of how much the local population can afford, and it doesn't matter how good the schools are. In highly competitive markets, there also may be many investors looking to invest, and they all could be justifying mediocre investments with the same reasons. Those investors are pushing prices even higher than what the local economies and buyer demand can support. There may be large hedge funds betting on that same appreciation to drive prices up. Just because a market has a great economy and high buyer demand does not mean prices will always rise. Prices may already be too high for the local economy to support.

Can you predict housing prices in stagnant, non-growth areas?

Predicting which housing markets will appreciate and when is very difficult, but it is easier to determine which housing markets will not appreciate. If an area either has no or negative growth, price increases will be almost impossible. Prices rise because there are too few houses for the number of people looking to buy. If supply exceeds demand, prices will fall—and continue to do so—until houses are demolished or converted or more buyers come to town. Many areas in the Midwest have very stable populations, and they see almost no appreciation because there is always an ample supply of houses for sale. Detroit has started demolishing or converting houses to decrease supply because so many people have moved away. It may be possible to predict which housing markets will decline, but it is tougher to predict which ones will go up.

Conclusion

Prices fluctuate constantly, and it is very hard for anyone to predict exactly when and by how much they will change. Prices may keep going up for one year, two years, or more, but they may also start falling in only a few months. The United States economy is healthy, but that could change very quickly based on the climate, oil prices, the world economy, and 1,000 other variables. The great thing is you can still make a lot of money relatively safely by buying below market value and planning for possible downturns.

CHAPTER 4

Which is Better: Renting or Buying?

Most people assume buying a house is better than renting one. Most would also assume I'd always recommend buying. After all, I own 16 rental properties, run a real estate team, and complete 10 to 30 flips a year. But despite my experience, I don't always think it is better to buy. You must consider your market, what you can afford, and your long-term plans. In some cases, renting may make much more sense, even if you have a goal to buy investment properties.

The first step when deciding whether to rent or buy is figuring out why you want a house. Do you want a rental property, a place to live, or a place to live that you eventually want to convert to a rental property? If you want a rental property, you obviously want to buy, but that doesn't mean you must buy the house you live in. You could rent the house you live in and buy the rental property. Or you could live in a house for a year and turn it into a rental property.

Where do you want to be in one, five, or even ten years? The longer you will stay in one location, the more sense it makes to buy. Real estate prices have historically always risen, but they can also decline in the short term. The longer you live in a house, the better the chance its value will rise. If you plan to move within one to two years, it may be smarter to rent. Here are some other considerations:

- **Selling a house costs money.** If you must sell, you need to sell for six to ten percent more than your original purchase price to break even.
- **Selling also takes time.** In today's market, houses are selling very quickly, but in a down market, it can take months. If you want to move quickly, buying can be a hindrance.
- **Can you qualify for a mortgage?** If you can't get a mortgage, renting is the obvious choice. To qualify, buyers need to have good credit, a steady job, and enough income to cover their current debt plus the

new mortgage. Many people don't realize that a large car payment or two can greatly affect their ability to qualify for a loan. Credit card debt and any payments that you make for appliances, furniture, or student loans all affect your ability to qualify.

How much does it cost to rent versus buying?

Some markets are better for renting and some markets are better for buying. Again, you must consider how long you want to live in a house. In my market, rental rates are extremely high compared to what you can buy a house for. Here are some numbers on renting versus buying in my area.

Buying a house for $200,000:

- Mortgage payment with 5 percent down: $962
- Taxes and insurance: $200
- Mortgage insurance: $200 (required on most loans where you put less than 20% percent down)
- Total payment: $1,362
- Total cash needed: $10,000 (assuming seller will pay for your closing costs)

Renting a house worth $200,000:

- Rental payment: $1,600
- Total cash needed: $3,200 (for first month's rent and deposit)

There are a lot of things to consider when making your decision. Monthly rent payments are higher, but you need more cash if you buy. Now, if you can use a VA or FHA loan, you may be able to put less money down, which could make buying a better option. When you buy, you do not have to make a payment until the second month. That would save you another $1,362 (for the extra month you live in there yet don't have to make a mortgage payment) over renting. Even though you need more cash when you buy, that cash is going towards paying off your loan. When you sell, you will get that money back, but you have selling costs like paying a real estate agent.

About $200 of your $1,362 mortgage payment will go towards equity pay down. After one year, you could be paying off $2,000 or more of your mortgage. Therefore, knowing how long you will live in a house is important. The longer you live in a house, the more equity you will gain through mortgage pay down and possible appreciation. When you buy, your interest part of the mortgage payment is also tax deductible. The savings from the tax deductions will vary based on your tax bracket, but for the average person, it's approximately $2,500 per year.

Looking at the numbers, buying a house costs $238 per month less than renting, and you gain $200 in equity pay down, $196 in tax savings, and $500 per month if your house appreciates three percent each year. That is over $1,100 per month in savings over renting. That savings more than makes up for the extra cash you must spend to purchase the house. There are, however, more things to consider.

What about the maintenance and repairs a house requires?

When you rent a house, you do not have to pay for maintenance and repairs. The landlord will pay to make repairs. When you own, you are responsible for all maintenance and repair costs. When an investor owns a rental property, a good rule of thumb is that 10 to 20 percent of the monthly rent income will be used for maintenance. I think that same figure can be used to determine how much maintenance your house will need. If your monthly mortgage payments are $1,300, you can count on annual maintenance and repair costs of at least $1,300. $1,300 is not a lot of money to spend on maintenance, but often, we want to improve or update our house. Improvements are a hard thing to value, but in most cases, they add value. In some cases, they will add more value than they cost, and in other cases they will add less. I will talk about this in much more detail later in the book.

Why buying will always beat renting if you do it right.

To this point, it looks like buying a house beats renting, but there are many factors we did not consider. In many areas, rental prices are not as high as they are in Northern Colorado, and it does cost less to rent in those areas. In some areas, house prices are extremely high, and rent control is in place which keeps payments low. Even in those areas, there is one thing that will always make buying a better option. If you can buy below market value, you can make thousands as soon as you sign the paperwork. When I buy houses, I want to buy them at 20 percent or less of what they are worth. For me, I aim to pay $160,000 for a $200,000 house, and that would make me a lot of money as soon as I close. To get a deal like that, I might have to make repairs, and it takes a lot of work and patience. If you are willing to do the work and find those deals, buying beats renting every time.

Another thing to consider is that when you buy, your mortgage payment is locked in. Your taxes and insurance may go up, but the actual payment to the bank will stay the same (unless you get an ARM, which we will discuss later). When you rent, the landlord can decide to raise the rent as soon as your lease is up. I have seen many renters who paid well below market rent for many years. They assumed rent would stay the same, but the landlord raised the rent or the property was sold, and the tenants had to find a new place. You can lock in your mortgage payment for 30 years, but you will have a hard time locking in a rent payment for more than 1 or 2 years.

Buying over renting may seem like an easy decision, but many people do not want to take the time to get a great deal. Many people also want to move within a year or two, and in these cases, it may make more sense to rent. If you can take the time to buy houses below market value and you consider the other advantages, buying is the clear winner.

CHAPTER 5

When Should You Buy a House?

We would all love to go back in time and buy a house when prices were at the bottom; however, we cannot travel back in time, and no one knows where the bottom is until it passes. How do you know the right time to buy? In 2017, prices are rising in most areas of the country, and many markets are higher than ever. Is it still a good time to buy if prices are rising? I think the decision lies more with the buyer than with the real estate market. You need to look at your goals and why you are buying. Can you afford it? Are you buying an investment? Where are you buying? If you are thinking of putting off buying a house, prices might go down again, but they could also go up.

The biggest reason I think it is still a great time to buy is the incredibly low interest rates that are available. I remember when we all thought 7 percent was a great rate for a mortgage. With most mortgage rates below 5 or even 4 percent, low payments are still well within your reach. Rates may go up soon, but much of that will depend on the economy and how well it does.

House prices are rising, but there are still opportunities.

We have seen an increase in prices across most parts of the country over the last few years. This has made it tougher to get great deals, but there are still many opportunities out there. In many areas, prices are still well below their historical average, even considering the recent upturn. If you buy below market value like I do, it is tough to lose money, even if the market drops. Just because prices are high does not mean there is not an opportunity for you. Colorado has one of the highest appreciating markets in the nation. I and many others still buy houses here. You always take risks no matter what you buy, but if you are smart when you buy, your risks is greatly reduced. Even with high prices, there will always be good deals.

Rental properties are in high demand

In many markets, rents are rising or staying stable. While banks have made it harder for investors to get loans, they have also made it harder for owner-occupied buyers to get loans. Since it is becoming harder to obtain a loan, there are more renters in the market than ever.

Many people have also lost their houses to foreclosure or sold them as a short sale. People who lost their houses will not be able to buy for at least three years in most cases. They have become renters and need a place to live. In my market, our rental vacancy rate is 1.6 percent, which is an incredibly low number. That means more people are renting, and rental rates will continue to be high. If you choose to rent instead of buy, you may be paying even more money every month!

The sooner you start buying real estate, the better off you will be

The sooner you buy a house, the sooner you will start paying down your mortgage. As with almost any investment, the sooner you get started, the better off you will be later. I wish I would have begun buying properties earlier than I did, as I would be in a much better financial position now. If you don't stretch your finances too thin and plan to hold a house for the long term if you have to, it will be a great investment.

Timing any market is tough. How do you know where the bottom or top is? You may be able to see it clearly two years later, but that does you no good. There are so many economic factors at play, and it is really tough to guess if houses will appreciate or not. Instead of timing markets, figure out if now is a good time to buy for you. If you learn the best ways to buy a house—and buy below market value—you will be in great shape.

CHAPTER 6

How Much House Should You Buy?

When you buy a house, lenders base your qualifications on the maximum amount you can afford to pay every month. The lender does not consider if you are trying to save money or if you will need to qualify for a rental property in the future. Many people who end up buying the most expensive house they can qualify for end up saving very little money and struggle to get ahead financially.

I love buying things that truly make me happy. I am not a person who preaches you should be as frugal as possible in every facet of your life. However, I don't think people should blindly spend money on everything they see. Be smart about what you spend your money on, and try to buy the things that truly make you happy or help you make more money. Having enough extra money to invest with is important. Our house is one of the biggest expenses any of us have. Most people need to look closely at how much they spend on their house and whether or not it allows them to save any money.

Buying a rental property is one of the best investments anyone can make. This book is not about real estate investing (I wrote other books on that topic), but I still love to talk about rentals and flips. If you buy the most expensive house you can qualify for, you won't be able to qualify for any rental properties. Many investors run into a roadblock when they try to buy a rental property because their debt-to-income ratio is too high to buy additional houses. The only solution is to make more money or reduce their debt.

How much house can you qualify for?

Most lenders, real estate agents and financial experts give a percentage for what is acceptable to spend on your primary residence. Many people say your payments should be 28 to 33 percent of your income. I think this ratio is why so many people live paycheck to paycheck. My current mortgage payment is about 10 percent of my income after taxes, and that is why I have so much to invest. I am very lucky and make a good living, but I also don't feel the need to constantly max out what I can qualify for when I buy a primary residence. Just because a lender says you can qualify for a certain mortgage payment does not mean you can actually afford the house.

You, and not your lender or real estate agent, need to decide how much payment you can afford. In our industry, we use the term "house poor" to describe people who buy the most expensive house they can afford. These people end up saving or investing very little money because all their income goes to their mortgage.

I could not afford my first house, although I did qualify for it.

I bought my first house in 2002, which was during the height of the real estate market in Colorado. When I purchased it, I bought the most expensive house I could afford, and I had no problem making my payments. I also managed to save almost nothing in 5 years, and I always had credit card debt. I couldn’t save any money because I spent it all on my house!

I lived in that house for 7 years and did not move until I found an amazing deal on a foreclosure. I ended up selling for less than I bought it for after spending $15,000 on repairs and upgrades. That was frustrating, but I bought my houses at the peak of the market, and in 2006 Colorado led the nation in foreclosures. I could make my payments, but I could not really afford that house because I didn't save any money. I also made the mistake of paying retail prices and didn’t get a great deal.

I spent much less on my second house.

I bought my second house at a foreclosure auction. I had to borrow money from my sister and my father-in-law since I needed the entire purchase price the day I bought it. I was able to refinance the home and pay everyone back a few months later. This was a steal of a deal, and we loved the house. I bought it for about $215,000 after factoring in the borrowing costs. Four years later, I sold it for $319,500 without spending much money at all on repairs. I think we painted the outside, expanded the deck, and did some landscaping work.

The third house we bought was more expensive than the others but still well within our budget. I used the money I made from my second house for the down payment on this house. We can easily make the payments and save enough money to invest in rental properties. I learned that I can save money, be happier, and be in a much better financial position if I spend less than I can qualify for.

Can you afford your house or just qualify for it?

Do you own your house because you love it or because it was the nicest you could qualify for? Did you weigh all the positive and negatives before buying it and consider how much you could save and invest? Buying the most I could afford for my first house was a mistake, and I didn't think about the financial sense of it at all.

If you made a mistake, don't beat yourself up over it. We all make mistakes, and mistakes are one of the best learning tools available. All we can do is move on and avoid the same mistake next time, or we can do our best to fix the mistake. I think spending 28 percent of our income on housing is a recipe for disaster; yes, you may make your payments, but can you save enough to invest in anything? Are you ever getting ahead in life if you spend that much? My new rule is to spend 10 percent of my income on my personal residence and no more. Depending on where you live and the housing market, this may not be possible, but at least think about what you are giving up before spending that much.

CHAPTER 7

How Does a Mortgage Work?

Houses are expensive, and most people do not have $200,000 in cash, which is the median U.S. price. Many banks will finance a house, and there are government-backed programs that encourage homeownership through low down payments. When you borrow money for a house, you most likely will use a mortgage. A mortgage is a loan that can be paid off over varying amounts of time. The most common mortgage has a 30-year term, meaning if a homeowner paid the minimum payments, they would pay off the loan in 30 years. There are 25-, 20-, 15-, 10- and even 5-year terms. The longer the term, the lower the payment. For every payment made, some money goes to the principal balance and some to interest. Early in the loan, much more money goes to interest than principal, but as the loan matures, more money will go to principal. The bank will base the loan amount on the value of the house, which is determined by an appraisal.

There are many things to consider when getting a mortgage:

- **What is the down payment?** Lenders will require the buyer pay a down payment. The down payment can vary from 3 percent (VA offers $0 down), to 5 percent, to 10 percent, or to as much as the borrower wants to pay. When you have a lower down payment, you will most likely pay mortgage insurance, which can add hundreds of dollars to your payment.
- **What are the closing costs?** Besides the down payment, the borrower will have closing costs. Closing costs consist of lender's fees, appraisals, pre-paid insurance, pre-paid interest, title insurance fees, and title company fees. Closing costs range from 2 to 6 percent of the loan amount. In some cases, the borrower can ask the seller to help pay the closing costs.

- **What is the payment?** The monthly payment is determined by an algorithm that includes the interest rate, the length of the loan, and any mortgage insurance. If you get a 15-year loan, the payment will be much higher than a 30-year loan. The lower the interest rate, the lower your payment.
- **How much house can you qualify for?** The lender will tell you how much you can qualify for. This does not mean you should try to max out that number! The lender is not concerned with how much money you can save, only whether or not you can make the payments.

How is the payment calculated?

Every month, part of your payment is used to pay interest and part is used to pay principal (the amount of your loan). Calculating your payment isn't easy because the amount varies based on the loan term and interest rate. For a 30-year loan on a $200,000 house, your monthly payment would be $1,755 at 10 percent interest. If the interest rate was 5 percent, the monthly payment would be $1,074. At 5 percent for 15 years, the monthly payment would be $1,582. The payment is much higher on a short-term loan because you have less time to pay off the balance.

On a $200,000 loan with a 5 percent interest rate, $249 goes toward principal and $833 toward interest in the first month. The cool part about mortgages in the U.S. is the interest is tax deductible in most cases. The longer you have the loan, the more of your payment will go toward paying it off and the less will go toward interest. In three years, $279 will go toward principal and $794 will go toward interest.

Every month, the principal and interest will change. You will pay much more interest in the beginning than at the end (online mortgage calculators can tell you exactly what your payment will be). Besides the interest and principal, most mortgages include taxes and insurance. Every property will have property taxes you must pay to the government, and the lender will require you to have homeowner's insurance.

Those costs are included in the payment because the lender wants to protect their investment. Tax rates can vary greatly between states. In some states, taxes and insurance might add $200 to your monthly payment, and in other states, they can add $800.

When do you have to make your payment?

When you first obtain a mortgage, the first payment is usually not due for two months. If you buy a house on December 15th, your first payment most likely will not be due until February 1st. Getting to skip a payment is good, but you still must pay the interest on the skipped payment up front (prepaid interest). Even though the payment is due on the first of the month, it is not considered late until the 15th of the month. You can safely make your payment on the 15th, pay no late fees, and still protect your credit with most loans. If you make the payment after the 15th, it is considered late. The lender will assess late fees, which will be detailed in your loan documents. The lender may report the late payments to the credit bureaus, which hurts your credit rating. If you start to consistently miss payments, you risk going into default. Laws are different in each state, but a lender can foreclose on a loan after a certain amount of missed payments.

Banks cannot immediately take the house away from borrowers after a couple of missed payments: they must foreclose on it. That means they must go to the courts, trustee, or sheriff (depending on the state you live in), show proof the borrower missed payments, and start the foreclosure process. The homeowner must be notified of the foreclosure and be given a chance to bring the loan current. In some states, foreclosure takes a few months, and in other states it takes years.

What are the different types of mortgages?

Not every mortgage is the same. There are private mortgages and government-backed mortgages. Government-backed mortgages were created to help more people buy homes with less money down. In the past, banks required a down payment of at least 20 percent. Now, there are many programs that allow people to buy for less than 5 percent down.

- **Conventional mortgage:** This is a mortgage from a bank and has no government-backed down payment assistance programs.
- **FHA:** This is a loan insured by the federal government. A regular bank will lend to the borrowers, but a certain amount of the loan is guaranteed by the government, allowing a lower down payment.
- **VA:** This loan is for veterans of the military and those on active duty. The loan is guaranteed by the government and requires zero money down.
- **USDA:** These loans are available in rural areas and allow low down payments backed by the government.
- **Local and state programs:** Many states and even cities have programs that give grants to homeowners.

What determines the down payment?

Typically, the lower the down payment the more expensive the loan. Banks are comfortable loaning 80 percent of the value of a house since the borrower supplies the other 20 percent as a down payment. Banks feel safe knowing the borrower has skin in the game (they are spending some of their own money), and if something goes wrong, banks have built-in equity. Luckily, for many borrowers who do not have 20 percent down, there are private mortgage insurance companies and government programs that will allow a lower down payment. FHA requires a down payment of as little as 3.5 percent, and some conventional loans require as little as 3 percent. With lower down payments comes higher costs. Both loans will have mortgage insurance, which can cost hundreds of dollars a month. VA loans require no mortgage insurance and no down payment but can only be used by active or veteran military personnel.

The best strategy depends on the borrower's financial position. If a borrower can get a conventional loan with private mortgage insurance, it is usually better than FHA. FHA loan costs are higher, and the mortgage insurance cannot be removed. However, insurance may be removed on conventional mortgages. The advantages of FHA loan are the borrower can qualify for more, even with a lower credit score.

If a borrower can put 20 percent down, that may be the best strategy to avoiding mortgage insurance.

How can you qualify for a mortgage?

Banks look at debt-to-income ratios when determining who can qualify for a loan and for how much. Someone who makes $100,000 annually may qualify for less than someone who makes $50,000 if the person making $100,000 has a lot of debt. Banks will look at monthly debt payments versus monthly income. High car payments, credit card payments, and child support payments can increase debt-to-income ratios, making it harder to qualify. For those with low income and little cash, an FHA loan coupled with a local down payment assistant program can be a great option. FHA allows higher debt-to-income ratios than conventional loans.

You should consider many other factors when applying for a loan:

- You must have worked at the same job—or in the same field—for two years.
- You must have decent credit (usually a score of at least 620).
- You cannot have had a recent short sale or bankruptcy.

What is the process for securing a home loan?

The first step is talking to a lender or banker. If you are looking to buy a house, many real estate agents can recommend a good lender. There are good lenders and bad lenders, and a bad lender can cost the borrower a lot of money. Do not assume any lender can get you the right loan and complete it on time.

CHAPTER 8

What Safety Issues Should You Consider When Buying a House?

Houses have become more than just structures to protect us from the elements. Houses have become luxurious, comfortable, expansive, and trendy places to enjoy our lives. While technology has made electrical systems, heating systems, and the structure itself safer, there are still dangers. Fires are a common occurrence; carbon monoxide can threaten lives; and radon gasses can cause cancer. Plus, if a house has been misused or neglected, things like mold, drug use or manufacturing, or other factors can cause you harm. When you buy, make sure you do everything you can to protect yourself and your family. Many states have laws in place to protect people, but those laws do not cover every danger, and not every law is followed. The more you know what to look for, the safer you'll be.

What are the biggest dangers?

Following are just a few of the dangers that could cause serious harm or even kill you:

- **Fire:** Fire can destroy a house quickly, even if it is contained quickly. Smoke can cause more damage than the fire itself. Smoke also kills more people than fires. Every house should have working smoke detectors.
- **Carbon Monoxide:** Colorado enacted a law a few years ago requiring all houses to have carbon monoxide detectors. The law was enacted because a family of five died from carbon monoxide poisoning while renting. Carbon monoxide can come from faulty furnaces and is odorless. Not all states require carbon monoxide detectors, but you should have them!

- **Natural gas:** Natural gas is odorless, but gas companies add an odor to make it detectable and warn people to evacuate before an explosion occurs. Most houses have natural-gas furnaces, hot-water heaters, and stoves. In rural areas, houses have propane may have propane, which can be just as dangerous. Breathing natural gas will not kill you, but it is extremely flammable, and if enough builds up, it will explode with any spark.
- **Drug use:** Some types of drugs will not only seriously hurt the user but also the people around them. Meth can be smoked, and in some cases, manufactured in houses. A meth house can be extremely dangerous due to the chemicals used. A meth house usually smells strongly of smoke and chemicals which can cause brain damage. To get rid of these chemicals, you may have to gut the entire house, including the walls, flooring, heating system, insulation, and even studs.
- **Mold:** Mold is everywhere: outside, inside, and in the air. Most mold is harmless, but too much mold or the wrong type of mold can be dangerous. Most dangerous mold is visible on drywall. It looks like black splotches and can make people very sick. Mold is caused by too much moisture in a house.
- **Radon:** Radon is a colorless, odorless gas. Many people have never heard of it, and most never test for it. Radon can cause lung cancer and is very common in Colorado. It's typically found in higher amounts in northern states and lower amounts in southern states. You can ask an inspector to test for radon.
- **Flooding/water damage:** Water causes the most damage to houses, although it is not always dangerous. Broken pipes, leaking roofs, and floods can all cause a ton of damage. If a house is in a flood zone, you will most likely have to get flood insurance, which is much more expensive than regular homeowner's insurance. Flash flooding can also kill

you, and you should be aware of how to escape if you are in a flood zone.

How can homeowners protect themselves from fires?

Fires can be devastating and extremely dangerous. All houses should have smoke detectors, which alert the occupants to a possible fire. Some smoke detectors are wired into the electrical system, and others are battery operated. If your smoke alarms start beeping, they need new batteries. Please do not disable the smoke detector—put new batteries in! In most states, smoke detectors are required by law.

The electrical system is a common cause of fires. Electricity is awesome, but it can also be dangerous, especially in old houses. Old wiring, aluminum wiring, and improperly installed wiring can all cause a fire. Homeowners do not need to know how to wire a house to be safe, but an inspector can give you an idea of any possible problems with an electrical system. There are no guarantees, since many wires are hidden behind walls, but an inspection can uncover many problems. If an inspector sees a possible problem, have a licensed electrician inspect the house to see if there is a safety issue.

There are many other causes of fires:

- **Candles:** Do not leave candles unattended!
- **Cooking:** We have all forgotten about a meal on the stove, but if you forget about it too long, it could cause a fire. Grease fires can spread quickly, and dumping water on them will only make it worse.
- **Garages:** Many fires are started in the garage. A poorly maintained car or certain electrical tools could ignite a fire. There should be fire barriers between a garage and the house, but large fires can still spread to the house.
- **Forest fires:** In Colorado and many other states, forest fires are common. If you live in an area with many trees, consider your comfort level with buying

in a high-fire-danger area. Looking for houses constructed of non-flammable materials and clearing trees away from your house can help protect it if a fire gets too close.
- **Fireplaces:** Fireplaces need to be cleaned and maintained often. A clogged chimney can cause either a fire or smoke damage.

Along with having smoke detectors, you should also have fire extinguishers. If you have a small fire, a fire extinguisher could easily put it out. But if you only have water, you may spread the fire, causing even more damage.

Make sure your family has a plan in case of a fire. If you have 2nd or 3rd story rooms that are too high to jump from, you might want to invest in safety ladders. Make sure your young children know where to go and what to do in case of a fire. They may try to look for mommy, daddy, or a pet instead of getting out.

How can homeowners protect themselves from carbon monoxide?

Carbon monoxide does not smell like natural gas, but it can be just as dangerous. Due to cracked heater cores or other problems, furnaces are the most common cause of carbon monoxide buildup. An inspector should spot indications of damage, and furnaces can be tested for carbon monoxide leaks. Because carbon monoxide is so dangerous, you need to have carbon monoxide detectors in your home. As you'll see below, not every state requires CO detectors!

CO detectors in homes:

- 26 states require carbon monoxide detectors in private dwellings via state statute: Alaska, California, Colorado, Connecticut, Florida, Georgia (via adoption of the International Residential Code), Illinois, Maine, Maryland, Massachusetts, Michigan, Minnesota, Nebraska, New Hampshire, New Jersey,

New York, North Carolina, Oregon, Pennsylvania, Rhode Island, Tennessee, Utah, Vermont, Washington, West Virginia, and Wisconsin. Certain states limit this requirement to buildings with fossil-fuel burning devices. Others only require the device be installed upon sale of the property or unit.
- Another 11 states require carbon monoxide detectors in private dwellings regulatory through the adoption of the International Residential Code or via an amendment to their state's building code: Alabama, Georgia, Idaho, Kentucky, Louisiana, New Mexico, North Dakota, Oklahoma, South Carolina, Virginia, and Wyoming.

CO detectors in schools:

- California, Connecticut, Illinois, Maine, and Maryland require carbon monoxide detectors in school buildings.

CO detectors in hotels and motels:

- Twelve states require installation of carbon monoxide detectors in hotels and motels under statute.
- Three of those states (New Jersey, Vermont, and Wisconsin) have complementary administrative regulations.
- Two states (Kansas and Washington) have requirements through administrative regulations alone.

Thank you for this information from:

http://www.ncsl.org/research/environment-and-natural-resources/carbon-monoxide-detectors-state-statutes.aspx

You need to have CO detectors in your house, even if your state does not require it. They are cheap, easy to install, and you will never notice them unless there is a problem. In

Colorado, the law states you must have a CO detector within 15 feet of every bedroom.

How can homeowners protect themselves from natural gas?

Natural gas is very flammable since it is used as fuel for furnaces, stoves, or hot water heaters. Natural gas companies make it smell like sulfur to alert people to problems. If you smell sulfur (a little like rotten eggs), there is a problem. Your house could literally explode if there is too much natural gas or propane built up. As soon as you smell natural gas, you should leave the house and call 911 so they can see what the problem is. I have had to call 911 a couple of times for houses I had listed that smelled like gas. I felt a little silly when the fire trucks pulled up and made a big scene, but I would much rather feel silly than lose a house to an explosion.

How can homeowners protect themselves from drug houses?

I have spent time in meth houses; it was not the healthiest thing I could have done. However, I did not know they were meth houses or how dangerous meth was. Meth is a drug manufactured from extremely harmful chemicals. If someone smokes meth in a house, the meth residue can seep into the walls and cause health problems. If someone manufactures meth in a house, it can cause severe health problems and destroy the house.

You won't know for sure if someone smoked or cooked meth in a house until you complete a meth test. Most inspectors or homeowners will not complete a meth test because it can take weeks to get the results. In Colorado, if someone finds out they are buying a meth house, they can cancel the contract at any time and get their earnest money back. Every state law is different, and there are some things you can do to ensure meth, or other illegal activities, did not occur in the house you're buying.

- **Security cameras:** Many people install a security system, but some people install them because they are paranoid about the police. If you see cameras all over the house, it's a sign the property may have been used for illegal activity.
- **Use your nose:** When I inspected houses where meth was manufactured, they had a very distinct smell. It smelled like a mix of cigarette smoke and chemicals. It also hurt my eyes, but I have a lot of allergies and am sensitive to that sort of thing. If a house smells really weird, it may be worth questioning.
- **Use your eyes:** Houses used for illegal activities are usually not well maintained. Houses where meth was used heavily may actually have stains on the walls. The chemical smoke can cause marks near or on the ceiling.
- **Ask the neighbors**: Neighbors usually know when something is going on or when neighbors are up to no good. Talking to as many neighbors as you can before you buy isn't a bad idea. They may talk to you about historical issues, any problems they know about, or any frequent police activity.
- **Check with the police:** If you suspect a house may be a drug house, the police may have record of arrests or complaints on the property. In Colorado, every house that was used for a meth lab is listed here: http://www.forensic-applications.com/meth/Properties.html

In Colorado, you can also sell a meth house that has been properly cleaned by a company licensed to clean them, without disclosing it was a meth house.

How can homeowners protect themselves from mold?

A lot of people are very scared of mold, but mold is everywhere. It is in the dirt, the air, and every house. Some types of mold are more dangerous than others. Many mold remediation companies will recommend a test for mold. If they detect any mold, they will recommend that you spend a lot of money to remove it. However, you can never remove all mold. If mold levels are dangerous, you can usually smell it or see it, although in some cases it may be hiding in the walls or may have been covered up.

Mold commonly appears on the walls, carpet, or any organic material like wood. Mold is also common in showers and bathrooms. If you see mold in the bathroom, you can most likely clean it without any health risks. If your walls have mold, you have a problem. Black mold is the most dangerous, and some people are allergic to it, which makes it even worse. An inspector can warn you about possible dangerous mold and its causes. You do not want to spend thousands of dollars getting rid of mold only to have it come back again because you never fixed the underlying issue.

Do not be afraid to get multiple opinions about any mold problems. Some companies will charge ten times what other companies charge for the same work because people get scared about environmental issues. A professional company can tell you how to treat the mold or if mold-infected areas need to be removed and repaired.

How can homeowners protect themselves from radon?

Radon gas can cause cancer. It is not one of those urban myths. High levels of radon gas can be very dangerous, and houses with too much radon should have a mitigation system. Most inspectors will not test for radon gas unless they are asked. The test can be expensive, but I suggest everyone do it. The test can take a couple of days, and a professional should perform it. A professional will use a test that measures the radon for an extended timeframe. The test can usually detect if someone is trying to tamper with the results. There are do-it-yourself tests, but they are not nearly as accurate and can be tampered with much more easily.

If you get a radon test and it shows high radon levels, you need to install a radon mitigation system. The radon mitigation system consists of pipes, vents, and fans that help circulate air around the house. These systems usually cost $1,000 to $2,000. If your house has never been tested for radon, you should have it tested to make sure you are not slowly poisoning yourself.

How can homeowners protect themselves from flooding and water damage?

If you buy a house in a flood zone, be prepared for floods! FEMA routinely changes and monitors flood zones. If you live in a flood zone, there is a good chance your house will flood at some point. When you live in a flood zone, you will be required to get flood insurance if you have a mortgage. Flood zones can add thousands of dollars per year to insurance costs. Floods can do incredible damage. It may seem like everything will be okay once the waters recede, but flood waters are not clean. A flood carries debris, sewage, and disease with it. When a house is flooded, it must often be gutted down to the studs and rebuilt before it can be occupied again. If you live in an area that is prone to floods, and for some reason you do not have flood insurance, your regular homeowner's insurance will not cover loss due to floods.

Non-flood water damage is also a huge concern for homeowners. Water damage can occur for many reasons:

- **Frozen or broken pipes.** When water freezes, it expands, and if it freezes in pipes, the pipes will rupture and leak. Never turn your heat off when there is the possibly of freezing pipes. If the water has been off for months or years, be very careful when turning it back on. This can cause massive damage to pipes. If you are worried that the pipes are frozen, you might be able to test them with pressurized air before turning the water on.

- **Leaking roofs:** Roofs should last about 30 years, but they are easily damanged by hail, wind, or neglect. A leaking roof can cause mold and attic damage long before you notice the leak. If you suspect your roof is damaged by hail or wind, ask your insurance company to check it out. They might replace the roof for you.
- **Sewage backups:** Sewer backups are one of the most disgusting things you'll encounter. Sewage lines can get clogged or blocked and back up into the house. Yuck. If your sink or toilet drains slowly, you may have a sewage problem. When you buy a house, you can get the sewer line scoped to detect any potential disasters. A broken sewer line can cost $10,000 or more to replace.
- **Poor drainage:** Poor drainage is one of the most common causes of a foundation problem. All houses should have rain gutters that direct water to downspouts that drain away from the home. Some houses have negative grade or no gutters, which causes water to back up against the foundation. The water seeps down into the foundation, weakening it. This causes water to seep into the crawlspace or basement. Foundation repairs are very expensive, and most can be avoided with proper drainage and grading away from the house.

Conclusion

Homeowners face many dangers. However, taking care of a house isn't terribly difficult. The older a house is, the more care and attention it will need, but you also must take care of newer houses. Before you buy, use an inspector, who can warn you of many problems. They can even give you some tips on how to prevent future problems.

CHAPTER 9

What Are the Tax Advantages of Buying a House?

One of the great benefits of buying a house is the tax advantages extended to homeowners by the United States government. Under our tax laws, homeowners do not pay income taxes on the sale of a house if they have lived in it as their personal residence for at least 2 out of the last 5 years (some restrictions apply and always talk to an accountant for specific tax questions). Also, the interest portion of mortgage payments is tax deductible. Here is the exact law from the IRS website:

https://www.irs.gov/taxtopics/tc701.html

How can you avoid taxes when you sell?

Because profits on the sale of a house are not taxed if you occupy it as your personal residence, buying below market value can be a huge advantage. You may have to buy a house that needs work, but you can repair it before moving in, or you can repair it while living there. Once you have lived in the house for two years, sell it...hopefully for a large profit. You won't pay taxes on the income as long as you do not make over $250,000, rent out the house, or use it for business. Once it's sold, you can repeat this process over and over.

You can use the profits as a down payment for your next house, which may allow you to keep buying more expensive houses. You could also buy the next house with as little down as possible and use the remaining cash to invest in rental properties or something else. The best part of this strategy is you don't pay taxes on the profit as long as you follow IRS rules. The taxes are not deferred like they would be with most retirement plans or a 1031 exchange; they are forgiven forever.

How do you choose the best house for this strategy?

The most difficult part of this strategy is finding the right house, especially for those of us with families. As many of us know, our families don't always want to move into a house that needs a lot of repairs or maintenance. We also may not have a schedule that's flexible enough to wait for a great deal. I knew about this strategy when I bought my first house and completely ignored it for a few reasons:

- The sellers market was very strong; there were not many fixer-uppers available; and I did not know how to find great deals like I do now.
- I was also very young and not as concerned about my future as I should have been.

We are currently seeing very strong sellers' markets in many areas, with multiple offers and low inventory. However, there are still many opportunities for owner-occupied buyers to find good deals. Many banks, and HUD, offer foreclosed houses to owner-occupied buyers before they offer them to investors. This gives owner-occupied buyers a huge advantage. Fannie Mae, Freddie Mac, and Wells Fargo also offer owner-occupied programs on their REO properties (foreclosures).

Continue the process over and over without paying taxes

This strategy can be used as many times as you can handle it. It is a great way to earn cash for investing or for a down payment on a nicer house. Yet for many reasons, this is a difficult strategy, which is why very few people utilize it. Often, a spouse or family member does not want to move into a fixer-upper, wait for a great deal, or must move every two years. If you can pull off this strategy a couple of times—or even once—the extra money can make a huge difference in your life.

Potential roadblocks to this tax-free strategy

Nothing ever works out exactly as we plan. There are a few things we have no control over that can delay or derail this strategy.

- A significant decrease in values can cause some serious delays or decrease profits significantly. If you buy a house you can afford below market value, you should be able to make a small profit, especially if you need to sell or ride out the market until prices improve.
- Selling your house before you have lived there for two years can also decrease the profit potential. You may have to sell early if you're transferred, have a great opportunity you can't pass up, or simply must get out of the town where you live. If you make a profit, you may have to pay taxes on that profit, but you will still make money and come out ahead. You would only pay taxes on the profit, so keep track of any repairs or improvements you make.
- Many people fall in love with their house and don't want to move. If this happens, there is nothing that says you must sell your house every two years and buy a new one. If you love your house and it means more to you than the money you would make from selling it, stay and enjoy it. The nice thing about this strategy is you don't have to follow it to a T to make it work. You can stay longer and change the plan as you go to suit your family's needs.

What other tax advantages does buying a house offer?

Besides avoiding taxes altogether as an owner-occupant, you also save money on taxes from your mortgage payment. The government wants people to buy houses. That is why they make tax laws so advantageous and encourage homeownership through government-backed, low down payment loans. When people buy houses, the economy does better.

When you have a mortgage on your personal residence—or even an investment property—the interest is tax deductible. Here is what the interest and principal would look like on a $190,000, 30-year loan, with a 5-percent interest rate:

- Total payment: $1,020
- Interest portion of the payment: $792
- Principal portion of the payment: $228

This payment does not include any mortgage insurance, taxes, or homeowner's insurance, which we will talk about later. The first month, $228 will go to principal (the amount left to pay on the loan), and $792 will go to interest (the income the bank makes from your mortgage). In the first year, you'll pay $10,216 in interest. That seems like a lot of money, but the interest portion will slowly decrease over time. That $10,216 is tax deductible, which means if you pay taxes in the 28-percent tax bracket, you would save over $2,800 per year. If you were renting, you would not be able to deduct any of the rent from your taxes.

Conclusion

It can be difficult to convince our families that moving is worth it, especially if the kids must change schools. It takes money and hard work to fix up a house, and houses that are good deals are not always our idea of the perfect house for us. If you can manage to pull this off even once, you can make a huge profit and pay fewer taxes. To many people, the extra money can be life changing and allow them to start investing and get ahead.

If you are looking for a way to save money on your taxes in other areas of real estate, please see a good accountant. They will save you much more money than it will cost to consult with them, and you will know you are doing it by the book.

CHAPTER 10

What Are the Costs Associated with Buying a House?

Buying a house is a goal for just about everyone. Even though lenders can finance up to 100 percent of an owner-occupied purchase, the buyer must still pay certain costs. The good news is that real estate agent commissions, title insurance, and other costs are usually paid by the seller. Buyers will have costs associated with getting a loan, closing fees, recording costs, and inspection costs. When buyers learn how much money they must bring to the closing once all costs are calculated, it can be a surprise, so in this chapter, I'll cover what you should expect.

Which costs does the seller usually pay?

The majority of the costs fall on the seller because they usually have more money to spend. The seller can use the equity in their house to pay a real estate agent, title insurance, and other costs. Most buyers don't have a lot of cash to spend on those costs, and having the seller pay them actually allows buyers to have more purchasing power, which raises house prices. Even though the seller pays more of the costs, the system benefits the seller because there are more buyers and higher prices.

The seller's real estate agent and title insurance can run six to eight percent of the selling price (all commissions are negotiable). In some cases, the seller may pay part of the buyers' closing costs as well, which could be another three percent of the selling price.

Which costs does a buyer pay before closing?

Even if a bank finances 100 percent of the house price, the buyer will pay something. Before the closing, a buyer may pay the following:

- **Earnest money:** Almost every seller will require earnest money when they accept an offer. That earnest money is usually refundable based on an inspection contingency, loan contingency, and other factors. The buyer will have to pay the earnest money to the seller, which is usually about one percent of the purchase price when all parties sign the contract. When the house closes, the earnest money will go towards the closing costs the buyer pays.
- **Inspection costs:** Most buyers should always get an inspection. Inspections run from a few hundred dollars to over $1,000 depending on the size of the house. On top of the money it costs to hire the inspector, on some listings...like HUD...the buyer will have to pay to have utilities turned on and the home re-winterized after inspection.
- **Appraisal costs:** Most lenders will require an appraisal to make sure the house is worth what the buyer is willing to pay. The appraisal can cost $400 to $1,000 and is paid by the buyer. In some cases, the seller may pay for the appraisal by paying the buyers' closing costs. However, the buyer may have to pay for the appraisal before closing, and if the house does not close they may get stuck paying that cost.
- **Repair costs:** A house may need repairs for a lender to loan on it, and the buyer sometimes must pay for those repairs. On HUD houses, it is illegal for the buyer to make repairs before closing, but in other situations, the seller may allow the buyer to fix items like the plumbing or electrical so that the lender will loan on the house. In many other cases, the seller may pay for these items to be repaired before closing.

Always get permission from the seller to fix anything on a house before you buy it!

- **Extensions:** On many REO and HUD listings, there is a specific amount of time you are given to close on a property. If you do not close on time, the seller will charge you a fee to extend the closing. The fee could be a daily number like $50 per day or a lump sum like $375 for 15 days. These fees will be laid out in the purchase contract you sign.
- **Total costs before closing:** $500, or up to $5,000 if repairs are needed.

What costs are involved with getting a loan?

There are many different loan options, which can vary greatly depending on whether you will be an owner-occupant or an investor. Most owner-occupant loans require the buyer to live in the house at least one year. Some loans, like those from the VA, will finance 100 percent of the purchase price for owner occupants. If you do not qualify for a VA loan, there are loans that will allow as little as three percent down.

Almost all banks will require investors to put down 20 percent or more. Whether you are an investor or an owner occupant, you will pay some loan costs.

- **Origination fee**: The bank charges this. It is their fee to complete the loan. The origination fee can be half a percent to two and a half percent. Some hard-money loans will have fees as high as six percent! Hard-money loans are used for flipping houses.
- **Lender's title insurance**: The lender will require title insurance to ensure they are in first position. Sometimes the seller will pay for this, but many times they will not. This cost is considered part of your closing costs and can be a couple hundred dollars or more.
- **Processing fees:** Some lenders will charge a processing fee of up to a few hundred dollars on top of the origination fee.

- **Flood certification**: If the house is in a flood zone, the lender will require additional flood insurance. Whether the house is in a flood zone or not, the lender will charge the borrower for a flood certification. There also may be credit report fees and other miscellaneous small charges that usually total less than $100.
- **Interest**: This fee can surprise many buyers because they don't expect to pay for interest on a loan they don't have yet. On many loans, the buyer does not make a mortgage payment until the second month after closing. For example, if the closing is May 15, the first payment is due July 1st, not June 1st. The lender makes this seem like a great benefit, but the buyer is still paying interest for that first month by prepaying it at closing.
- **Prepaid insurance and taxes**: Another surprise for many buyers is they must pay their insurance on a house upfront. The lender will usually escrow the insurance and property taxes, meaning the costs are added to the mortgage payment. The lender does this to protect the house to make sure the loan can be repaid if the house burns down. If the owner does not pay property taxes, the state could auction off the property, which the bank does not want!
- **Mortgage insurance**: There will be mortgage insurance on FHA loans and many other low-down-payment loans. Mortgage insurance is required on most loans where less than 20 percent is put down (except VA) and protects the lender if the buyer defaults. With FHA loans, some of the mortgage insurance is paid at closing in addition to every month.
- **Down payment**: Not all loans have zero down payments like VA loans do. The buyer will have to pay the down payment on top of the other loan costs discussed.

You can expect to pay total loan cost of $2,500 to $5,000 based on a $100,000 purchase price.

As you can see loan costs can add up very quickly. Just because a loan is advertised as three percent down does not mean the buyer will only be bringing three percent of the purchase price to closing.

What are the closing costs when buying a house with cash?

Any buyer will have to pay cash at closing, whether they get a loan or pay cash. For a buyer getting a loan, these costs would be on top of the costs we already discussed above.

- **Closing fee**: The title company completing the closing will charge a closing fee. In Colorado, typical fees range from $200 to $500, but some states use attorneys to complete closings, and the costs can be much higher. It is common for this fee to be split between buyer and seller.
- **Recording fees:** When a closing is completed, the deed and other documents must be recorded. When a buyer gets a loan, many more documents must be recorded, and the fees will be much higher. Recording fees can be up to a couple hundred dollars.
- **HOA fees**: If a home has an HOA (Home Owners Association) the seller may agree to pay transfer fees or it may be agreed to split the transfer fees. These can be minimal or hundreds of dollars.
- **Taxes and transfer fees**: In Colorado, we do not have tax fees for most real estate transactions. That is not true in every state and these can be paid by either party as well. The transfer tax could be as high as 2 percent of the purchase price in some areas.
- **Title insurance**: Most sellers will pay for title insurance, but some sellers do not. HUD does not pay for title insurance and neither does VA when they sell their foreclosures.

- **Costs without a loan: $300 to $5,000**

The total cost to buy a house can range from less than $1,000 if paying cash, to well over $10,000 if you are getting a loan. These costs are based on a purchase price of $100,000 with a low-money down loan. The costs would go up significantly on more expensive houses. Because the costs vary so much in different states and with different loans, you need to talk to your lender or agent about costs as soon as possible.

How can you bring less cash to closing when buying a house?

As you can see, the costs to buy a house can run into the thousands of dollars very easily. Many buyers do not have the cash needed to pay these costs on top of the down payment. In some case,s the seller is allowed to pay closing costs for the buyer to bring down the amount of cash needed. HUD will pay up to three percent of the buyers' closing costs, and some sellers will pay even more.

You must remember: when you ask the seller to pay your closing costs, you are asking them to take less money. If you offer $100,000 with the seller paying $3,000 in closing costs, that is basically a $97,000 offer. In a competitive market ,buyers sometimes have to offer more than list price, especially if they are asking the seller to pay closing costs. An offer of $103,000 with the seller paying $3,000 in closing costs would be the same to the seller as an offer of $100,000 with the seller paying no closing costs.

Most lenders will not let the seller pay any part of the down payment amount or anything besides closing costs and prepaid items. If you want to buy a house for $100,000 and finance $120,000 to pay for repairs, you are going to be limited to very specific loans like a FHA 203K or hard money. You cannot ask the seller to pay the down payment for you, just the closing costs.

Conclusion

As you can see there are a lot of involved in buying houses, especially with a loan. If you are interested in buying a house, talk to a lender right away as they will give you an estimate of these costs, and let you know if any of them can be financed into the loan. There is no guarantee the seller will pay title insurance or the agent fees either, but usually they will.

CHAPTER 11

How Much Does It Cost to Sell a House?

Selling a house can be a fantastic experience if you buy below market value and are aware of all the costs involved. Selling can also be a disappointing experience if you are not aware of all the costs involved and do not make as much money as you hoped to. Knowing selling costs upfront will make the experience much more enjoyable. You will most likely have to pay a real estate agent, title insurance, recording, and closing fees.

Costs can vary greatly based on real estate commissions, closing fees, closing costs, title insurance, and more. For a rough estimate of the cost of selling with a real estate agent, count on 7 to 10 percent of the selling price. This figure can be quite shocking to many sellers, but it costs money to get top dollar for your house.

The biggest cost is paying real estate agents.

By far the biggest cost is what you pay real estate agents. There is no set commission, but HUD pays a six percent commission: three percent to the selling agent and three percent to the listing agent. I will use HUD's commission structure as an example throughout this book, but you can try negotiating fees with your agent.

A six percent commission seems like a lot of money, but I believe it's a necessary cost. The agent knows the market and is an expert at selling houses. If you do not use an agent, you could underprice or overprice your house, which could easily cost you more than what the agent charges. An agent also knows the contract process, how to market, how to negotiate, how to handle inspections, how to handle appraisals, how to stage your house, and much more. Trying to figure out everything on your own can take a lot of time and cost you a lot of money.

The seller usually pays title insurance.

In most states, the seller customarily pays for title insurance. Title insurance is a guarantee to the buyer that a house has clear title. It guarantees that all loans are paid off and all liens, judgments, and title defects have been settled. It is always wise to get title insurance when you buy. In Colorado, it costs between $600 and $1,200, depending on the price of the house. This cost can vary by state, as some states have different laws regarding title insurance.

The seller must pay closing fees, recording fees, and more.

Title insurance is just one cost. Many others apply. The closing company charges a fee to handle the closing, which can range from $200 to $800 (usually on the lower end). In some states, you must use an attorney to close. In Colorado, the closing fee is typically split between the buyer and seller, but that can be negotiated as well.

There are also recording fees for the deed, recording fees for any mortgages, wiring fees for loan pay-offs, and many banks charge to provide pay-off figures. These fees can range from $50 to $500 depending on the number of loans and pay-offs involved.

You may also pay for taxes and utilities.

When you sell, you must pay the taxes and utilities up to the day you close in most cases. In Colorado, we pay property taxes, but you usually don't have to pay transfer taxes or local taxes. Even though your mortgage company may be paying your property taxes through an escrow account, you may owe taxes at closing. These taxes must be paid before the house is sold, and if the escrow account holds extra money, it will be returned to the seller after closing.

An escrow account is used for water bills in my area as well. The water account balance must be brought zero before closing. The title company will typically escrow a small amount for the water bill so they can pay the final water after closing, and any unused money will be returned to the seller.

Taxes and the water escrow can range greatly depending on the price of the house. Colorado property taxes are low, around .05 percent of the sales price in my county. A water escrow may be $100. In other states, property taxes can be ten times higher than in Colorado.

If you lived in your house for two of the last five years, you most likely will not pay any income taxes if you profit on the sale. If you are selling an investment property, the taxes for gains are much more complicated.

HOA costs can be a huge surprise to sellers.

When you live in a neighborhood with an HOA, you must usually pay a monthly fee. HOAs may have additional costs and payment structures. I just sold a house which had an HOA but had no monthly HOA payments. The HOA collected money by charging a .05 percent fee on the selling price, which was split between buyer and seller on every house sold in the neighborhood. The sellers did not know this policy and were quite surprised at closing.

Most HOAs do not work this way, but many do charge transfer fees or fees for a status letter. These fees can be $20, $150, or more. The purchase contract will determine who pays these fees. The fees could be split, paid by the seller, or paid by the buyer.

What are the total direct costs involved in a sale?

Costs discussed up to this point have been direct costs. On a $200,000 house, the costs may be as follows:

Real estate agent commissions:	$12,000
Title insurance:	$1,000
HOA transfer fees:	$150
Recording Fees, pay-off fees:	$150
Water escrow:	$100
Prorated taxes:	$750
Closing fee:	$200
Total:	**$14,350**

Your mortgage payoff may surprise you at closing.

The mortgage payoff surprises many people when they see how high it is. The payoff and taxes are figured to the day of the sale. When you receive your statement, the principal amount listed is calculated after you just made a payment on the loan. That number is almost always less than the actual payoff. Every day after that principal amount is calculated by the bank, the interest increases. A $180,000 loan balance at five percent interest will accrue interest of about $25 per day. If you decide not to pay your last mortgage payment because you are closing on the 5th of the month, there could be 30 days of interest that accrue on that loan before it is paid off. That adds up to $750 dollars and can be a shock to sellers who expect their payoff to be the same as their last mortgage statement principal balance.

Which closing costs may the buyer request?

In some instances, buyers may need the seller to pay closing costs so the buyer can qualify for a loan. Closing costs can range from two to four percent of the price of the house, and many times, buyers do not have the cash to pay these costs. The seller commonly to pay three percent of the closing costs for the buyer, but in some cases the price of the house is increased to make up for the closing costs. Closing costs are negotiable, just like the price of the house. Sellers should be aware that many buyers using owner-occupied financing may ask for closing costs, which will decrease the seller's bottom line.

Fix-up costs.

Most people want to get the most money they can when they sell their house. The best way to get the most money is ensuring your house is in great condition. If you have lived in a house for any amount of time, there is a good chance wear and tear has occurred. If you have kids like me, *a lot* of wear and tear may occur! Most buyers want a house that is in great shape and will not need any work. Some buyers want houses that need work, but they also expect to get a great deal when they buy those houses. Some sellers may think they can just deduct the price of the repairs from the price of their house so they can avoid spending extra money. However, the worse the house's condition, the fewer buyers who will want and qualify for it. If your house needs $10,000 in work, you won't get $10,000 less than it is worth after repairs. You would probably get $20,000 or even $25,000 less than it is worth. It almost always makes sense to fix up your house before you sell it.

Conclusion

It takes a lot of money to sell a house, but remember—the person you bought the house from paid those costs when they sold it to you. When you add real estate commissions, closing costs and fees, and money for repairs, total costs can be significant. If you plan to use the proceeds from the sale to buy a new house, make sure you calculate the correct amounts and are not shocked when you get your figures for closing!

CHAPTER 12

How to Find a Great Real Estate Agent

Choosing a great real estate agent is usually the first step to making the buying or selling process fun, exciting, and a wise financial decision. The problem is there are millions of agents in the United States, and they're not all good. A great agent will help you find the perfect house at a great price, and they will show you how the process works. A bad agent can cause you to lose your dream house, lose earnest money, lead you to buy a bad house, or even open you up to a lawsuit. There are ways to find a good agent, and there are ways to tell how good your current agent is.

How can a real estate agent, whether good or bad, affect a house transaction?

Most buyers do not know exactly how the house-buying process works. A lot must happen:

- The buyer must get a loan.
- The buyer must find a house.
- The buyer must write an offer and negotiate.
- The buyer must complete an inspection.
- The buyer must complete the loan process.
- The buyer must avoid doing anything to mess up the deal like buying a car right before closing.

A real estate agent can help with these items, and the great thing for buyers is the seller usually pays for their agent! However, you must choose your agent wisely. If an agent messes up one thing, the whole deal can fall apart and cost the buyer or seller a lot of money.

You can easily spot bad agents looking for a lack of communication, knowledge, honesty, and timelessness.

- **Communication:** One of the most important things an agent must do is communicate often and openly with everyone involved in a transaction. The agent needs to check with lenders, title companies, inspectors, and appraisers to make sure everything goes well. Not all lenders are great either, but a great real estate agent will be in constant contact with the lender to make sure they are doing their job.
- **Knowledge:** Real estate agents need to know what they are doing! That may seem obvious, but every real estate transaction is different. The best agents have experience and have worked in the business for a long time. However, that does not mean new agents cannot be great if they have a team or a mentor to help them.
- **Honesty:** One of the worst things an agent can do is lie. Most lies occur when agent does not know something, so they make things up instead of admitting they don't know. This book should give you guidance on spotting a knowledgeable, honest agent.
- **Timeliness:** In today's hot real estate market, the agent must also communicate quickly. If it takes an agent two days to return calls, it can easily cost the buyer a deal. The agent must also make sure the inspection, appraisal and other items are completed on time so the buyer does not lose their earnest money.

A solid agent will not only do their job but will go above and beyond for their client. Real estate can be one of the best investments if you buy the right house. An agent can help buyers research values, advise on items to look out for, and find an overall awesome deal.

What are some signs that your real estate agent may be good or bad?

Many buyers will have no idea if their agent is any good unless something goes wrong. By that time, it may be too late to switch agents or save the deal. Here are some things to help you determine if an agent is good or bad:

- **How much experience do they have?** New agents are not always bad, but they have a better chance of messing something up. On the other hand, new agents can be a great resource for investors or someone looking for a great deal. Often, new agents make up for their lack of experience by having more time and more drive than experienced agents. I would not write off new agents, but make sure they have a team or a more experienced agent helping them learn the business.
- **Are they part or full time?** Many real estate agents work part time. They have a full-time job and try to work their real estate career around it. This can earn the agent extra money, but it can hurt their clients. Real estate agents need to be available almost all the time. They do not have to work all the time, but they must be on call. Some buyers want to view houses during the week, some at night, and some on the weekend. When a good deal comes up, most buyers cannot afford to wait a day or two to view it. When there is a problem with a loan, the lender may not be able to wait all day to reach of the agent. If an agent works part time, it does not mean they are bad. You must make sure they have a flexible schedule or that they have help if they are not available.
- **How fast do they respond?** I have searched for real estate agents myself when looking at out-of-state properties. I have also searched for real estate agents to refer to clients. In my experience, most agents are not very good at communicating. I estimate that 1 out of 3 real estate agents return my calls. If an agent doesn't respond to you, via phone or email, do not use them! If it takes two days for someone to get back to you, you probably should not use them. The best agents will answer their phone or get back to

you within an hour or two. That is not always possible, but if an agent takes a day to get back to you every time you contact them, it's not a good sign.

- **Do they know the market?** You may not be able to tell if an agent is knowledgeable. There are many terms that buyers may not be familiar with, and there is a lot going on behind the scenes. A buyer can still ask their agent questions to see how knowledgeable they are about neighborhoods or houses. Real estate agents who know what they are doing should know the answers to these questions or be able to look them up very quickly. If they have problems answering them, they may not be very experienced. Here are some questions you should ask:
    - How old is this house?
    - Are most houses in this neighborhood the same age?
    - Is there an HOA fee, and how much is it?
    - Is the house priced at, above, or below market value?
    - Would this house qualify for a loan based on its condition?
    - How much would an inspection cost?
    - Have you had any problems with houses appraising in this market?
    - How long does it take to close?
    - What are the costs associated with buying a house?

What are the best ways to find a real estate agent?

There are many real estate agents, and they advertise everywhere. One sign of a good agent is they advertise because active advertising means they are making enough money to market themselves. Here are some tips for finding a good agent:

- **Ask friends and family who they have used**. A referral from someone who has used a great agent is a good place to start. If someone suggests you use a certain person, ask them if they used that agent. They could refer their friend or sister, but if they have never used them, it is tough to know if they are any good.
- **Zillow or other online real estate sites.** Zillow, Realtor.com, Trulia, and other sites all recommend agents. These sites charge agents to advertise. The problem with these sites is if you ask to be put in touch with an agent, 5 agents may call you at once. You can still find good agents on those sites, and you should be able to contact those agents directly without submitting a request for someone to contact you.
- **Ask professionals in your area**. Most people have an accountant, doctor, chiropractor, lawyer, or another professional they can ask. The nice thing about asking them for a referral is they don't want an agent to make them look bad. Hopefully they refer agents who do a good job or refer someone they have used themselves.
- **Calling real estate offices.** Most real estate offices have "floor time." Agents can sign up for floor time, and whenever the office gets a call or visit from a client who does not have an agent, the floor agent gets the lead. When you call a real estate office and ask for an agent, you will most likely get the floor agent, who may or may not be any good. This is probably not the best way to choose an agent.
- **Calling on listings or going to open houses**. Another way to contact agents is to go to open houses or call the numbers on yard signs posted at listings you may be interested in. I think this is slightly better than calling an office because you know these agents have a listing or are working an open house to get clients.

- **Calling agents who run advertisements in local publications**. You will see agents on billboards, in grocery stores, on bus stops, and in local magazines. Advertising in these publications can be expensive, and it is usually a good sign when agents advertise. They have some money to market, which means they sell houses.

The more you see an agent's name around town, the more likely it is they will have experience. Advertising does not guarantee they are a great agent, but it tells you they sell houses and might be good.

Should you use friends or family when choosing an agent?

Many people have a brother, a sister, a mother, a cousin, or a friend who is an agent. Working with friends and family can be a nightmare, or it can be awesome. Don’t use friends or family just because they are friends or family. Use the same criteria as you would a stranger. This is a huge financial decision, and you don't want to pick a bad agent to avoid hurting someone’s feelings. Some friends have chosen not to use me as their agent, and I did not take it personally. In some cases, my friends handled it in brilliant ways.

If your friend or family member is a good agent, use them! If you have multiple friends or family who are good agents, put their name in a hat and choose one. Tell everyone how you decided to pick and that it was nothing personal. Some friends of mine have decided to pick someone they did not know to avoid business transactions with friends or family. Remember, real estate agents and lenders will learn a lot about your finances. If you don’t want friends or family learning about how much money you make, you may not want to use them. You could always pick the person you think is the best agent, and tell the other people you drew names out of a hat. You don't have to lie—just make sure every name in the hat is the person you want to work with! After all, this is the biggest purchase of your life.

Conclusion

Finding a great agent can make the difference between finding a great deal or paying way too much. Choosing the wrong agent can mean missing out on your dream house or even getting sued! You could also be in for some big surprises regarding how much it costs to buy a house or how much the lender will charge. If you need help finding an agent, I know of some great ones across the country, and I can refer you to them. I also have an awesome team of agents who can help you out in the Colorado area. If you are looking for an agent, email me at Mark@investfourmore.com.

CHAPTER 13

Should You Work with More Than One Real Estate Agent?

Working with more than one real estate agent may seem like a great way to find a house. You have multiple people working for you and a better chance to find the right place. However, working with more than one agent can often hurt more than it helps. As an agent myself, I can give the real estate agent's perspective on how we operate and the best way to work with us.

How do real estate agents get paid?

Agents are paid in many ways, and there are no standard commissions or structures. I will outline the most common scenario in my area.

In most real estate transactions, two real estate agents are involved: one for the buyer and one for the seller. Usually, the seller pays the commissions for both agents. We will use the HUD commission structure for this example, which is 3 percent for the buyer side and 3 percent for the seller side. That seems like a lot of money for one deal, but agents have a lot of expenses, and you would be surprised how much does not go in their pockets.

- Real estate agents must carry a lot of insurance. I carry E and O, general liability, and umbrella policies.
- Real estate agents must pay fees for their license, MLS and office expenses, and office space.
- Most Real estate agents don't keep their entire commission. They pay a percentage to their broker. In turn, the broker pays for staff, advertising, or other expenses. Commission splits can range from 50/50 to 90/10 depending on what the office pays for and the number of transactions the agent closes.

- Agents do not receive any benefits! They pay all their health insurance costs and have no matching 401Ks or other benefits of a corporate job.
- Real estate agents are self-employed and may pay more taxes than those who are employed by someone else.

After accounting for these expenses, agents don't make as much as most people think. An agent usually only gets paid when they sell a house. They may make $5,000 on one sale, but they may have also spent 20 hours with a client who never bought a house, and therefore they earned nothing for their time.

The reason I am outlining the way agents get paid is to show you that agents want to make sure the people they work with are serious. Agents do not want to work for free! If the agent or agents you work with do not think you are serious, they will do a poor job. The best way to annoy or put off an agent is to work with multiple agents at the same time.

Why don't agents want their clients working with other agents?

A good agent will flat out ask any buyer if they are working with another agent. In ethics class, they are taught not to steal other agents' buyers or sellers. It is drilled into our heads that it is very bad to "step on another agent's toes" by showing houses or writing contracts for a buyer that has already looked at houses with another agent. Agents only get paid when they sell a house, and they do not want to spend two months with a client just to see them write an offer with an agent they just met.

Because of this training, most agents will naturally shy away from any buyer that says they have viewed houses with other agents, are receiving listings from other agents, or are working with more than one agent in any way. This doesn't mean agents won't help people who work with more than one agent, but they probably won't put a lot of effort into it. If you want an agent to do a great job, choose one and stick with them. If you do not like your agent or want a new one, be honest and upfront with everyone. Tell your old agent you are done and you will not be working with them anymore. Tell your new agent that you fired your old agent, told that agent they were fired, and need a new agent.

What if you signed an agreement?

Many agents want buyers to sign a buyer agency agreement. This agreement states the agent will perform certain services for the buyer, and the buyer will not use any other agents. The agreement can last a couple months or even a year. Before you sign an buyer agency agreement, make sure you like the agent!

If you happen to choose an agent, but they're performing poorly, you can still get out of your buyer agency agreement. Be honest. Tell them why things are not working and why you want out. Most agents will let you out of the agreement, and you can move on. If an agent does not want to let you out of the agreement, you can ask to talk to that agent's broker (if they have one). The broker oversees the agent and may convince that agent it is best to let a client go rather than fight them.

If you sign an agreement with Agent A but use Agent B when you buy, you may still owe commission to Agent A. Even if you do not sign an agreement but view houses with Agent A and then use Agent B to buy the house, you may still owe commission to Agent A! If it is decided that one agent was the procuring cause of a sale and you used another agent, the first agent is owed a commission. In these cases, it is not the seller that pays the commission but the buyer because they caused the problem. Not only can working with multiple agents hurt your chances of finding a house, it can also cost you thousands of dollars.

Should you work with more than one agent for investment properties?

Many investors like to work with more than one agent to find properties for them. They feel the more agents looking for properties, the better chance they have of getting a good deal. They will talk to many agents all over town and tell them they are a serious investor looking to make some purchases. This strategy can work in some cases, but it can also backfire. Most agents can sense when an investor or buyer is going to work with more than one agent.

The only time an investor succeeds using these strategies is when they can find deals themselves and only need agents to complete paperwork. It also helps when the investor communicates that they use multiple agents. It also makes sense to use multiple agents if a buyer is looking in a large geographical area and one of the agents is not an expert in that entire area.

Conclusion

Investors may successfully work with more than one agent, but most people looking for a personal residence are better off using one agent. I suggest you find one hard-working agent and stick with them.

CHAPTER 14

What Is the Difference between a Realtor and a Real Estate Agent?

Throughout this book, I may refer to both real estate agents and Realtors. Many people feel that a real estate agent and a Realtor are the same thing; however, there are some big differences. Realtors have different ethical responsibilities than agents. Realtors generally have more ethical responsibilities than agents, but does that really make a difference to a buyer or seller? I was a Realtor for 15 years, but I recently switched to being an agent only.

Why would an agent want to be a Realtor?

Being an agent involves getting licensed in the state you want to work in and hanging your license with a broker. As of March 25th, 2016, there were 1,150,141 Realtors compared to approximately 2,500,000 agents. Being a Realtor comes with many perks besides just being able to say you are one.

Being a Realtor also gives you access to many organizations.

- **NAR:** National Association of Realtors
- **State Board of Realtors:** Most states have a state board of Realtors
- **Local Board of Realtors:** Most areas have a local board of Realtors specific to market location

I work in Northern Colorado and once belonged to CAR (Colorado Association of Realtors) and GARA (Greeley Area Realtor Association). When I was a member of those boards, I could attend local meetings, luncheons, classes, and charity events put on by those boards. I could also run for leadership roles.

How much does becoming a Realtor cost?

One drawback to becoming a Realtor is it costs more than being an agent. Here are the fees I paid to various boards. These will vary based on the board you belong to and the state you are in.

- NAR: $120 annually
- NAR: $35 special assessment annually
- CAR: $165 annually
- GARA: $209.17 annually
- **Total: $519.17 annually**

These fees are separate from any MLS dues or other fees. As you can see, being a Realtor is expensive, and I also pay for the agents on my team to be Realtors, which costs me thousands of dollars each year. This is one reason I am no longer a Realtor.

Why would buyers and sellers prefer to work with a Realtor?

Realtors are also supposed to be held to a higher level of ethics.

Below are the pledges a Realtor makes that a real estate agent is not required to make:

- Pledge to put the interests of buyers and sellers ahead of their own and to treat all parties honestly.
- Shall refrain from exaggerating, misrepresenting, or concealing material facts, and is obligated to investigate and disclose when situations reasonably warrant.
- Shall cooperate with other brokers/agents when it is in the best interests of the client to do so.
- Have a duty to disclose if they represent family members who own or are about to buy real estate, or if they themselves are a principal in a real estate transaction that they are licensed to sell real estate.
- Shall not provide professional services in a transaction where the agent has a present or

contemplated interest without disclosing that interest.

- Shall not collect any commissions without the seller's knowledge nor accept fees from a third-party without the seller's express consent.
- Shall refuse fees from more than one party without all parties' informed consent.
- Shall not comingle client funds with their own.
- Shall attempt to ensure that all written documents are easy to understand and will give everybody a copy of what they sign.
- Shall not discriminate in any fashion for any reason on the basis of race, color, religion, sex, handicap, familial status, or national origin.
- Expects agents to be competent, to conform to standards of practice, and to refuse to provide services for which they are unqualified.
- Must engage in truth in advertising.
- Shall not practice law unless they are a lawyer.
- Shall cooperate if charges are brought against them and present all evidence requested.
- Agree not to bad mouth competition and agree not to file unfounded ethics complaints.
- Shall not solicit another REALTOR'S client nor interfere in a contractual relationship.
- Shall submit to arbitration to settle matters and not seek legal remedies in the judicial system.

Realtors can market themselves as abiding by these standards, where real estate agents may not have to abide by these standards (depending on state laws). In my experience, many Realtors and agents have practiced unethically. I have not seen a difference in one or the other being more ethical. When we have had problems with unethical Realtors, the boards did not do much to help us out.

While Realtors can advertise that they are held to a higher level than just agents, I do not think it makes much of a difference to a buyer or seller.

Why did I stop being a Realtor?

Being a Realtor was costing me thousands of dollars per year and was not very beneficial. Most buyers and sellers did not care if I was a Realtor, and I had a few issues with how NAR handled some problems. My primary business is listing foreclosures for banks. I worked hard to build my business with banks and REO companies. I worked for years to build relationships and earn an awesome reputation. I built my business up to where I was selling 200 homes per year. A few years ago, NAR decided that REO brokers like myself had too much business and that every agent should be able to list REO houses without putting the work in. NAR lobbied to force banks and REO companies to include more agents and take business away from the existing agents. That did not sit well with me, and I thought a few other decisions they made were questionable as well. I personally did not see the value in being a Realtor, and I do not think cancelling my membership hurt my clients in any way.

Conclusion

The difference between a Realtor and a real estate agent may not matter to most buyers and sellers. I happen to think being a Realtor does not make you a better agent. I would base my search for a great agent on the criteria I listed previously over whether someone is a Realtor.

This concludes the first part of this book. From here on, I provide much more detail on every subject I discussed to this point! I delve into buying houses, financing them, and maintaining them. If you learned just a little bit from this section of the book, it will be an enormous help in the buying and selling process.

Part II: Buying a House

Buying a house is one of the biggest financial decisions most people make. You should treat it as such! Buying the wrong house for too much money can be a nightmare, which puts you in a hole for years. Buying the right house at a great price can bring you financial freedom and make life so much easier. The trick is learning how to buy houses below market value. When you buy below market value, you can make a lot of money and end up in a great financial position.

Most people never try to buy houses below market value or learn what it takes to get a great deal. They may ask their real estate agent to find them a good deal, but they never confirm how good their deal is, nor are they patient enough to find one. Getting a decent deal is not too hard: most agents can find those. But finding an awesome deal is tougher. When you find an awesome deal, have the right financing in place, and are realistic about your expectations, it is an awesome experience. A good deal to me is one that is at least 20 percent less than the market value. Sometimes you must buy a house that needs work or a house that may not be perfect for you. But getting a great deal will make it much easier to get your perfect house in the future.

In this section, I will also talk about how much to spend. Lenders are not financial advisors; they should not tell you how much to spend. They can tell you how much you qualify for, but that does not mean you should buy the most expensive house you can!

CHAPTER 15

How Much Should You Spend on a Starter House?

Many people dream of the day they can buy a house they can call their own. Houses are expensive, and many people start out by purchasing a starter house. There are many perks to homeownership, such as tax advantages, possible appreciation, equity growth, and control over your living situation. However, a lot of people do not take the time needed to research the house-buying process.

A starter house is typically a smaller, low-cost property. Most people cannot afford to buy a mansion right away. Whether you should buy a starter house, a larger house, or even rent instead of owning will depend on many factors.

Why don't most first-time homeowners take the house-buying process more seriously?

Buying a house is a big deal! With low-down payment loan options and 30-year mortgages, houses may not seem very expensive. Plus, most people are expected to buy a house. We're told to get a good job, get married, have kids, and buy a house (not always in that order). Because of this expectation, most people buy a house. Since it does not take that much money to buy a house, I think many people take the process lightly.

Buyers will often let real estate agents and lenders tell them what kind of house to buy and how much to spend. Getting an awesome deal on a house you love can be extremely beneficial. It takes some work and time to figure out how much house you can afford and how to get a great deal.

How much house can you afford?

I believe the main factor that should guide a first-time buyer is how much house can they afford, which is different from how much they can qualify for. Most lenders and agents will tell buyers they can afford up to a certain amount. Buyers assume this is how much they should spend because that is what the lender tells them they can qualify for. But the number the lender gives is the most they can buy based on many financial factors. That max number comes from how safe the bank feels the buyers are and how confident the bank is that the buyers can pay back the loan. If the bank were to lend more money, there is a pretty good chance the buyers would default on the loan. Do you want to spend so much money on a house that you find yourself on the edge of not being able to pay back the loan?

The number the lender gives buyers also has nothing to do with the buyer's comfort level, spending habits, or saving habits. In the industry, we call those who spend all their money on a house and have nothing left to save or invest "house poor." Lenders do not care if you have an emergency fund, how much you are saving towards retirement, or your kids' college. Lenders care if you can make the house payment. Do not rely on a lender to tell you what you should spend.

I love the advice a lender gave on one of my podcasts: "Figure all of your expenses, make sure you can save 20 percent of your income, and see how much you have left over for a house payment." When you get an idea of how much you can spend on a house and still save money, you know how much house you can afford. I like to spend less than 10 percent of my income on my personal residence.

What if you cannot afford to buy any houses in your area?

Once you figure how much you should spend, you need to research prices in your area. If you live in San Francisco, New York City, or other popular cities, you may not be able to afford anything. If you live in the Midwest, you may be able to afford an awesome house with a lake. Usually, to be able to afford to live in a very expensive city, you must make a lot of money. You may need to choose between being house poor or moving to a different area.

Renting is also an option if prices are too high in your area. There is nothing wrong with renting if it makes more financial sense. If you really want to buy a house or live in an expensive area, try to cut down on as many of your other expenses as possible.

If you decide to spend most of your money on a house because you live in an expensive area, getting an important deal is even more important.

Why is it important to get a great deal?

When most people look for houses, they want to make sure they aren't paying more than the house is worth. When I buy houses, I want to make sure I am paying *much* less than they are worth. One of the advantages of real estate is you can buy houses below market value. Some houses need work, the seller needs money right away, a bank wants to get rid of it, or other circumstances occur which cause a house to sell for less than market value. Buying below market value is not easy, and most people are not willing to put work and time into the process. If you can buy a house that is a great deal, it will do wonders for your financial health. Buying below market value brings:

- **Instant equity**. If you buy a house valued at $100,000 for $75,000, you immediately earn $25,000 in equity.
- **Ability to remove mortgage insurance.** Many low-down-payment loans have mortgage insurance, which can add hundreds of dollars to the monthly payment. On some conventional loans, you can get the mortgage insurance removed after a couple of years. The house must have enough equity for the mortgage insurance to be removed, and getting a great deal helps tremendously.

- **Easier to refinance.** When you have more equity in your house, it is much easier to refinance it. You may be able to take cash out with the refinance.
- **Easier to sell.** If you buy a house at fair-market value but must sell quickly, you may lose money. When you sell, you must pay agent commissions, recording fees, title insurance, and in some cases, attorney's fees and transfer taxes. These costs can easily comprise 10 percent or more of the value of the house. If you pay market value, you must bring money to closing to sell quickly, but if you get a great deal, you may still make some money.
- **When you sell your personal residence, you might not pay taxes**. When you sell a house you have occupied for at least two years, you may not have to pay any income taxes on the profit.

Conclusion

If you are in the market to buy your first house, do not blindly trust your real estate agent and lender to buy it for you. You need to figure out how much you can afford, where you want to live, what type of house you want, and how good of a deal you need to get. You may end up with a starter house, something much better, or you may end up renting. None of those are bad options depending on your financial situation. I will go into much more detail on how to find a great deal later.

CHAPTER 16

How Long Does It Take to Buy a House?

If you decide you want to buy a new car, you can go to a car dealership, test drive some vehicles, choose the perfect ride, get a loan, and drive away in that new car the same day. The house-buying process is a little different. If you are buying a house, you may be able to close on the deal in a few days if you have no contingencies and cash. Most people do not buy houses with cash, and most people want to make sure the house they are buying is in decent shape. It can take 30 to 60 days to complete the buying process. On average, it takes about 45 days to close in Colorado because slow appraisals are causing delays.

What is the fastest way to buy a house?

Even if a buyer has cash and is ready to buy today, closing a deal takes time. The buyer will want to make sure they get clear title to the house, which requires a title company or attorney to provide title insurance. The quickest title insurance can be obtained is usually a couple of days. A closing time must be set up, and if there is a loan on the property, a payoff must be ordered from the bank. In reality, it takes at least a week to close on using cash and no contingencies.

How long do contract contingencies add to the timeframe?

When I buy houses, I often remove all contingencies except for clear title. I want to make sure I am not buying a house with a $100,000 judgment I do not know about. I am a very savvy buyer and have been buying houses professionally for the last 15 years. Most buyers will want to perform an inspection, will have appraisal contingencies, and will have loan contingencies.

Inspection contingencies can take from 3 days to 20 days. Most inspection contingencies range from 7 to 14 days. The shorter the inspection, the better for the seller because if there is a problem, they will not waste as much time before they can put the house back on the market. One way for a buyer to make their offer more appealing to the seller is to shorten the inspection period if they need one. Once the inspection contingency period is over, additional time may be needed to negotiate any problems discovered during the inspection. If you need an inspection, the quickest you can buy a house would be about two weeks.

How long can it take to buy a house when a loan is involved?

The biggest delay in this process is getting a loan. A few years ago, loans closed in under 30 days, but things have changed greatly in Colorado and across the country. New laws require more disclosures from lenders. This was meant to protect consumers but added delays. If a buyer is getting a loan, it almost always takes at least 35 days to close, and in some areas where there is an appraiser shortage, even longer.

Loan approval takes time because the lender must verify all the buyers' information. When a buyer is disqualified from a loan, they give basic information to the lender and their credit is pulled, but the lender does not verify all the details. When the buyer's contract on a house is accepted, the lender checks out everything in the buyers' financial history to make sure they are making what they say they make and they have no hidden debt. The lender also rechecks credit and makes sure the buyer's financial position did not change since first qualifying for the loan. All this verification can take from two to four weeks depending on the lender and the type of the loan. If the buyer uses some sort of down payment assistance program, the process can take longer because the entity giving that down payment assistance will want to verify all of the buyers' information as well.

In Colorado, appraisals currently take 3 weeks to 4 weeks—and sometimes longer for properties outside of the main towns. Once a contract is accepted, it is vitally important the lender orders the appraisal as soon as possible to get the deal closed in 45 days. If the lender waits a week or two, the process may take two months! How quickly an appraisal can be done varies depending on your area. In some parts of the country, it may only take a couple of days, but in areas like Portland, it may take two months.

CHAPTER 17

How Do You Choose the Right Neighborhood?

A real estate agent may seem like the perfect person to recommend a good neighborhood. However, as an agent, I can't tell my clients or anyone else what a "good" or "bad" neighborhood is. Telling someone a neighborhood is good or bad is considered steering and is illegal.

The reason it is illegal for me to recommend neighborhoods is because my opinion of what a good neighborhood is will be different from someone else's. If people used my judgement, they would all buy houses in the same areas. If everyone bought houses in the same neighborhoods, it would push up values in some places and lower values in others.

What can a real estate agent tell you about neighborhoods?

Not only do real estate agents shy away from offering general opinions about neighborhoods, but many also do not talk about crime rates, school ratings, or demographics like ethnicity. It is illegal for agents to talk about many of these characteristics. If you are frustrated that your real estate agent will not give you the neighborhood information you want, it isn't because they are a bad agent...it is because they can't legally do it.

What should you look for?

Since a good neighborhood is relative for each buyer, it is up to each buyer to figure out what a good neighborhood is to them. A buyer needs to determine what they want in a neighborhood first. Neighborhood characteristics a buyer should consider are:

- Crime rates.
- School ratings.
- House prices.
- Age of houses.
- Size of houses.
- Size of the town.
- Proximity to large population areas.
- Local economy.
- HOAs.
- Types of houses (multifamily or single family).
- Tax rates.

How can someone determine what a good neighborhood for them is?

- Call the local police department. Often, the local police will tell you what the crime rates are and even tell you which neighborhoods have high crime.
- Drive through neighborhoods on the weekends and in the evening. Driving through neighborhoods will give you an idea of the houses' conditions and the traffic situation.
- Check websites, like City Data, that give neighborhood information statistics.
- Ask friends or people you know who live in the town you want to buy in. If you don't know anyone in that town, try to meet some people! Non-agents can give you much more information about neighborhoods.
- Talk to people in the neighborhoods. When you are driving around looking at houses and you see someone doing yard work or walking their dog, ask them what they think of the neighborhood.

Conclusion

It is not easy to determine what the best neighborhood for you is. Each person's idea of the perfect neighborhood will be different. If you don't know a town or neighborhood well, make sure you do your due diligence before you buy.

CHAPTER 18

Should You Get an Inspection?

Most buyers are given a certain amount of time to complete an inspection. Most people complete some type of inspection when purchasing a house, but is it always necessary? In my professional opinion, 95 percent of buyers should get an inspection. An inspection is not needed in a few cases, and in some cases, declining an inspection will actually give you a better chance at getting a great deal.

How does an inspection work?

The inspection typically occurs right after the house goes under contract. Buyers are given a specific amount of time to either inspect the house themselves, have a friend inspect it, or have a contractor or a professional inspector review the house.

Buyers should be allowed to check out everything in a house, including the major systems, utilities, and minor cosmetic issues. In some cases, like with HUD homes or some REO sellers, many utilities cannot be turned on. If the pipes on a HUD home do not hold pressure when HUD inspects the house, the buyer will not be allowed to turn on the water for inspections or appraisals. Houses that are in poor shape may not have the electric or gas turned on if it is not safe to do so. On a HUD home, buyers are usually responsible for ordering and paying for the inspection, and it gives them a chance to ensure the house is in satisfactory condition before they buy it. On most real estate deals, the buyer is not responsible for turning on utilities for the inspection.

How much does an inspection cost?

Inspection costs can vary greatly. Smaller houses are cheaper to inspect than larger one. Costs vary depending on the region of the country and its living costs. Different inspectors also charge different rates.

For a rental property I would buy that is about 2,000 total square feet, I can get an inspection done for about $300. On my personal house, which is close to 6,000 square feet, the inspection was $600, and the inspector did not even get a chance to look at everything in the house (even after 5 hours). I can get slightly lower rates because I am an agent. As a regular buyer, expect to pay a little more than I do.

Besides using an inspector, you can also use a contractor. Use caution when using contractors because they might tend to underestimate the seriousness of some repairs. If they convince you not to buy and they know you will use them to fix it up, they cost themselves a job. I had a local roofing contractor look at a flip for me last year that had major structural problems. He said it looked like an easy fix and not to worry about it. After started the job, the easy fix turned into almost a complete roof rebuild!

What happens to earnest money if a contract is cancelled due to an inspection?

Most contracts are written so that the buyer can cancel the contract and get their earnest money back if certain things happen. If a buyer has an inspection contingency written into the contract, they have a certain amount of time to complete an inspection. If the buyers cancel their contract because of the inspection and they notify the seller before their inspection contingency expires, they will usually receive their earnest money back (HUD is an exception I cover in more detail later).

Is a contract automatically cancelled after a failed inspection?

If you find major problems after an inspection, you do not automatically lose the house. There are many options for the seller and buyer to save the deal. The outcome will depend on how serious the problems are and how motivated the sellers and buyers are.

The buyer will be given the opportunity to ask the seller to make repairs, to ask the seller to renegotiate the contract terms, or to cancel the contract. Here are a few ways inspection issues can be resolved.

- **Buyer agrees to purchase the house as-is**. In some cases, the buyer will decide to proceed with the purchase even if there are major problems. Sometimes, the buyer will have no choice because the seller will not make repairs or change the contract (HUD).
- **Seller agrees to make repairs**. Often, a seller will agree to make repairs after the inspection. The seller may agree to make all the repairs the buyer requests or negotiate to make some of the repairs.
- **Seller agrees to lower the price or renegotiate other terms**. The buyer may ask the seller to lower the price, or the seller may offer to lower the price after the buyer requests repairs be made. The seller can also agree to lower the price and make some repairs.

Buyers can ask the seller to repair whatever they want or lower the price to whatever they want, but the seller does not have to agree to anything. If the seller and buyer cannot come to an agreement on what to fix or how much to renegotiate, the contract will fail.

Why would a buyer waive an inspection?

In most circumstances, it makes sense to perform an inspection. Most buyers do not have the expertise to know what problems they may encounter. A professional contractor or inspector can discover problems and determine their severity. An inspection also gives a buyer the chance to ask for repairs or renegotiate the contract. I recommend almost all buyers request an inspection.

Having said that, I have not ordered an inspection or asked for an inspection contingency on the last ten houses I have bought. When you waive your inspection contingency, your offer becomes much more attractive to the seller and, your offer has a better chance of being accepted. This is a great tactic to use in a very competitive market when there are few deals. It is also a great tactic to use in a multiple-offer situation.

Do not waive an inspection if you are not very experienced with buying houses, knowing what repairs are possible, or knowing how much they will cost!

Why do I feel comfortable buying houses without an inspection?

I have a lot of experience with repairs. I even repaired a flip myself a few years ago, which did not go as planned but sure taught me a lot! Houses can have many problems, and you must know what to look at:

- Foundations
- Roofs
- Plumbing
- Electrical
- HVAC (heating and cooling)
- Mold
- Asbestos
- Siding
- Wood rot

These are just some of the areas serious problems can occur. You should review each of these areas. These issues do not include cosmetic or obvious visual problems like:

- Kitchens.
- Baths.
- Fixtures.
- Paint.
- Carpet.
- Doors.

- Windows.

Not only do you have to be able to tell when there is a problem, you must also know how much it will cost to repair these items. When I buy flips or rental properties, I buy them at huge discounts. When I estimate the cost of repairs, I always budget extra money for things I may miss or discover during the rehab. I never assume a house only needs the work I can see, which is another reason I feel comfortable buying houses without an inspection.

Why are HUD inspections different from traditional sale inspections?

HUD homes and some REO sales have much different guidelines than traditional sales. HUD homes are government-owned foreclosures. For owner-occupants, HUD allows the buyer a 15-day inspection period. The buyer must pay for the utilities to be turned on for the inspection, and in some cases, HUD will not allow the water to be turned on. HUD orders pre-inspections on their houses, and they do a pressure test on the plumbing system. If the plumbing system does not hold water, HUD will not allow the water to be turned on for the inspection or appraisal.

The inspection HUD orders before listing the house provides some information, but the utilities are not usually on when that inspection is done. I would never rely solely on the HUD inspection; I would get my own inspection on HUD homes. HUD publishes the findings of that inspection (it is called the PCR) on Hudhomestore.com under addendums. This is important to know because if HUD lists something on the PCR that requires repairs, the buyer cannot use that as a reason to get their earnest money back. If the buyer of a HUD home finds an inspection problem and they want to cancel, it must be due to a new problem that HUD did not disclose.

HUD will also not make any repairs or lower the price based on the inspection, and investors are treated differently than owner occupants. An investor will not get their earnest money back due to any inspection problems on a HUD home.

Is it safe to waive an inspection if a house is pre-inspected?

I have already talked about why you should not trust a HUD inspection and should have your own done. Some traditional listings will advertise that they are pre-inspected. I think pre-inspections are a good sign, but again, it is best to request your own inspection. Inspections are relatively cheap compared to the cost of the problems they uncover. Even if a house is pre-inspected, order your own to confirm nothing was missed.

Is it wise to use an inspection contingency as a negotiating tool?

If you find major problems you did not know about, requesting repairs or asking for a lower price makes sense. Some buyers will make an offer with the intention of asking for a price reduction no matter how the inspection turns out. I never do this, and I find it to be dishonest and unethical. For investors who buy many houses, it can also hurt your chances of getting a great deal.

I have seen some deals fall apart because buyers tried to use this tactic, and it made the sellers and real estate agents very unhappy. When investors buy a lot of houses, they will make offers to the same agents repeatedly. If I notice a buyer always asks for ridiculous inspection items or price reductions, I will let my seller know before they accept their offer. If a buyer or real estate agent gets a reputation for renegotiating every offer on inspection, it will make it harder for their offers to be accepted.

A buyer on one of my REO listings asked for every single item listed in the inspection report. They asked the bank to repair 40 items. The bank responded "no" to everything. Had the buyer asked for repairs on a few major things, the bank most likely would have agreed. But because the buyer asked for everything, it hurt them. The funny thing, is once the bank said no, the buyers continued with the contract and bought the house!

How to find a great inspector.

When you use a real estate agent, they should suggest inspectors in your area. You can also find inspectors online, but I would use a professional's recommendation. There are many inspectors, and in some states, they do not need any training or licenses.

I would interview any inspector before you use them, and make sure you are comfortable with their knowledge and services. Some inspectors will nitpick even minor issues, and some will not be very thorough and could miss major issues. A good real estate agent can help you choose the right inspector as well as help you review the report.

Conclusion

Inspections are very important to buyers who don't buy many houses. Even if you buy multiple properties, if you waive an inspection, you must know what issues to look for and how to estimate repair costs. If you waive your inspection, you can get out of a contract but may lose your earnest money in the process. My advice to most is always request an inspection.

CHAPTER 19

What Is Title Insurance and Who Pays for It?

When buying or selling a house, it is important to know what title insurance is and how it works. Typically, the seller pays for the title insurance, and it guarantees the buyer will get clear title. Clear title means there are no other liens or loans from the previous owner that are not paid off at closing. There are different types of title insurance coverage and different types of deeds a buyer can get when purchasing a house. Every state has different laws, and it is important you check with local experts to make sure you know how title insurance works in your area and what the costs are. There are also some instances where you cannot get title insurance, which greatly increases the risks for a buyer.

Why does a buyer need title insurance?

Buyers should get title insurance to ensure a lien or loan they are not responsible for is not attached to the property. A contractor can attach a lien to a property if they are not paid for a completed job. If someone does not pay a credit card bill, a judgement can be placed against the person and their house. When you get a loan on a house, the lender uses your house as collateral. If you sell that house, the loan must be paid off. If a loan, judgement, lien, or any other encumbrance is still owed when a house it sells, the new buyer will have to remove that encumbrance before they can sell or refinance.

If a buyer is a getting a loan, the lender will almost always require title insurance. The lender requires this to make sure there are no liens or judgments that could still be owed on the house. Those liens have priority over the new loan if they are not paid off before the sale. Property taxes almost always take priority, and if they are not paid, someone could buy the house through a tax auction. This would wipe out any loans, and the lender would lose all their money.

When they issue title insurance, title companies guarantee all the liens or previous issues on the title are clear before the buyer takes ownership. If the title company misses anything, they will fix the problem at their own cost. As an agent and investor myself, I have seen a few cases where the title company missed problems with the title. In one case, HUD did not actually own a house when they sold it! HUD found the mistake 6 months after selling the house. Luckily, the buyer paid for title insurance, and the title company fixed the problem.

Why does the seller pay for title insurance, and how much does it cost?

Different states have different title insurance rules. Some states, like Texas, mandate how much title companies can pay for insurance. Title insurance in Texas is much more expensive than it is in Colorado. In some states, attorneys may be used for closings and in others, title companies may be used. It is important to talk to your real estate agent to see how title insurance works in your area and how much it costs. In Colorado, title insurance for a $200,000 house might cost $1,000, but in Texas, it could cost twice that amount. In states that use attorneys, the cost could be even higher.

The seller typically pays the real estate commissions and title insurance. The seller pays for these costs because buyers usually do not have much extra cash. The seller will earn money from the sale. The more costs a seller can cover, the more buyers there will be and the higher house prices will be. Even though the seller pays for this cost, it benefits them in the end because housing prices will be higher than if the buyer paid for those costs.

When doesn't the seller pay title insurance?

The law does not require the seller to pay for title insurance, but this practice has been adopted in most areas.

HUD does not pay for title insurance when they sell houses. If you buy a house from some auctions or foreclosure sales, you may not receive title insurance from the seller either. The buyer can still get title insurance in most cases, but they will have to pay for it themselves.

With some bank REOs (foreclosures), the bank will agree to pay for title insurance if the buyer uses their title company. Typically, the seller chooses the title company who will close a transaction, and the buyer usually picks the same title company. If the buyer decides to use the bank's title company, the bank will pay for title insurance, but if the buyer chooses a different title company, the bank will not pay for any of the title insurance or closing fees. Usually, the buyer and seller split the closing fee, which is what an attorney or title company charges to complete a closing.

A seller might wonder: if banks and HUD do not have to pay for title insurance, why should I? Most REO properties and HUD homes are priced below market value, so the buyer gets a good deal. If you want to sell your house for less money and avoid paying title insurance, you could do that, but it doesn't make much sense.

Buyers must be very careful about buying houses from foreclosure auctions. Usually, there is no title insurance guaranteeing title on these houses. There is even the chance a buyer could purchase a house at a foreclosure sale that has other loans against it that must be paid. You could pay $50,000 for a house at the foreclosure sale thinking you got an awesome deal but later find out you are responsible for an additional $150,000 loan!

Why do different sellers offer different types of deeds?

Another thing to watch out for when buying houses is the type of deed the seller offers. In most cases, a general-warranty deed is used, which transfers all the sellers' rights to the new owner and guarantees full title. A special-warranty deed could also be offered, but that only guarantees title for any liens that occurred since the current seller took ownership of the property. Most REO sellers offer a special-warranty deed, and although it sounds a little risky, I have never had any problems with a lien from the previous owner showing up later. Banks foreclose on properties they own, and the foreclosure process wipes out almost all liens. The title company still can find any liens that do survive (property taxes and city liens usually survive a foreclosure), and they're not a secret to the buyer.

The riskiest type of deed is a quit-claim deed, which guarantees nothing. Most title companies will not insure a quit-claim deed. REO sellers, in online auctions, sometimes offer these. All this deed does is transfer title from one owner to another, and it does not require any liens to be paid off. The owner could owe $500,000 and quit-claim that house to someone else without paying any of those liens. The liens stay with the house. This is basically the same deed that is given to someone who buys a house from a foreclosure auction. A foreclosure auction is the auction the sheriff, trustee, or courts conduct to complete a foreclosure. An REO auction is an auction that is conducted on houses that have already gone through the foreclosure auction and are already owned by the bank.

On most transactions, the buyer will receive a general-warranty deed, and they will not have to worry about the other types of deeds. When you get title insurance, the title company or attorney can advise the buyer what protections they will receive with the title insurance. As you can see, figuring out how different deeds and liens are handled can be complicated.

What are some other things to consider with title insurance?

Some states also have basic and extended-coverage title insurance. Basic title insurance insures against any recorded liens, and extended coverage insures against unrecorded liens. Extended coverage costs extra, and some sellers will not pay for it (HUD, REO), but it is usually a good idea to get full coverage on any house you buy.

If you are flipping houses, some title companies will offer hold-open policies, which allow someone to buy a house and pay more for the policy. If the buyer sells that house within a certain timeframe, that same policy can be used without purchasing a new policy. This can save the buyer a lot of money on title insurance.

Conclusion

Title insurance can be confusing, but the title company or attorney you use to buy or sell can walk you through how it works in your state. Most buyers will never have an issue with title insurance or deeds, but you must be very careful when buying from auctions—or when buying without a title company or attorney.

CHAPTER 20

What Is Earnest Money and Who Pays It?

When a buyer agrees to purchase a property, the buyer usually pays the seller earnest money as a deposit on the house. This amount varies based on the type of deal and the price of the house. In most cases, the earnest money is also refundable based on certain contingencies. Those contingencies may involve an inspection, an appraisal, the buyer's loan, homeowner's insurance, a survey, or many other items. Usually, the earnest money tends to be about 1 percent of the purchase price. Using earnest money and contingencies is very common with real estate in the United States, and there are many ways to use earnest money and contingencies to a buyer's or seller's advantage.

How much is the earnest money on most houses?

The earnest-money amount varies based on the buyer, the seller, and the deal. The amount can also vary based on location or the state. Typically, earnest money totals about 1 percent of the price of the house, but not always. For houses in the $100,000 to $150,000 range, the earnest money usually totals $1,000. For houses in the $200,000 to $300,000 range the earnest money might be $2,000 to $2,500. The minimum earnest money amount usually totals $1,000, although I have seen it as low as $500.

In some instances, the earnest money could be more. With some REO sellers (banks selling foreclosures), the earnest money could be as high as 10 percent of the price of the house. Fannie Mae requires 10 percent earnest money on offers made with cash. A buyer could also increase the earnest-money amount if they want to make their offer appear better than others.

How is earnest money paid?

Earnest money is usually paid within a couple of days of all parties signing the contract. Most sellers will accept personal checks, but some may require certified funds. HUD and some banks that are selling their foreclosures will require a cashier's check or money order. The company holding the earnest money check will cash it as soon as they receive it. You cannot ask them to hold it until you have enough money to cover it. If the seller does not receive the earnest money in a timely manner, they can cancel the contract. Some sellers, before they even look at an offer, will also require the earnest money check with the offer.

What if the buyer does not have enough cash for the earnest money?

Some buyers can qualify for loans with very little money down. VA loans require no down payment, and the buyer will sometimes get money back at closing. Sometimes, a buyer must sell their house before buying another, and they must use the proceeds from the sale to pay for both the new house and the earnest money. The buyer may just need to wait until they get paid again before they can afford earnest money. There are ways to get a seller to accept a contract without paying the earnest money right away.

Buyers can use what is called a promissory note, which is basically a loan from the seller to the buyer. The buyer will agree to pay the earnest money at some point in the future. Even though you can write an offer with a promissory note, seller doesn't have to accept it. When a buyer uses a promissory note, the seller may have serious questions about the buyer's ability to buy the house. If the buyer cannot pay the earnest money, will they really be able to afford an entire house? I think it is best to avoid using promissory notes if at all possible.

Who holds the earnest money?

The buyer does not pay the seller directly. In Colorado, and in many other states, title companies handle all transactions. The title company or attorney will hold the earnest money until the sale closes or it is released to one of the parties. The real estate agent's office, or other parties, may also hold it.

Is the earnest money non-refundable?

Earnest money is typically refundable. The buyer has many opportunities to back out of the deal and still get their earnest money back. When a buyer (usually the buyer's agent) presents an offer to the seller, it contains contingencies. Contingencies are things the buyer or seller must be satisfied with by a certain date for the contract to continue. If one party finds something they deem unsatisfactory, they must notify the other party in writing of their objection by the date listed in the contract. Here is an example of the process:

- The buyer has until July 15th to complete their inspection.
- The buyer learns the roof is bad, and they want it fixed.
- The buyer must send the seller (usually seller's agent) an inspection objection notice by July 15th or sooner notifying the seller that they must agree to repair the roof by the time the house closes or the contract will terminate.
- If the seller agrees, the contract continues, the seller must get the roof fixed, and everyone is happy.
- If the seller refuses to have the roof fixed, the contract will terminate and the buyer will get their earnest money back as long as they notified the seller by the contingency date.
- The seller can also counter the request with another solution.

There also could be contingencies for many other items:

- **Title:** This ensures the seller has clear title and can sell the house legally.
- **House insurance:** In some cases, insuring a house can be tough if there have been too many claims in the past.
- **Appraisal:** Most lenders will require an appraisal, which values the house and notes if there are any repairs needed for the loan.
- **Survey or ILC:** Some lenders will require a survey or Improvement Location Certificate (ILC) to show exactly where the lot lines are and make sure there are no boundary problems.
- **Loan approval:** The buyer must get their loan approved or give notice that they cannot get their loan.
- **Conditional sale:** When a buyer must sell their house before they can buy a house themselves, they sometimes will have a contingency for when their house must sell or go under contract.

There can be many other contingencies having to do with HOAs, leases, disclosures, and much more.

What if the buyer cannot meet some of the deadlines?

If the buyer needs more time for loan approval, they do not have to terminate the contract. They can ask the seller for more time by sending them an extension. The seller does not have to agree to the extension, but it gives notice to the seller that they must sign the extension or the contract will terminate and the buyer will get their earnest money back. Usually, the seller will agree to extensions if they are reasonable and there is a valid reason behind the extension.

What if the buyer just wants to get out of the contract?

If the buyer decides they either should not or do not want to buy a house, they can usually get out of the contract. In Colorado, if the buyer is still in the inspection period, they can terminate the contract without any reason or without giving the seller a chance to fix anything and get their earnest money back. This has happened to me during a sale, and it can be frustrating, but there is nothing the seller can do.

If the buyer is past the inspection deadline, they may still be able to get out of the contract and get their earnest money back. They could ask their lender to say they no longer can get the loan or use another contingency to wiggle their way out. This is not exactly ethical, but it does happen.

What happens if the buyer and seller cannot agree on who gets the earnest money?

Occasionally, earnest money disputes—where the buyer and seller cannot decide who gets the earnest money—arise. In some cases, a date was missed but the buyer thinks the seller was not acting in good faith. The seller may not have fixed something, and the buyer thinks they should have fixed it due to an inspection request. Or one real estate agent may not have sent a timely notice to another agent. If there is an earnest money dispute, the party holding the earnest money will not release to either party until a solution is reached. If there is an active dispute, the seller will not be able to sell to another party, which puts the seller at a disadvantage.

If there is a dispute, most contracts allow the buyer and seller to agree to go to arbitration or mediation. If the buyer and seller cannot come to an agreement regarding the earnest money, they will have to pay a third party, who will determine the recipient. The cost to involve a third party is usually as much as the earnest money. It is very rare for both parties not to come to some type of agreement on the recipient of the money.

How can you use earnest money to get a better deal?

When I buy investment properties, I will waive my inspection and all contingencies...except for clear title. This lets the seller know I am serious about buying the house, and this often means my offer will be accepted over higher offers that contain more contingencies. When I remove my contingencies, the seller knows that if I back out of the contract, they will get my earnest money. Other buyers who have contingencies may keep the house under contract for weeks, and the buyer could back out and get their earnest money back.

Increasing the earnest money amount and removing your contingencies is another strategy. This really lets the seller know you are serious about buying the house if your offer is accepted.

Earnest money is a requirement in almost every transaction. You can try to get away with avoiding it, but it will make your offer much less desirable. In today's hot real estate market, I try to make my offers more desirable. I don't nickel and dime the seller. In most cases, if you are working with a good real estate agent and lender, any problems should result in you earning a refund of your earnest money.

CHAPTER 21

What Must the Seller Disclose?

Sellers must disclose any known material facts, which are physical flaws in or on the house. The seller typically uses a seller's property disclosure to disclose these facts. Sellers, by law, do not need to fill out a disclosure in all states, but it is commonly used. Sellers provide this disclosure to any potential buyers, or they can wait to provide it until the house is under contract. The homeowner must disclose what they whether they use a property disclosure or not. In some states, you must disclose more than just material facts, like if someone passed away in the house.

Why must sellers disclose these facts?

Houses can be very complicated, with heating systems, electrical systems, plumbing systems, structural systems, and much more. You can see many parts of the house, but you cannot see everything. An inspection won't even cover everything. You cannot tear off the drywall to see how much insulation there is or to view the wiring. You may not be able to see the foundation walls due to a finished basement. You may not know the basement floods every time it rains because it has not rained for weeks. You may not be able to tell there was a fire in the attic because access is blocked. Because a potential buyer cannot know everything about a house, laws are in place that require the current homeowner to disclose what they know. The laws are different in every state, but for the most part sellers must disclose material facts.

What is a material fact?

The definition of material facts can vary from state to state. Typically, a material fact is something physically wrong with a property. Here are some examples:

- The roof leaks
- The basement floods
- The house has a severely cracked foundation
- The furnace has a cracked heating exchange
- The neighbors' garage partially extends onto the property
- The house does not legally conform to the lot
- There are high radon levels
- There are excess levels of mold

Many other items that can be considered material facts. "Material" means the fact is important to whomever is making a decision about the property. A homeowner does not have to disclose every single thing they know if it is not important. You probably don't have to tell the new buyers that an outlet cover is cracked or that some of the trees need to be trimmed. Material facts are major or even minor problems that someone would want to know about when buying the house.

When I bought my house a few years ago, we later learned the outside water line that runs under the deck was broken. The sellers did not disclose this, but it would have been nice to know, and it was a material fact.

If there is a problem but the seller fixes that problem, they may not have to disclose that fact. In Colorado, if a house was used to manufacture meth but was cleaned correctly, the seller may not have to disclose it.

Why do different states have different laws?

Every state has different laws regarding what a seller must disclose. States get to make their own laws for real estate transactions and real estate agents. It is very important you check with your local laws or real estate agent to see what must be disclosed in your area. In some states, you must disclose if someone passed away in the house, but in others you do not. Some states require that you disclose whether someone was murdered, but not if they passed away from natural causes. You may even have to disclose if your house is haunted! In New York, the courts ruled that a seller should have disclosed their house was haunted. However, in that case, the seller told everyone the house was haunted, including Reader's Digest. Since the seller very publicly stated the house was haunted, the courts decided the seller should have also told the buyer.

What is a seller's property disclosure?

Many states allow the seller to complete a property disclosure form, which provides buyers information about the house. The seller should complete this form on their own, without help from their real estate agent. The form includes information about all the major systems in the house, any problems with them, how old they are, etc. Many homeowners don't have this information or knowledge, and that is okay. You can mark that you don't know. Just make sure that you really don't know the answer if you mark it as such. Otherwise, it will seem like you're trying to hide something.

I have seen some sellers mark the entire property disclosure with a giant "X" and refuse to answer any question. They claimed they never lived in the house and didn't know anything about it. Technically, even if you never lived in a property, you still might know material facts. As a real estate investor with many rental properties and flips, I still fill out a property disclosure for every house I sell. Even though I may mark "I do not know" on most questions, I still take the time to complete one. I can also indicate when something was replaced, that the roof is new, that the appliances are new, etc., which may make the buyer feel better about the house. If you do not fill out a property disclosure or refuse to answer any questions, the buyer may think you are hiding something.

If a seller chooses not to complete a property disclosure, they're not absolved of the responsibility to disclose material facts.

What happens if the seller does not disclose material facts?

The tricky part to disclosing material facts is determining what a material fact is and then determining if the seller knew that fact. I think it is reasonable to assume that if the seller knows something is wrong that would cause most buyers to rethink the purchase, they should disclose it. Disclosing deaths or a haunting depends on state laws.

If the seller does not disclose something like a leaking roof, the buyer could sue them for damages. Whether the buyer wins the case or not would again depend on state laws and the magnitude of the issue. As a seller, it is important to remember that buyers have your house inspected. If the inspection reveals major problems and the contract fails, the seller may be required to disclose those problems to new buyers.

Conclusion

I think it is wise to over-disclose anything you know about your house. If you try to hide a major problem, the buyer will discover it eventually. You may end up in court, and it will cost you much more in the end than it would have if you were honest. If you have any questions, make sure you ask your real estate agent or attorney about local laws and local disclosure requirements.

CHAPTER 22

How Do HOAs and Covenants Work?

Most new neighborhoods have HOAs (homeowner's associations) and covenants. Covenants are neighborhood rules and guidelines that an owner must abide by. HOAs charge fees to enforce covenants, maintain parts of the neighborhood, or even maintain the houses themselves. HOAs and covenants are almost always attached to condos and townhomes and also to many single-family houses If you buy an older house, you may find there is no HOA, but you will still have to follow local government rules. There are pros and cons to HOAs and covenants. Some people like the rules because they keep the neighborhood looking nice, while others do not like someone telling them what they can and cannot do.

Why do HOAs and covenants exist?

Most cities and counties require any new subdivision (built in the last 20 years) to have an HOA and covenants. The local government wants new subdivisions to be visually appealing, have similar properties, and not be a blight on neighboring properties. HOAs help enforce the covenants, and they also maintain any common areas in the subdivisions. Almost all new subdivisions will have some form of common grass, walking areas, roads, fences, etc. that are not maintained by the city or county, but also aren't part of anyone's lot. Someone must maintain that property, and the HOA is the entity responsible.

People who can look for violations, account for fees, and approve any new projects run the HOA. With most newer subdivisions, if you want to build a garage, a shed, change your landscaping, or even change the exterior paint color, you might have to get approval from the HOA. The covenants will help guide the HOA on whether they should approve new projects or paint colors.

Our house was built in 2005, and our subdivision has an HOA. We are rebuilding our deck, have added a basketball hoop in our driveway, and have added a concrete patio and sidewalk. We needed HOA approval for all those projects. If we did not get approval and the HOA decided those projects were against the current covenants, the HOA could make us take out or redo the projects.

What legal right does the HOA have to enforce their rules?

HOAs are handled differently in every state, but most HOAs have the right to enforce their rules via fines. If the homeowner does not pay the fines, the HOA can place a lien against the house. If the homeowner does not pay the HOA dues, a lien can also be placed against the house. When a lien is placed, the house usually cannot be refinanced or sold until that lien is paid off. A lien can also show up on someone's credit and prevent them from getting a car loan or buying another house.

What kind of rules and regulations do most HOAs have?

Most local governments require new subdivisions to have basic building and outbuilding requirements. The houses, lots, and outbuildings must be somewhat similar in size and design. The city does not want a 1,000-square-foot ranch mixed in with a 5,000-square-foot, 2-story house. The city does this because a 1,000-square-foot house may decrease the value of the larger house next to it. A huge shop on a quarter acre lot will most likely block the view of the neighboring houses. Crazy paint colors can also detract from values in a neighborhood. In my opinion, I also think having every house look the same can detract from values. I think it is good to have some restrictions, but too many restrictions make a neighborhood boring.

Most HOAs will have these basic rules:

- Size of houses
- Size of lots
- Type of outbuildings allowed (no sheds are allowed in my neighborhood)
- Landscaping requirements (most HOAs require landscaping)
- Proximity to other houses and lot boundaries
- Restrictions on visible trash or debris
- Restrictions on parking RVs, work vehicles, or even outside parking for regular cars
- Fencing requirements (type of fence and size)
- Maintenance requirements (must mow your lawn, pull weeds, shovel snow, paint your house, etc.)

HOAs might have even more rules depending on the neighborhood:

- Paint color
- Type of roof shingle and color
- Number of trees in your yard (minimum or maximum)
- What percentage of your yard must be grass
- How many pets are allowed and what type

Some HOAs will have as many restrictions as they possibly can, while others will have very few. When you are buying a house, you should have the chance to review the HOA covenants to see what they do and do not allow.

What are the pros and cons of HOAs?

Some people love HOAs and some people hate them. The pros of HOAs are they keep a neighborhood looking clean and force homeowners to maintain their houses. If you live in a neighborhood with beautiful houses—except for the one right next to yours—it can greatly affect the value of your house. You can tell the difference between neighborhoods with HOAs and those without. Neighborhoods that do not have an HOA tend to have more outside debris, parked vehicles, and non-conforming houses. Some people love to have the freedom to park all their cars and trailers wherever they like, while others prefer a neighborhood with more restrictions.

HOAs also come with higher costs and fees, since the HOA must charge the homeowners for the services they provide.

How much are HOA fees?

HOA fees can be as little as $25 per year (there are a few HOAs in my area that have no fees) to thousands of dollars per month. Typically, an HOA will charge relative to what they provide. Many HOAs provide very basic common area maintenance. Other HOAs may include a pool, tennis courts, a gym, security, trash, water, exterior maintenance, and even insurance. Most of the extra services are provided on patio homes, town homes, or condos. It is very important to understand what the HOA will cover and what the fees run because it can affect how much of a loan you can qualify for.

Can HOA fees increase, and what are special assessments?

HOA fees can increase every year, but HOA members must usually vote on any changes. I have seen a local HOA increase their fees from $100 per month to over $200 per month in only a few years. They claim they need the extra money for maintenance, even though similar HOAs in the area charge around $100 and offer more services than the HOA charging $200.

HOAs must have a certain amount of reserves for repairs and maintenance. They must disclose what their balance sheet looks like, and with the help of an agent, you should be able to tell how healthy the HOA is. If they keep raising their fees every year, there is a good chance they will continue to raise them.

Special assessments are another big concern for people who live in an HOA. A special assessment is a one-time fee that an HOA can charge to every homeowner. Special assessments usually occur in HOAs where the association maintains buildings or a lot of land. If every condo needs a new roof, the HOA may not have enough money in reserves to pay for the roof. They can ask for a special assessment to be placed on every property. If the assessment is approved, everyone must pay that assessment, whether they voted for it or not. I have seen special assessments as high as $15,000 in my area and heard of much higher assessments in other parts of the country. The condition of the unit is something else to look out for if you are considering a townhome, condo, or patio home where the exterior maintenance is paid for by the HOA. If they need new roofs, siding, or paint, a special assessment may be in the works.

How can you avoid living in an area with an HOA?

Even though most new subdivisions will have an HOA and covenants, you do not have to live with an HOA. If you buy an older house (1990 or older), there is a good chance it will not have an HOA. If you buy a new house that is in the country and not part of a subdivision, it may not have an HOA. Even if you live in a house that is not covered by an HOA, that does not mean you can do whatever you want. Cities and counties will have their own building codes and maintenance requirements.

Most cities and counties have codes for lawn maintenance, weeds, parking, building size, etc. The government codes may not be as restrictive as HOA covenants, but they still must be followed. The government can also fine homeowners for code violations and place liens on properties.

Conclusion

HOAs and covenants have a purpose, but some HOAs go a little overboard. If you live in a townhome or condo, you also need to be wary of special assessments. Even without an HOA, you still must abide by local building and maintenance codes. Make sure you do your homework on any house you are considering that has an HOA.

CHAPTER 23

How Do You Buy Real Estate Below Market Value?

One of the keys to my strategy is to buy houses below market value. This is not easy to do and you cannot just call up a real estate agent and ask them to find you awesome deals from the MLS. It takes patience, hard work, the ability to act fast, and nerves. If you learn how to buy right, it is a lot of fun and you will make a lot of money.

I have bought every house I have owned, except for the first one, below market value. I bought my first house in 2022. I was 22, and I bought it for $188,000. I put at least $10,000 in materials and a lot of sweat equity into it over seven years. In 2009, I managed to sell it for $190,000. Talk about a huge disappointment! I learned that I could not depend on the market to increase to make money in real estate. I had to buy below market value and force equity into the property.

My next purchase was a foreclosure from the Public Trustee. We bought this house for $220,000 by borrowing money from my sister and father-in-law (I had to pay cash at the sale). I was able to refinance the property and pay them back in full. My wife and I lived in that house for three years, and thanks to an awesome deal and some market appreciation, we sold the house for $350,000. That was a tax-free profit since I lived in the house for at least two years. I used that money for the down payment on our current house.

Some of the techniques I describe in this section of the book may seem confusing, but you do not have to understand everything. You can get a great deal just using one of these methods. As you gain knowledge and confidence, you might be up for trying other methods to get even better deals.

How do you determine market value?

Determining market value is one of the most important factors in spotting a good deal. When you are fixing and flipping houses, market value is obviously the most important factor for determining profit. Actually, ARV (after repaired value) is the most important factor because you want to know what the house will sell for when it is fixed up. When you are buying long-term rental properties, the market value may not be as important as it is on a fix and flip. When you are buying a house as your primary residence, market value is extremely important.

You need to know the market value because you may have to sell one day. You may have to sell for many reasons, even though you may not plan to when you buy. You could have a financial setback, a medical problem, a relationship issue, or some other emergency. You may decide you do not like investing in rentals, or you may need the money for an incredible opportunity. I eventually want to own 100 rental properties, but if a better opportunity comes along and I need to sell some of my rentals, I will have no problem selling them for much more than I bought them.

The best way to gain equity is to buy houses below market value. The more equity you have in a property, the more money you will be able to take out when refinancing. I have refinanced 7 rental properties over the last four years and taken out over $200,000 in cash. They still have great cash flow even after the refinance because I got great deals on them. If I would have paid market value, I would not have been able to take out nearly as much money.

The easiest way to determine market value is to hire a professional. As an agent, I provide comparative market evaluations for sellers all the time. I also provide values for investors and buyers. The tricky part is convincing an agent that you are a serious and are not wasting their time

My advice is to be perfectly honest with agents. Tell them you are new and you are trying to figure market values. It helps if you have done some work first and can ask them if the value you came up with seems accurate. Then buy them lunch or give them something in return. Simple gestures like buying lunch can make a huge difference in convincing someone to help you.

Do not ask the agent for ridiculous things or make huge requests. Do not ask for 100 values or sales comps from the last two years for an entire town. I recently had an investor ask me for all the cash sold comps in the last year for metro Denver. Then he wanted me to put them all on an Excel sheet and email them to him. I had never talked to this investor prior to this request, and I was just a little put off that he expected me to put in hours and hours of work for him. He gave me no reason to do this work and did not even tell me why he wanted this information. To top it all off, I am not even in the Denver market!

If you're not an agent, how do you determine value?

I mentioned that it would be good to have your own value in mind when talking to an agent, but how do you come up with a value yourself? It is not easy to value a house unless you use a website like Zillow. However, Zillow is not always accurate. Some of the values were as much as 40 percent off when I compared my own values to theirs! I would not trust Zillow to provide a value, although you can get some great information from them.

I use sales comparables to determine property value. I compare multiple sales from the last six months that are as similar as possible to the house I am valuing. As an agent, I can easily pull up any sold comps I want from MLS. If you are not an agent, finding sold comparables isn't as easy. You can find sold comps online at Zillow and a few other websites, but you do not get all the information you need with those.

Zillow uses all the sold comps it can find: foreclosures, short sales, and sometimes trustee sales. The reason this is important is you do not always know if those were market sales or just sales. A trustee sale price could simply be the amount the bank was owed and not a market value. You also do not know what the condition of the sale was, what concessions there were, or the financing terms. You do not know how long a house was for sale, how many price changes there were, or if it was a short sale or REO. These are vital details for making an accurate valuation.

An investor who is not an agent may be able to determine a range of values from online comps, but you still need to talk to an agent to make sure your values are accurate. If you have a great agent, they will probably offer you sold comps in an area and make your life much easier!

It's also possible to use active listings to value properties. This method isn't easy because if a listing is active, it still may not sell for the asking price. In fact, it may not sell at all. Active comps do give you an idea of what is for sale in a neighborhood and what the competition is. I use active comps along with sold comps to value properties. You can use active comps for a broad value but not a solid value. The best way to use active comps for values is to track them over time. Keep track of the asking price, when they go under contract, and for how much they sell. When you know the history of a sale on a website like Zillow, that comp becomes much more valuable.

Adjusting for values

When you find sold and active comps that are similar to your subject, your work is not done. You then must decide if you need to adjust for the differences between the comparables and the property you are valuing.

If you are valuing a house with a one-car garage, and the sales comps have a two-car garage, you must make an adjustment. If the bedroom, bathroom, or room count is different, if square footage is different, if views, location, or anything else is different, you need to make adjustments. Coming up with the adjustment amount is the tricky part. Pricier houses have different adjustment amounts than less expensive ones. Different areas of the country put more value on certain amenities than other parts of the country. I cannot tell you exactly how much your adjustment should be because I am not in your market.

Again, a real estate agent can help you figure out how different amenities add value. When you look at enough homes and comparables, you should start to get an idea of how value features and size add. Getting to know your market and accurately figuring values and adjustments will take time.

Here are a few adjustments I would make on properties in the $200,000 price range:

- 1-car versus 2-car garage: $4,000 to $7,000 adjustment
- 3-bedroom versus 2-bedroom: $4,000 to $8,000 adjustment
- 1,500 square feet versus 1,200 square feet: $9,000 to $18,000 adjustment

A $4,000 adjustment for a bedroom does not seem like very much, but you must consider the house has more square footage that would add value as well. You should look at the entire picture when adjusting make sure the amounts make sense.

Adjustments are not an exact science, and you do not have to be exact. You should be able to tell what a house is worth within 5 percent of the value. If you can find houses that are 10 to 30 percent below market value, you will be in great shape.

What are the different ways to buy houses below market value?

There are many ways to purchase below market value, including buying REOs, short sales, estate sales, HUD homes, off-market properties, and even regular sales. Getting a great deal takes time, work, and the ability to act quickly. Knowing the market value is the first step in making sure you are getting a great deal.

CHAPTER 24

How to Buy Bank-Owned Properties (REOs) Below Market Value

REO (Real Estate Owned) is a term for properties banks have taken back through foreclosure. REO properties are usually listed in the MLS (Multiple Listing Service) by an REO listing agent. I am an REO listing agent myself, and I can tell you that each bank handles their REOs very differently. Some banks repair houses before they list them, and others do not fix anything. Some banks are willing to negotiate prices quite a bit, and others will hardly budge.

REOs are getting harder and harder to find due to the improving housing market. There are still some great deals, but usually the deals involve houses that need many repairs.

If you find a great deal on an REO, do not be surprised if you find yourself in a highest-and-best situation. Many banks ask for highest and best when they receive more than one offer. There is a ton of competition for REO properties right now, and multiple offers are not rare. Highest and best gives every buyer who made an offer a chance to raise his or her offer and hope it is good enough to get the property. In many highest-and-best situations, the winning offer is higher than the actual asking price. I will discuss highest and best in more detail later in this chapter, as many sellers now use it.

Many banks prefer a cash offer and sometimes they actually prefer an owner-occupant buyer. Sellers like Fannie Mae, Freddie Mac, and Wells Fargo only allow offers from owner-occupant buyers at the beginning of the listing period. This can be frustrating for investors looking for a good deal, but there is no way around their owner-occupant restrictions. It is against the law to pretend to be an owner-occupant when you will not be occupying the property.

You need a real estate agent to buy almost any REO property. Buyers see vacant REO properties and think that if they can just talk to the bank, the bank will sell it to them well below market value. The truth is that banks have strict house-selling requirements, and they almost never sell houses without putting them in the MLS system. Trying to contact the bank to get them to sell to you is almost always a huge waste of time unless they are a very small local bank.

Getting a great deal on REOs has become tougher as banks have strict requirements regarding who can bid and when they will review offers. A lot of my techniques do not work well on bank-owned properties because speed is not always important. However, banks will negotiate much more on properties that have been on the market an extended period. If a property has been for sale for 60 days or more, banks will sometimes look at low offers.

CHAPTER 25

How Can You Get a Great Deal on a HUD Home?

HUD (Department of Housing and Urban Development) homes can be an incredible opportunity for investors looking for a great deal. However, some investors are apprehensive about bidding on HUD homes because purchasing a HUD home is much different from purchasing a traditional listing or even an REO. HUD also gives owner-occupant buyers priority over investors. Once you know the HUD system, submitting bids and buying HUD homes becomes very easy. I happen to be a HUD listing broker, and I know the HUD system very well.

HUD homes are properties that have been repossessed by the bank after going through foreclosure. HUD homes were previously purchased with government-insured FHA loans. Many houses that have FHA loans and go through foreclosure return to HUD. When HUD becomes the owner, they sell the houses through local listing brokers such as myself and list them on www.hudhomestore.com. Hudhomestore.com lists all HUD homes for sale that are not currently under contract. Once a HUD home has an accepted bid, it is taken off Hudhomestore.com and the status in the MLS is changed to "under contract." HUD homes are sold in an online-auction format, and all bids must be submitted online by a licensed agent who is registered with HUD.

When can investors bid on HUD homes?

HUD has very strict owner-occupancy restrictions on the houses they sell. HUD has two main classifications for their properties: FHA insurable and uninsurable. On FHA insured HUD homes, only owner-occupants, nonprofits, and government agencies can bid the first 15 days that the house is on the market (typically called the owner-occupant-only period). For uninsured houses, the owner-occupancy-only bid period is the first five days. Investors can bid on HUD homes on the sixteenth day for insured properties and on the sixth day on uninsured ones.

When a HUD home goes under contract, HUD stops the daily count for it being on the market. If a HUD home goes under contract on the eleventh day and that contract falls apart, the house goes back on the market 11 days into the bid period. Therefore, some HUD homes have been for sale for 30 days but are still in the owner-occupant period. An investor can see whether a HUD home is insured or uninsured on the Hudhomestore website.

If a house is listed as only available to owner-occupants, an investor can see when they can bid by looking at the period deadline. The period deadline will tell you when the last bid will be accepted.

HUD typically changes the price on HUD homes every 35 to 50 days it is actively on the market. HUD does not begin a new owner-occupant bid period when they change the price. Investors can bid the first day after a price change.

What are the penalties if investors bid as owner-occupants?

A HUD home is federal property, which means that any crime committed involving a HUD property, is usually considered a felony. HUD is very clear that any investor who bids as an owner-occupant is **subject to two years in federal prison and up to $250,000 in fines**. HUD prosecutes investors who have been caught buying during the owner-occupant period. HUD also may take away the ability for the real estate agent representing the buyer and their office to sell HUD homes. HUD and other investors watch these properties looking for and reporting investors who break those rules.

Investors who make repairs to a HUD home or move anything onto it before closing are also committing a felony. Because HUD prefers owner-occupant buyers, it can be a great opportunity for regular buyers. It can be tough for owner-occupants to compete with investors for great deals because some investors can offer cash. HUD does not care what type of financing a buyer uses and gives preference to owner occupants.

Why are HUD homes a great way to buy below market value?

HUD orders an appraisal on each of their houses before listing them. That appraisal usually becomes the list price and determines how much HUD will take for the house. For whatever reason, many HUD appraisals come in very low compared to market value. Uninsured HUD homes (houses that need more than $5,000 in repairs) do not qualify for FHA loans. The more repairs that a HUD home needs, the better its chance of making it to the investor bid period. Investors are much more likely to buy uninsured houses. I have sold many HUD homes to investors who were able to flip the house or get a great deal on a rental property because the house needed a lot of work.

HUD uses different formulas in different areas of the country to determine how much less than list price they will accept. In Colorado, HUD usually does not take less than 90 percent of the list price unless the house becomes an aged asset. HUD considers a house to be an aged asset if it's actively been on the market for more than 60 days. In my market, once a HUD home becomes aged, HUD may accept 80 percent of the list price. If a HUD home is on the market for an extended period, they may take even less. However, discounts are figured on a case-by-case basis, and there is no across-the-board rule. In other parts of the country, I have seen HUD sell houses for 80 percent of the list price in the first month. On some aged assets, investors are getting HUD homes at 50 percent or less of list price.

If HUD receives a bid that is close to the price they will take, they may counter a buyer. It never hurts to submit a low offer to HUD; the worst they will do is reject your bid. HUD does not blackball investors who submit multiple offers; in fact, HUD encourages all bids be submitted no matter how low. The only exception is when an investor submits the same bid every single day. There is no need to resubmit a bid over and over, which may annoy HUD. HUD keeps track of the bids and usually notifies buyers of a price change or if they will now consider a bid that was too low in the past.

Speed is the key to an investor getting a HUD home. Many investors are waiting for HUD homes to make it to the investor bid period, and most good deals will be bid on the first day investors are eligible.

Investors can also use a trick on uninsured houses to gain an advantage over other investors. HUD opens bids the next business day after the five-day owner-occupant bid period expires. HUD does not open bids first thing in the morning; they usually open them mid-morning or later depending on how busy they are. At the beginning of the sixth day, an uninsured HUD home will be available for investors to bid on, even though HUD may be accepting an owner-occupant bid later in the day. Investors should always try to get their bid into the system on that sixth day because HUD homes tend to fall out of contract more than other properties.

If an owner-occupant cancels their contract, HUD moves on to any acceptably priced backup offers in their system before they put the house back on the market. If the contract is cancelled, an investor who bid on the sixth day could have their bid accepted before any other investors get a chance to bid.

Buyers should always have their real estate agent mark "yes to backup position" when bidding on a HUD home. There is no penalty to buyers if they mark "yes to backup position" and later decide they do not want the house. There is also a chance that HUD will accept an investor's low bid if HUD changes the price, making that low bid fall into an acceptable range to HUD.

How does HUD handle inspection periods?

A very important point to remember is HUD does not give earnest money back to investors if they cancel their contract. HUD very clearly states they consider investors "savvy," and if an investor cancels due to inspection items, the earnest money is forfeited to HUD. If an investor is using financing and their loan cannot be completed, they may get half of their earnest money back. I always tell investors to expect to lose their earnest money if they cancel a HUD contract. HUD also does not pay for title insurance or any closing fees that other sellers typically pay.

Owner occupants have a much easier time getting their earnest money back but still must be careful. HUD will not make any repairs even if the lender requires them. If you want to cancel due to an inspection issue, it needs to be something not already disclosed by HUD's inspection.

Conclusion

HUD homes can be a great deal for those who know how the system works. Getting used to the system and learning all the HUD dates and procedures can take some time. Many buyers shy away from HUD because it is different and can be confusing. This creates more opportunity for the people who are willing to learn the HUD system. My best advice is to find an agent who knows the HUD system very well.

CHAPTER 26

How to Buy Short Sales Below Market Value

Short sales are another great way for investors to find deals. Short sales are owned by private sellers who are selling the house for less than they owe the bank. In order to sell the home, the bank has to agree to take less money than what they are owed.

Historically, short sales could take up to six months or even a year to close because lenders were so slow to make a decision. In the last couple of years, banks have gotten much quicker at making decisions, and some short sales are approved in two weeks or less (some banks still take months). With many short sales, the first party to make an offer will get the house. You must act very quickly when a great short-sale deal comes on the market. Remember, even if the seller accepts your offer, there is no guarantee the bank will approve the offer. It is wise to wait to perform an inspection or start the loan process until you have written approval from the seller's bank that your short sale offer is accepted.

You must be careful when buying off-market properties as short sales. Banks are very strict about offers they accept. If a buyer and seller are using a short sale to sell a house but not disclosing all the terms to the bank, it could be considered fraud. A couple of years ago, short-sale fraud was the most investigated crime by the FBI. Most banks require that short sales be listed on the MLS by an agent, the buyer and seller cannot be related, and the properties sell for close to market value. A good real estate agent can help buyers navigate the short sale process.

CHAPTER 27

How to Buy Fair-Market Sales Below Market Value

Fair-market-sale houses are owned by a private seller who has enough equity to sell without having to involve the bank in the decision-making process (not a short sale). Finding great deals on fair-market sales is harder because sellers are usually not in a huge rush to sell below market value. In some cases, you can find a great deal on a fair-market sale.

I have purchased properties that were great deals from estates. Often, estates just want to get rid of the house because they have issues or creditors that need to be paid quickly. I have also purchased a house that the seller had recently bought as a foreclosure. It needed a lot of work, and the sellers did not have the money to complete the repairs. The market appreciated enough that they could sell the house.

Another way to buy below market value is to look for investor-owned houses. Investor-owned houses are usually rented out, and although it may be perfect for a first-time homebuyer, the first-time homebuyer cannot wait three months for the tenants to move out. The only choice for the investor is to sell the house to another investor at a discount. Investors also try to flip homes yet run out of money and must sell before the house repaired. As an owner-occupant buyer, if you have flexibility, you may be able to get a great deal on these types of houses.

Buying houses in rapidly appreciating markets also creates opportunity. Some real estate agents may not keep with current prices. I have bought multiple houses where the agent underpriced the property and I was the first to make an offer.

I buy many of my flips and rentals as fair market sales. We will talk about strategies for buying these properties later.

CHAPTER 28

How to Get Great Deals from the MLS

Some people will tell you that it is impossible to find great deals on the MLS (Multiple Listing Service). I buy almost all my flips and rentals from the MLS. Even if you are not an agent, you can still get deals from the MLS, but you must have a great agent helping you (more on that later). You can buy short sales, REOs, fair-market listings, and estate sales from the MLS. We have talked about what those properties are, but this section will go into detail on exactly how to buy them.

Many deals exist on the MLS if you know how to find them, and in my opinion, it is easier to buy from the MLS than from other places. I used to buy many of my fix-and-flips from trustee sales (foreclosure auction), but there is so much competition that prices are higher at the trustee sale than on the MLS! I would rather buy from the MLS, where I can complete an inspection, see the house, and get a loan.

I still buy REOs and short sales, but more of my purchases have been traditional or estate sales. Prices are rising in many areas of the country, and that creates opportunity for buyers. With rising prices, more fair-market sellers are able to sell their homes.

Some of those homeowners need to sell a house that is in poor condition. A house that needs repairs creates opportunities. The more work that is needed, the bigger discount it takes to sell. My fifth rental property was a fair-market sale. It needed a lot of work and was a great deal. I bought it for $88,000, and two and a half years later, it was worth $170,000. You can find detailed numbers about and videos of all my rentals on https://investfourmore.com.

How can rising prices create opportunity on the MLS?

With rising prices, real estate agents or sellers sometimes underprice houses. I recently bought a couple of houses that were underpriced, and either my offer was accepted right away, or I won a multiple-offer situation. Houses may be underpriced because the real estate agent did not know the true value of the house, either due to an increasing market or because the seller wanted to sell quickly.

My 9th and 10th rental properties were underpriced fair-market sales. I purchased the 9th rental property for $130,000, and with only $3,000 of work, it was worth $180,000. I purchased the 10th rental property for $99,000, and with a minimal amount of work, it was worth $150,000. Investors may see opportunity if a real estate agent is not paying attention to market-price increases, if a house needs some work, or if the sellers simply want to sell their house quickly.

Some sellers get into trouble and cannot make their payments for various reasons. If the market is stagnant or declining, these houses must be sold as short sales or they become foreclosures. When the market is strong, sellers are able to sell, but if they must do it quickly, they may be very motivated.

Being a real estate agent gives me a huge advantage when quickly submitting offers. I check MLS many times per day. As soon as I see a great deal, I look at the house as soon as possible. If I like it, I have my assistant write up an offer and send it to me with DocuSign, which allows me to sign the contract electronically on my phone and send to the seller almost immediately. By being an agent, having an assistant, and using DocuSign, I can send an offer less than an hour after a house is listed. Acting quickly is one of the most important things you can do when buying from the MLS.

Many REO sellers will not accept an offer right away, but many short- and fair-market sales will. Most banks, when selling their REOs, wait five days or longer before they will review offers. HUD, and some banks, use owner-occupied periods when a house is first listed. During this period, only owner-occupants can make offers. This is why short sales and fair markets sales can sometimes be better deals than REOs for investors, but owner-occupants have an advantage with REOs and HUD homes.

No matter what you do, it takes longer to submit an offer if you are not an agent. One way to speed things up is to ask your agent to set up property alerts for you. In my MLS, I can set up alerts to send an email as soon as specific properties that meet my given criteria are listed. I set these alerts so I will not miss a great deal on the MLS. I was able to buy my last fix-and-flip thanks to a property alert that told me the house was back on the market. Buyers can use sites such as Zillow and Realtor.com, but their listings are not always current. May listings that show for sale on Zillow are actually under contract. The best way to be able to submit offers quickly is to either have a great real estate agent or be one.

Offer the most you can in multiple-offer situations.

If you find a great deal, do not be cheap! Do not try to lowball an already great deal. Offer the most you can while still making it a great deal for you. You also do not want to stretch your limits. It does not make sense to buy a house that will not make you money.

I may try to offer a little less than I want to pay if I think I can get my offer in before any others. If the house is an amazing deal, I offer full price or sometimes more, hoping that the seller will sign my offer before any other offers come in.

When some sellers (most REOs) get more than one offer, they will ask for highest and best. They want every buyer who sent in an offer to make their very best offer, and the seller will choose the best offer. In a multiple-offer situation, I do not pay attention to the list price. I offer the most I can that will still make me my desired profit. Sometimes, I offer less than the listing price and sometimes I offer more. Do not be scared off by a multiple-offer situation!

Buyers always tell me they do not want to get in a bidding war. Why not? A bidding war means that a house is priced great and many people want it. Why would other people being interested in a house make you not want to buy it? I think too many people let their emotions get in the way, and they feel the seller should have just accepted their offer and ignored the other offers. Do not let your emotions stop you from getting a good deal! It makes no sense to withdraw your offer in a highest-and-best situation.

Make your offer more appealing to a seller by using cash or fewer contingencies

I am an experienced investor, and I am positioned to offer cash on a property if necessary. I also have a great portfolio lender that does not require an appraisal on loans under $100,000. Most sellers want quick and easy closings, so a cash offer is usually the most enticing to them. If you must use financing, use as few contingencies as you can. I am able to remove the appraisal contingency on most of my financed offers, and often I will even remove my inspection contingency.

By removing my inspection contingency on most of my transactions, I know that helped my offers be accepted. This is risky for someone who does not know what to look for in a house, but if you are getting a good enough deal and know what to look for, it may be a good strategy. A cash offer with no inspection contingency will often be accepted over a higher offer with financing and inspection contingencies. However, some sellers, such as HUD, only care about the net price to them and do not care if you use cash or a loan.

Use real estate agent mistakes to your advantage on the MLS

I have bought many houses from the MLS that were listed incorrectly. I bought a house from HUBZU, and the listing said there was no basement when in fact there was a full, finished basement with two bedrooms and a bath. I recently bought a rental that was listed as a three-bedroom, two-bath house, but it was actually a five-bedroom, two-bath house. You must know your market, pay attention to the listing photos, and confirm the information in the listing. Do not be afraid to look at many houses to find the few that are listed incorrectly. The more market knowledge you have and the more experience you gain, the easier it will be to spot the mistakes.

You need to be flexible when buying from the MLS

In some cases, the buyer cannot occupy some houses until months after the sale because there are tenants. In these situations, competition is reduced because most owner-occupants will not want to buy a house they cannot move into right away. Often, when you are trying to show the house, tenants can be difficult, or they may not keep the house presentable, which decreases the amount the seller can get. The worse the tenant is, the better deal a buyer can get!

How do you know when one seller is more motivated to negotiate than another?

When you flip houses or buy rentals, you must get an awesome deal to make any money. Ninety-seven percent of the houses on the MLS will not work for flipping because there is not enough profit after all the costs are considered. Some houses listed on the MLS can be awesome deals, but the list price does not indicate how much the seller is willing to take. I do not advocate submitting low offers on every house hoping one seller will accept 50 percent of list price. However, some sellers will take significantly less than asking price if you know what to look for.

- **Aged listings**: Some houses sit on the market for months without selling. Often, the sellers priced the house too high, it was hard to set up a showing on the house, the house needed major repairs, or other factors caused the house not to sell. Not every aged listing can be bought for much less than asking price, but some can. HUD homes that are on the market more than 60 days can sometimes be bought at a significant discount. Some sellers will not lower their price when their house does not sell but may take less than asking price. Submitting low offers on houses that have been on the market a long time doesn't hurt, but look for other signs as well.

- **MLS comments**: Some comments in the MLS descriptions shout: ***make a low offer!*** If you see the words "as-is," "seller motivated," "quick-close preferred," "cash deal," "no financing," "will not go FHA," "out-of-state owner," "needs work," "needs TLC," or anything else that indicates the house needs work and the seller wants it gone quickly, they may be more willing to negotiate.
- **Fast price changes**: If a house does not sell right away, the seller will usually lower the price. I see house prices lowered at around the 30- to 60-day mark in most cases. However, occasionally I see a house pop up on the market, and in only seven or ten days, the price changes. This indicates to me that the seller wants it gone quickly! The bigger the price change, the quicker they want it gone.
- **Back on the market**: Houses go under contract and then come back on the market all the time. However, in some cases, a failed contract can indicate a house with major problems, or it can also motivate the seller. When I see a house come back on the market at a decent price, I will ask the agent why it came back on the market. Sometimes the agent will indicate it was buyer financing or a problem with the inspection. In some cases, the agent will indicate the seller wants to get rid of the house because they were expecting it to sell and the contract fell apart. A house coming back on the market and the price changing at the same time indicates a very motivated seller! If a house repeatedly goes under contract then

comes back on the market, the seller may be motivated by a cash offer with no inspection to get the deal done.

How low should your offer be?

As I mentioned earlier, if the house is already an awesome deal, do not be afraid to offer list price or higher if the numbers work. Many of my deals were houses that I bought well below list price because I saw some of the situations mentioned above and knew that the sellers were motivated.

I rarely, if ever, submit an extremely low offer. I have never submitted an offer that was 50 percent or less than list price. When I submit a low offer, it is usually about 70 to 80 percent of list price. Offers lower than 70 percent of list price usually offend the seller, and even a 70 percent offer might offend them. I do not submit low offers on every house on the MLS, but I select listings that I think will be more likely to negotiate.

When I make my first offer, I do not offer the most I can pay. I leave some room for negotiation because the seller most likely won't accept my low offer. I recently bought a house listed for $109,900. This was a good price, although not for a flip because of the work needed. Seven days after the house was listed, the seller lowered the price to $104,900. I noticed in the comments that the house needed TLC, was dirty because previous tenants had just moved out, and would not qualify for financing. This was music to my ears! I knew the seller was motivated because they would not spend $150 to clean the house. I offered $80,000 with no inspection and a cash-closing in 20 days. The seller countered at $85,000, which I happily accepted. Often, the seller will want to negotiate at least a little so they feel like they got the most money they could.

What if the seller will not come down low enough to make a deal?

Not every offer I make is accepted. In fact, I don't end up buying most houses I make offers on. If you want to get a great deal, you cannot be afraid to have your offer rejected or to see someone else get a deal you were hoping to buy. The best way to get into trouble is paying too much. If the seller will not come down to a price that makes sense for you, do not force the issue and pay too much! Even if the seller does not accept your offer, you still may get the house later.

If I make a low offer, I can usually tell how motivated the seller is. If the seller rejects my offer or acts offended over it, I forget about the house and move on. It is not worth my time to negotiate back and forth if the seller won't come close to my price. If the seller comes down significantly from their list price, I know I have a chance of getting something together. Sometimes we cannot get together on the price or they accept another offer. In those cases, I am always polite and ask their agent to let me know if anything changes or if the seller is interested in my offer later. Often, the first accepted offer falls apart because it was an owner-occupant who later realized how much work the house needed, or maybe a wholesaler got the house under contract but could not find a buyer. Do not give up if another offer is accepted, and do not burn bridges.

Should you try to negotiate inspection items with the seller?

When I make offers, I do not ask for an inspection period. I have enough experience to know what major issues to look for and what repairs are needed. I would suggest proceeding with the inspection if you are not very experienced. Waiving the inspection period gets me many deals, especially when a house comes back on the market. Many of the houses I am interested in have motivated sellers who want to sell fast. If they put the house back on the market due to inspection problems, it costs them time and money. Every time a house comes back on the market, buyers wonder what is wrong with it, and the seller will not get as high of a price.

If I make an offer without an inspection or financing contingency, the seller knows they will get my earnest money if I do not buy. This gives me an advantage, and I have bought many houses at a lower price than other investors were offering because I waved my inspection.

They assume they will be able to use the inspection to ask for a lower price and get the house cheaper. I do not do this because I feel it is not operating in good faith. While this tactic may work a couple of times, it will also give the buyer a reputation of always asking for a lower price on inspection. Another reason I get so many deals is agents know me and know I do not play games. If I write a contract for a certain price, I buy the house at the price I say I will. Building a good reputation will give you a better chance of having your offers accepted in the future. If you are only going to buy a few houses, it may make sense to negotiate hard. If you want to be a serious investor, negotiating too hard can hurt you in the long run.

Buying from the MLS is not impossible; it is actually my favorite way to buy houses. In my market, which is one of the hottest in the country, I still get deals all the time. You cannot use the excuse that buying from the MLS does not work in my market. There will always be deals on the MLS if you know how to spot them and can act quickly.

CHAPTER 29

How to Get Great Deals Below Market Value from Auctions

Buying a house from a foreclosure auction is another way to get a great deal, but this comes with risk. Auctions tend to have less competition because they have stricter requirements for buyers, and often you cannot inspect the house or even see the inside of it before buying. I have bought many houses from auctions over the years and made money on most, but I have also lost money on a few.

The fewer people you must compete with, the better chance you have of getting a great deal. Auction companies usually have strict criteria:

- **Cash purchases:** Many auctions require the buyer to pay cash. Foreclosure auctions may require the buyer to have cash the same day they bid or even before they bid on a property.
- **No inspections:** Many auctions do not allow buyers to inspect a house before they bid. In some cases, a house may be occupied and the buyer cannot inspect the interior until they buy. I am currently buying a house that is occupied, and I have never seen the interior. If the house is occupied, you cannot just kick out the occupant. You must evict them or possibly honor their lease if they have one.
- **Non-refundable earnest money**: With an auction property, if you back out of the contract for any reason, you usually do not get your earnest money back.
- **Short notice:** Some state foreclosure sales give buyers very little time to know what houses will be up for bid or what the starting bids will be. Other online auctions give buyers much more notice before an auction. In Colorado, we are given the sale list for properties two days before the sale.

- **Clear title**: Many foreclosure auctions do not guarantee clear title. There is no guarantee you are even bidding on the first loan.

These factors make it tough for most buyers to purchase houses from auctions. The majority of homebuyers are owner-occupants who need to get a loan. Most investors also need a loan to buy property, and auctions that require cash eliminate those buyers as well. Many buyers fear auctions because of the possibility of losing earnest money, the lack of inspections, and other issues. That usually leaves experienced investors to battle over the properties. The experienced investors know how much they can pay, can handle the risk, and still make money. Some online auctions are less risky than foreclosure auctions, which can provide opportunities for less-experienced buyers.

How does the foreclosure auction work in Colorado?

Different types of real estate auctions come with varying degrees of risk. The riskiest are local foreclosure sales because they require the quickest payment with the least amount of due diligence available. Every state has different laws regarding foreclosure auctions, which makes it very tough for inexperienced buyers. Make sure you know your local laws before bidding!

A foreclosure auction gives the public a chance to buy houses the bank or other lien holders are foreclosing on. Before the lien holder can take possession of the house through a foreclosure, they must offer it up for auction. The bank or lien holder will make a starting bid, which may be what is owed on the loan including late fees and interest. The bank can also start the bidding at less than what is owed.

If no one bids on the house at the foreclosure sale, the house will go back to the bank. However, investors—or even owner-occupied bidders—can buy houses at the foreclosure sale if they bid more than the banks bid (assuming the bank is not bidding as well, which is possible). I used to buy most of my fix and flips at the foreclosure sale in Colorado, and I even bought a personal residence at the foreclosure sale. For the most part, we stopped buying at the foreclosure sale because competition has increased, pushing prices too high. In my area, I can get a better deal on the MLS than I can at the foreclosure sale.

How the foreclosure sale works in Colorado:

- The pre-sale list, which lists the properties going up for sale, along with their starting bids, is published every Monday afternoon.
- The foreclosure sale occurs Wednesday morning at 10 a.m. You can call the public trustees office on Wednesday before the sale to see if the properties you are interested in are still going to auction.
- The auction is conducted at 10 a.m., and all bidders must register in person at the public trustee office before the auction. The auction is live and goes very quickly.
- The winning bidders have until noon on Wednesday to come back to the office with a cashier's check for the full amount of the bid. If the winning bidder does not show up, the second highest bidder is notified and given a chance to buy the property at their highest bid.
- There is a short redemption period (8 days) for junior lienholders. A junior lienholder can redeem the property by paying off the first bid amount in full plus interest.
- In Colorado, there is no guarantee you are bidding on a first loan or that you will get a clear title. The day before the sale (Tuesday), we would get an O & E (Ownership and Encumbrance report) from the title company, check out the house as much as we could, and decide if it is worth bidding.

What are the foreclosure laws in other states?

The process I outlined is only for Colorado. Other states have much different laws, and each state handles their auctions differently. Here are a few differences you may run into:

- Some states require proof of funds before the auction. This requires bringing cashier's checks for the amount you want to bid.
- Some states give much less notice about which houses will go up for sale and what the starting bids will be. I have heard that, in some areas, you have only a few hours to research properties before they are sold.
- Some states have an owner-redemption period, where the previous owner has a certain amount of time to pay off whoever won the bid and get the house back. Some states have redemption periods of up to six months!
- Make sure you know exactly how the foreclosure auctions in your state work before you bid. I have seen many new investors watch auctions for weeks to learn how they work. I have also seen new investors bid on a second loan, not realizing there was a first loan. That investor was still responsible for paying off the first loan!

How did I lose money on houses I bought at the foreclosure sale?

I have made a lot of money from houses I bought at foreclosure sales, but I have also lost money because of the nature of the auction.

On one deal, we were the winning bidder. We had an O & E that showed we were bidding on a first-position note, and we viewed the house before the sale. We looked through the windows and the house appeared to be completely vacant. After winning the property, we learned the previous owners had filed a lawsuit against the bank claiming the bank did not foreclose correctly. The lawsuit had not yet been recorded and we had no way of knowing about it. In the end, the lawsuit was thrown out, but it took the judge a year to look at the case, and we had to hold the property that entire time. After interest and carrying costs, we ended up losing money.

In many instances, I had to buy a house without seeing the interior. There are no open houses or showings when you buy at foreclosure sales. Some investors try to get into houses before the sale, but if caught they can be charged with trespassing or even breaking and entering.

You must consider how much repairs might cost if you're buying a house you can't view beforehand. I usually bought houses from the auction for purposes of flipping, so I knew what my repair budget could be to make a profit. I always assumed a house needed new flooring, paint, appliances, fixtures, and at least $5,000 in other repairs, depending on its age. Sometimes we got lucky and houses needed less work, but sometimes they needed more.

I also tried to talk to the occupants before the sale to get as much information as I could. Talking to someone about a house they're losing through a foreclosure is not a fun situation. Most people are actually friendly, and they will at least tell you if they are renting or if they own. Often, they have no idea how the process works, and you can build rapport by telling them how it works and what the timelines are.

Foreclosure auctions versus online REO auctions.

There are many types of auctions, and some banks use another auction to sell the house once they have completed the foreclosure. HUBZU, Homesearch.com, Auction.com, WilliamsandWilliams.com, HudsonandMarshall.com, Xome.com, and many more sites hold auctions for REO properties that the bank already owns. These auctions have much different terms than foreclosure sales, and it is much easier to buy from them. Online auctions for REO properties sometimes:

- allow financing.
- allow inspections.
- allow appraisals.
- give title insurance.
- pay a real estate agent commission.

Online auctions have different terms for different properties, and you must be very careful about what you are bidding on.

Buying a house at the foreclosure auction can be scary and very risky. I stopped because prices increased to a point where the risk was no longer worth the reward. Foreclosure inventory in Colorado has dropped significantly, and I think investors who counted on foreclosure sales for inventory had to increase the prices they pay because they did not know any other way to buy. I would not rule out buying from foreclosure sales, but I would also make sure you have multiple ways to get great deals as the market changes.

CHAPTER 30

How Can You Get a Great Deal from Real Estate Wholesalers?

Recently. I have been buying most of my properties from real estate wholesalers. I usually buy from the MLS, but I had a goal last year to find wholesalers so I could diversify my business. It took some time to find good wholesalers in my area (or let them find me). It can be frustrating because there are a lot of people who call themselves wholesalers who never wholesale a house. You must be diligent if you want to find wholesalers who actually have great deals.

What is wholesaling?

Wholesaling involves a real estate investor finding a great deal, getting it under contract, and usually finding another real estate investor to buy the property. A wholesaler could use a double close or an assignment to transfer the property to the new investor. The wholesaler usually does not do any work on the properties, and they do not use their own money to buy the property.

A double close involves the wholesaler buying the house and then selling the house the same day to another investor. The wholesaler does not need any money to buy the house because the title company uses the money from the end investor to pay the original seller. Not all title companies will do this, but some cater to investors and will. I have bought most of my wholesale deals using this technique.

An assignment is when the seller signs a contract to sell their property to the wholesaler, and the wholesaler then assigns that contract to another investor. The wholesaler will most likely use their own contract and not a state real estate contract with the seller. Not all contracts can be assigned. If you are dealing with REO properties or short sales, it is unlikely you can assign those contracts. Wholesalers make their money by charging more to the end investor than what they agree to pay the seller.

How does buying a house from a wholesaler work?

When a real estate investor buys a house from a wholesaler, it is much different from buying a house from the MLS. The investor does not have much flexibility on how long they have to close or other terms. Often, the investor must put down a non-refundable deposit, and they get no inspection. The houses are sold as-is, and no repairs will be made. These terms can make it tough to get a loan on a wholesale deal, especially if the lender needs an appraisal. It is tough to buy a wholesale deal as an owner occupant because of these restrictions.

Wholesale properties are not advertised on the MLS because most wholesalers are not real estate agents. They also do not want to pay real estate commissions. The wholesaler will find as many interested investors as they can and let them know whenever they have a deal. The wholesaler will usually send an e-mail to all their investors listing the price, repairs needed, terms, and their valuation of the house. I never trust these numbers and always verify everything myself. The wholesaler compiles a list of investors who want to see the property and meets the investors at the house (usually more than one at a time).

Every wholesaler does business a little differently, the way they choose the investor who gets the house can vary. In some cases, the first investor who says they want the house for the asking price will get it. Some wholesalers will use online forms to submit a contract, and the highest offer gets the deal. If there are not enough investors who want the deal, the wholesaler may negotiate their fee or try to get the seller to come down in price.

When I look at a property with other investors, I make sure to tell the wholesaler I want the deal as soon as possible. You cannot be timid and wait for the wholesaler to talk to you or finish talking to other investors. If you want it, tell them right away.

Why do most wholesalers never complete a deal?

The tricky part in dealing with wholesalers is they never do a deal. A lot of people who call themselves wholesalers because it is the most common type of investing taught, and many programs promise big money without using any of your own. A wholesaler sells houses to investors who want a great deal. They pay cash, waive the inspection, and must be very flexible on many of the terms. Investors who buy from wholesalers want a huge discount over MLS deals or it is not worth their trouble. The wholesaler must get an awesome deal that leaves room for them the investor to make money. Finding these deals takes a lot of time, effort, and marketing. I estimate that 90 percent of wholesalers never find a deal good enough to sell. Here are some problems I see with many wholesalers:

- They may find properties they think are deals, but they do not know market values well. They overestimate market value, underestimate the repairs, and don't really have a deal.
- They do not know how much profit an investor needs. Many flippers go by the 70 percent rule, and many wholesale prices do not have that much room for profit.
- They assume the repairs are the only cost and forget about carrying costs, selling costs, etc.
- They do not know how to market or have the money to market like they need to.
- They will not tell investors they have never done a deal, so when looking for a wholesaler, you must be very careful. You can waste a lot of time with wannabee wholesalers who will never send you a deal. If you find the right wholesaler they can be an awesome deal source.

How do you find a great wholesaler?

There are many ways to find wholesalers, but they are not all effective. Here are some of the ways I have found wholesalers and ways I have heard of others finding them:

- **Real estate investor meetups:** Most areas of the country have real estate investor meetups, and they can be a great place to network. I have met many wholesalers at meetups and have never seen a deal come from any of them. I am not saying that you cannot find a good wholesaler at a meetup, but that is where many new investors go.
- **Search online:** Many wholesalers set up websites for investors looking to buy deals. You can search online for wholesalers in your area, but again, whether they actually have deals can be hit or miss.
- **Ask around:** Some of the best ways to find wholesalers is to network with other investors, but they may not be keen on giving you their source. Besides investors, ask real estate agents, title companies, and other people in the business. Many wholesalers will e-mail real estate agents to find buyers.
- **Look for marketing:** If a wholesaler is marketing, you know they are at least trying to find deals. Instead of looking for wholesalers, look for their marketing. Look for bandit signs, billboards, Craigslist ads, Facebook posts, and call their number. Most wholesalers market by advertising they will buy houses fast for cash. Tell them you don't want to sell your house but you want to be on their buyer's list. If you receive a letter from someone wanting to buy your house, do not throw it away. Call them back and tell them you are a buyer.

I found the wholesalers I bought houses from by accident. One of them sent me an email because they wanted to know if I had clients who were interested in buying their deals. Two other wholesalers found me online through my blog. I spent a lot of time actively looking for wholesalers, and the only ones that worked out found me!

Finding a wholesaler is not easy, but it can be a great source of deals. Investors tell me there are no good wholesalers in their area. While most wholesalers may not be very good, almost every market (if it is decently sized) will have active wholesalers. If you are looking to buy in larger markets, I may even know some awesome wholesalers I can introduce you to.

Owner occupants can also buy deals from wholesalers, and they often use their own real estate agent to help them get the deal done. The main wholesaler I work with offers a commission to real estate agents who bring buyers.

Final Thoughts on Buying below Market Value

Buying below market value is the key to almost any successful real estate investing strategy. If you want to make money flipping or through rental properties, you will need to buy below market. If you are purchasing a personal residence, buying below market value gives you a huge financial advantage. While it is tough to buy below market value when starting out, you can still get a deal without waiving your inspection, without paying cash, and without looking at a house hours after it has been listed. However, getting those deals will be tougher if you cannot act quickly, waive an inspection, or pay cash.

If you are new to buying real estate, I don't recommend waiving inspections. Knowing whicn repairs are needed and knowing how much of a profit margin you need in order to absorb extra costs that may occur takes a lot of experience. When I buy flips or rentals and waive my inspection, I assume the house will need more work than what can be seen. Houses usually need more repairs than you think they will after you start working on them and uncovering things.

While cash deals are a great enticement to many sellers, some sellers, such as HUD, do not care. HUD does not care if you pay cash or use a loan. All they care about is the net price they receive. Often, I get approved for a loan, even though I make my offer in cash. I put a clause in the offer that says I have the cash to pay for the house if needed but may use financing from a portfolio lender.

If you learn anything from this book, it's that you should try to by all your houses below market value!

Part III: How to Get the Best Loan

Getting a loan is one of the most important parts of buying a house. Most people do not have the cash to buy a house outright, and even if you do have the cash, paying cash may not be the right move. A house can be a great investment, but it is not easy to sell or to get your money out of. If you pay cash, it takes time to refinance, take cash out, or sell to get cash out. If you want to refinance, there is no guarantee you can get a loan, even if you own the house free and clear. Many people who bought houses with cash have told me horror stories because they assumed they could refinance later but could not qualify for the refinance.

To refinance, you need to qualify for the loan just like you would if you were buying a house. You must have good credit, a good job, good debt-to-income ratio, and more. If you think you will want to get a loan on a house at some point, it is best to get the loan from the very beginning. You can usually get the best terms and rates on a first mortgage than you can on a refinance.

This section covers everything you need to know about getting a loan, the available loan options, and much more. It will also cover refinancing, lines of credit, and other options for financing your house. Most of the programs I talk about are for owner occupants. The loan rules for investors are very different. Keep in mind that, as an investor, you will have to put more money down, have better credit, and there will be limits on how many houses you can buy from traditional banks. There are ways to get more loans from non-traditional banks, but those subjects are covered in my books: Build a Rental Property Empire and Fix and Flip Your Way to Financial Freedom.

CHAPTER 31

How to Buy a House with Little Money Down

To buy a house in the past, you had to put at least 20 percent down. Government programs and private-lending programs now provide loans with much less money down. An owner-occupant can get into a house with less than 5 percent down, and in some cases, no money down. There are many loan options that offer a low down payment, but they are not available to everyone. This chapter will explain the different loan types and how they work.

Which loans allow for a smaller down payment?

Many owner-occupant loans allow for a small down payment. Most investor loans will require at least 20 or even 25 percent down. An owner-occupant has many more low-money-down options.

- **FHA loans:** FHA loans are government-insured loans that can be obtained with as little as 3.5 percent down. You can only have one FHA loan at a time unless you have extenuating circumstances like a job relocation. You must pay mortgage insurance, which I will discuss later. There are limits to the mortgage amount, which vary by state and even city.
- **USDA loans**: A USDA loan is a loan that can be used in rural areas and small towns. The loan can't be used in medium-sized towns or large towns/metro areas. The loan is for those who qualify and want to buy in the designated areas. USDA loans can be obtained with no money down but have mortgage insurance as well.
- **VA loans:** VA loans are run through the United States Veterans Administration. You must be a veteran to qualify for the loan, but they also can be

had with no money down and no mortgage insurance! VA loans are a great option for those who qualify because the costs are so much less without mortgage insurance.

- **Down payment assistance programs**: Many states have down payment assistance programs. In Colorado, we have a program called CHFA. The program helps buyers get into owner-occupied houses with very little money down. CHFA actually uses an FHA loan but allows for less than a 3.5 percent down payment. Later, I dedicate an entire chapter to down payment assistance programs.
- **Conventional mortgages**: For owner occupants, conventional mortgages offer down payments as low as 3 percent. You will most certainly have to pay mortgage insurance with any conventional loan that has less than 20 percent down.
- **FHA 203K Rehab loan:** An FHA 203K rehab loan allows the borrower to finance the house and finance the repairs they would like to complete after closing. This is a great loan if a house needs work yet the buyer has limited funds for completing those repairs. There are more upfront costs associated with this loan because two appraisals are needed and lenders charge higher fees. The same down payments and mortgage insurance will be needed as with a regular FHA loan.

Besides the down payment, what loan costs does a buyer need to consider?

With almost any loan, you will have more costs than the down payment. The lender will charge an origination fee, appraisal fee, prepaid interest, prepaid homeowners insurance, and possibly prepaid mortgage insurance. Plus, you may have costs like a closing fee, recording fee, and possibly title insurance. In most cases, the seller pays for title insurance, but with HUD and VA foreclosures, the buyer must pay for title insurance. These costs can add up to another 3.5 percent of the mortgage amount...or sometimes more. When you talk to a lender, they can give you an estimate of exactly how much these costs will be before you get your loan.

Reduce the amount of money needed to buy a house by asking the seller to pay closing costs.

Even though the lenders and title company will charge you more than just the down payment, you may not have to pay those fees up front. You can ask the seller to pay closing costs for you. If you can get the seller to pay your closing costs, you may obtain VA and USDA loans with no out-of-pocket cash. You may still have to put down an earnest money deposit, but that can be refunded at closing in some cases. When you ask the seller to pay closing costs, the amount of money they receive from the sale is reduced, so you might actually be paying more for the house than if you didn't ask for closing costs. But in my mind, paying a little more for the house and financing those costs to save cash is better than paying more money out-of-pocket for a little cheaper house.

For example, an offer of $102,000 with the seller paying $2,000 in closing costs is the same to the seller as an offer of $100,000 with the seller paying none of the closing costs.

How much does mortgage insurance add to monthly payments?

Mortgage insurance is an upfront fee paid at closing, a monthly premium paid on top of mortgage payments, or both. Mortgage insurance protects your lender when your down payment is less than 20 percent. Loans with a lower down payment are typically riskier, so the lender charges mortgage insurance to protect themselves in the event you default on the loan. Each loan type has different mortgage insurance amounts and time frames. With some loans, mortgage insurance can be removed after you have enough equity in the house.

A lower down payment increases the monthly payment.

Whenever you get a loan and put down less than 20 percent, your monthly payment will be higher. Not only does your payment increase because the loan amount increases, but the mortgage insurance will add even more to your mortgage payment. Often, the difference between a 20-percent-down loan and a 5-percent-down loan can be hundreds or thousands of dollars per month.

CHAPTER 32

Which Loan is Better: FHA or Conventional?

Owner-occupants looking to buy a property with little money down have several options. The government does not back conventional loans, but conventional loans offer low-down-payment options. In fact, conventional loans offer down payments of as low as 3 percent, and they also come with other advantages, such as lower mortgage insurance.

What are the advantages of an FHA mortgage?

FHA mortgages are federally insureds, and because of that, the down-payment requirements are low. Borrowers with a credit score as low as 580 can qualify for an FHA mortgage. Borrowers can also have a debt-to-income ratio of up to 52 percent. As I mentioned earlier, FHA mortgages allow for down payments as low as 3.5 percent. FHA is a great option for people with low credit scores and little money. Remember, just because the lender says you can qualify for a mortgage, it may not be a wise financial decision.

One downside to a low-money-down loan is you will almost always have mortgage insurance. On FHA loans, mortgage insurance is charged both when you first buy and every month thereafter. The cost for mortgage insurance on an FHA loan is 1.75 percent of the loan amount up front and between .8 and 1.05 percent of the loan every year. The mortgage insurance on an FHA loan can never be removed.

What are the advantages of a low-down-payment conventional loan?

The down payment on conventional mortgages for owner-occupied buyers can be as low as 3 percent. The great thing about some conventional mortgages is the mortgage insurance is lower and can be removed after a few years in some cases. Conventional mortgages have higher credit-score and debt-to-income requirements. With many conventional mortgages, the borrower's debt-to-income ratio cannot exceed 45 percent and their credit score cannot be lower than 620.

While it is tougher to get a conventional mortgage, the costs are usually lower and the mortgage insurance can be removed. If, after three years, the loan amount drops below 80 percent of the value of the house, many conventional loans will allow the mortgage insurance to be removed. The cost for mortgage insurance on conventional loans ranges from .5 to 1 percent of the loan amount, and usually it is not charged up front.

What if a house needs repairs that make it ineligible for a typical loan?

In some cases, a house may need repairs that will disqualify your ability to obtain a typical loan. FHA and conventional loans for owner-occupied buyers both require the house to be in livable condition. If a house needs a new roof, the plumbing won't work, or there are holes in the walls, it may not qualify for FHA or conventional loans. If you are buying a HUD home, a short sale, or an REO property, there is a good chance the seller will not fix these items.

Sometimes the best deals need the most work, which makes things difficult for owner-occupant buyers. However, there are ways for owner-occupants to qualify in these situations (more on that later).

Conclusion

Those looking to buy with little money down have many options. The scope of repairs, your credit score, your debt-to-income ratio, and other factors will determine which loan is best for you. Make sure you talk to your lender about your options and ask about down payment assistance programs as well.

CHAPTER 33

What is the Monthly Payment on a $200,000 house?

As a real estate agent, many people ask me how much their payment will be, whether the house is $100,000, $200,000, or $300,000. There is no one-size-fits-all answer because many factors will increase or decrease a mortgage payment. The down-payment amount, interest rate, terms, mortgage insurance, property taxes, and other factors will all determine your payment amount. Knowing your payment amount is very important because lenders will qualify borrowers based on their monthly income and monthly payments.

How are the principle and interest calculated?

The interest on a mortgage is not calculated strictly on the interest charged. With a basic-interest loan, a 10 percent interest rate on a $200,000 house is $20,000 per year, or $1,667 a month. However, mortgages are structured so you slowly pay down the principal as well. Your payments will be higher than the $1,667 monthly figure because you will also pay part of the principal each month. So, based on a 30-year mortgage, your monthly payment will be closer to $1,755. You pay less principal at the beginning of the loan than at the end. This is an amortization table that outlines the monthly payments for the first few years of a mortgage:

https://investfourmore.com/2016/05/02/how-much-would-my-payment-be-on-a-200000-house/

In this example, within two years the monthly principal amount increases from $88 to $108. Initially, you pay off the principal very slowly. The more time that goes by, the more you pay to principal and the less you pay to interest. In year ten, you'll pay close to $250 per month to principal.

Why are low interest rates important?

The lower the interest rate, the lower your mortgage payment. However, an interest rate of 5 percent does not equate to half the monthly payment over a rate of 10 percent. If the interest rate on a $200,000 loan is 5 percent (which is close to today's rates) your monthly payment will be $1,074. If your rate was 10 percent, the monthly payment would be $1,755. You pay almost $700 less per month in this example, but why isn't the payment even lower? After all, 5 percent is half of 10 percent, so shouldn't the payment be half as much? With the 5 percent interest rate, you pay monthly principal of $240 from the very beginning. The actual interest you pay is 50 percent less on the 5 percent loan, but you pay much more in principal.

Not only does a low-interest loan mean a smaller monthly payment with more going to principal, but you can also qualify for a more expensive house. Lenders qualify buyers on their debt-to-income ratios. The debt-to-income ratio is the percentage of monthly debt (credit cards, car payments, mortgage payments, etc.) compared to your monthly. Assuming an interest rate of 10 percent, your payment on a $200,000 mortgage would be $1,755. Maybe you can qualify for an $1,800 mortgage (counting principal and interest only), so at 10 percent you can qualify for a $200,000 loan. If rates were 5 percent, you could qualify for $330,000, and your monthly payment would only be $1,771. The higher interest rate, the more house you can qualify for. The really cool thing is that you will be paying off almost $400 per month in principal with the 5 percent, $330,000 loan, compared to only $88 per month with the 10 percent, $200,000 loan.

What else do you need to consider when calculating your monthly payment?

Up to this point, I have only talked about principal and interest; however, there is more to a payment. You must pay property taxes, homeowners insurance, and possibly mortgage insurance.

- **Property taxes:** This is how much the state, county and city charge you to own a house. These taxes pay for schools, roads, etc. Some states charge higher taxes than others. In Colorado, I pay about $1,000 to $1,500 per year in property taxes on a $200,000 house. In New Jersey you may pay $5,000 to $10,000 on a $200,000 house. That's a difference of $600 per month, just in taxes!
- **Insurance:** When you get a loan, the lender will require that you carry homeowners insurance. This protects the bank in case the house burns down or is destroyed by a tornado. Insurance varies by state based on the risk of weather or natural disasters. If the house is in a flood zone, the insurance can be very pricey.
- **Mortgage insurance**: Mortgage insurance can be hundreds of dollars a month and carry upfront costs as well.

When you factor in these costs, the payment on a $200,000 house will include much more than just the principal and interest.

- Principal and interest: $1,074
- Property taxes: $200
- Insurance: $70
- Mortgage insurance: $175
- **Total payment: $1,519**

Knowing your insurance, tax, and mortgage-insurance amounts is very important. These costs greatly affect your mortgage payment and your ability to qualify for a loan. If you put 5 percent down and live in a flood plain in New Jersey, you may pay $2,000 per month for your mortgage. If you put 20 percent down and you live in Colorado, you may pay $1,300 on the same loan amount.

What would your mortgage payment be on different loan amounts?

Payment amounts vary based on the size of the loan. Here is a chart outlining different principal and interest amounts on a 5 percent, 30-year loan.

Loan Amount	Payment
$50,000	$268
$100,000	$537
$150,000	$805
$200,000	$1,074
$250,000	$1,342
$300,000	$1,610
$500,000	$2,684
$1,000,000	$5,368

Remember, you should add the other costs I discussed to that payment amount to get your true payment.

How does a 15-year loan affect your mortgage payment?

Many people get 15-year loans because you pay less interest and pay off the loan more quickly. If we took that same $200,000 and used a 15-year loan instead, here is what would happen:

	30-year loan	15-year loan:
Payment	$1,074	$1,582
Principal	$240	$748

With a 15-year loan the payment and the amount of monthly principal paid every month increases by $508. That doesn't seem like a huge advantage, but the interest rate on a 15-year loan is usually lower than on a 30-year loan. Instead of paying 5 percent interest, you may only pay 4.5 percent, which lowers the monthly payment to $1,53, and increases the monthly principal paydown to $780.

Getting a 15-year mortgage may seem wise if you can afford it. However, I personally think 15-year mortgages are a bad idea for most people, especially if you want to invest in real estate. The higher payment makes it harder to qualify for more houses, you have less flexibility, and I don't think the savings is worth it. I also could invest that extra $500 per month into something that makes me much more money than what I would save over the life of a 15-year mortgage.

Conclusion

Monthly mortgage payments can vary greatly depending on the interest rate, taxes, insurance, and mortgage insurance. If you choose to get a 15-year mortgage, your payments may increase dramatically. I think it is obvious that no matter which loan you choose, today's low interest rates are a huge advantage.

CHAPTER 34

How to Qualify for a Loan

Qualifying for a loan is the first step in the house-buying process. It is often the first thing a potential buyer should do. It determines how much you can afford. Obviously, if you don't qualify, you cannot move on with the process. Banks review a few things during the qualifying process, including credit score, income, debts, and financial history.

The basics of qualifying for a mortgage

When qualifying you, most banks review multiple items:

- **Debt-to-income ratios:** This is your monthly income compared to your monthly debt payments. The percentages a bank will be comfortable with depend on the loan.
- **Time at job:** Most banks want to see a borrower working the same job for two years before approving a loan. Banks may be comfortable with you switching jobs yet staying in the same field. Banks verify income, which makes it very hard for retirees to get a loan.
- **Credit score:** Some loan programs allow credit scores under 600, but the lower your score, the more fees and costs you will pay.
- **Tax returns:** Banks will verify your income using tax returns. Getting a loan may prove difficult if you claim very little income.
- **Financial history:** A short sale, bankruptcy, foreclosure, or judgement on your record can greatly affect your ability to get a loan.

If you think you will have problems qualifying, the best thing you can do is talk to a lender as soon as possible. They can tell you what you need to fix, how long it will take to fix, and they will do this for free! There are many very expensive credit-repair companies out there, and most of them are not worth it. A lender can tell you if your credit is bad enough to warrant using a credit-repair company. The lender can also recommend a good company. Don't be scared to talk to a lender right away.

Is it harder for investors to qualify than it is for owner-occupants?

With new lending regulations, it is harder for investors to get a loan. If you are an investor and want to get a loan on more than four or more than ten properties, it really gets difficult.

One of the biggest issues investors run into is they must qualify for two houses if they have a loan on their personal residence. Because of this, it is very important to avoid buying the most expensive house you can qualify for. You must have a low debt-to-income ratio to qualify for a new loan whether you are an owner-occupant or an investor. If you max out your qualification on your personal residence, it will be very difficult to qualify for a loan on an investment property because your debt-to-income ratio goes up.

Most banks require at least 20 percent down on an investment property. Banks want investors to put more skin in the game. The origination fees, appraisal fee, and other loan costs may also be more expensive depending on the type of investment property you are buying.

Investors must also have more money in the bank than an owner-occupant. Most banks require at least six months in reserves for mortgage payments on all houses an investor owns, including the new loan. If you have a $1,000 mortgage payment on your personal residence and want to get a loan on an investment property with a $500 mortgage payment, you will need $9,000 in the bank on top of the money you need for the down payment and closing costs.

Most banks require investors looking to buy rental properties to have a higher credit score. After you have four mortgages, conventional lenders require at least a 720 credit score from investors. While some owner-occupied loans may allow a credit score under 600, do not expect to get a loan on an investment property with a credit score under 620.

CHAPTER 35

How to Lower Your Debt-to-Income Ratio

A high debt-to-income (DTI) ratio is one of the biggest obstacles to qualifying for a mortgage, whether on a personal residence or an investment property. Most lenders require DTI ratio of 45 percent or lower. Even my portfolio lender, who has very lenient lending requirements, will not lend to people with high DTI ratios. So how do you lower yours? Either make more money or pay down debt.

How is DTI calculated?

Your DTI ratio is calculated by taking your monthly debt payments and dividing them by your gross income before taxes. If you pay $2,000 to debt and earn $5,000 in gross income, your DTI ratio for the month is 40 percent ($2,000/$5,000 = 40 percent). That is a very simple equation, but other items factor into the DTI ratio.

You must also count the new mortgage payment. Even though your DTI ratio may currently be 35 percent, a new mortgage payment may push that number to 45 percent. The DTI ratio will generally be the deciding factor for the amount you can qualify for. The highest payment you can qualify for on a new mortgage is the payment that pushes you to the maximum DTI ratio allowed by the lender. If a lender allows a DTI ratio of 40 percent, and a $1,000 payment pushes you to 40 percent, that is the highest payment you could qualify for.

Banks pay attention to your monthly income and monthly debt payments...not your total balances. If you owe $2,000 on a credit card, you may think that affects your ability to qualify for a loan. But if your monthly payments are $200, that will have much more impact on the amount you qualify for. A $200 dollar monthly reduction in mortgage payments can reduce the amount you qualify for by as much as $40,000!

What expenses and income are included in DTI?

If you are applying for a loan, everyone who will be on the loan will have to include these debt payments:

- Minimum credit card payments
- Auto loans
- Student loans
- Consumer loans
- Other financial obligations including child support and alimony
- Your current mortgage payments (these do not count if you are going to sell the house before you buy the new house. If you are keeping the house you need to count the payments as debt.)
- Your estimated future housing expense, which includes principal, interest, taxes, insurance, and any HOA fees.

To calculate your income, you use:

- Your gross monthly salary before taxes, plus overtime and bonuses. Include any alimony or child support received that you choose to have considered for repayment of the loan.
- Any additional income like rental-property profits. This is tricky because some lenders will not count any rental income until it shows up on your taxes. Other lenders will count 75 percent of your rental income if you are an experienced investor or have leased out the house.

Usually, calculating your DTI ratio is a little tricky because different banks calculate things differently. It is best to let whatever lender you are using calculate the DTI for you. If the bank comes up with a DTI that seems very high, double-check their calculation method to see if they are doing something strange or put a wrong number in somewhere. Some banks will count depreciation of investment properties against you, even though that depreciation is not a monthly expense.

Why do different banks use different DTI ratios?

Different banks and different loan programs use different DTI ratios. VA and FHA typically limit borrowers to a DTI ratio of 52 percent, but in some circumstances, they may slightly increase that percentage. Fannie Mae allows a DTI ratio of up to 45 percent on some loans, but you must have great credit. Typically, if your credit score is below 700, your DTI ratio should be under 36 percent (unless you go FHA).

As you can see, this can all get very confusing. The best thing to do is to talk to a lender, and if your DTI ratio is high, work on lowering it.

How can you lower your DTI ratio?

The easiest way to lower your DTI ratio is to make more money. The more gross income you make, the higher your DTI ratio will be, but that is not the only thing lenders look at. It is not easy to simply start making more money, but many investors and self-employed individuals or business owners claim very little income on their taxes. Claiming little income is great if you don't want to pay much in taxes. If you want to qualify for a loan, claiming little income can make it nearly impossible to buy a house. You may think you are making $10,000 per month, but if your taxes show you making $2,000 per month, your DTI ratio could be much higher than you think. Claiming more income on your taxes will mean you must pay more taxes, but it may be worth it if it means you can buy a house.

Reducing debt is another way to improve your DTI ratio. Remember, DTI ratios consider all monthly debts that show up on your credit report. Your shortest debts usually hurt you the most because they have the highest payments. Even though you think you are doing the smart thing by getting a 15-year instead of a 30-year loan on your primary house, this will actually hurt your DTI ratio. A three-year car loan will make your DTI ratio higher than a six-year loan. I am not saying you should always get the longest term possible on your debt, but the lower your minimum payments are, the lower your DTI ratio will be. You can always make extra payments if you want to pay off your loans quicker.

- **Minimum credit card payments:** Credit cards typically have very high interest rates and high monthly payments. Paying off credit cards will greatly improve your DTI ratio, but you must pay off the entire balance.
- **Auto loans:** car loans can destroy a DTI ratio! A $600 car payment is equal to a $120,000 mortgage and will reduce your ability to qualify for a mortgage by $600 per month. Do you need a new car every three years if it means you can't buy a house?
- **Student loans**: Student loans may have low interest and low payments, but they still hurt your DTI ratio.
- **Consumer loans:** Do you have a loan for a TV, furniture, home equity line of credit, or any other monthly payments that show up on your credit? Even a home equity line of credit that you are not using can count against your DTI ratio.

If you don't have the money to pay off your debt, you may be able to consolidate it with a larger loan against your house that would have a lower interest rate and monthly payment.

What is the best way to pay off debt?

If you have a lot of credit card debt, car loans, and consumer debt, the best way to pay it off is one at a time as quickly as possible. The payments will stop affecting your DTI ratio once they disappear from your credit. That is why paying off one at a time will improve your DTI ratio more quickly.

When you pay off one debt, you can use the money you spent on those payments to pay off the next debt more quickly. Pay off the debt with the lowest balance first. If you have a $2,000 debt with $200 monthly payments, pay that off before you pay off a $5,000 debt with $300 monthly payments. You will pay off the $2,000 faster and then be able to use that extra $200 per month to pay off the next debt...and so on.

If you have a huge car payment, don't be afraid to sell the car and buy a cheaper one. I have never bought a new car. My daily driver for ten years was a 1991 Mustang that I bought with cash. Now that I make a living through real estate investing, I own nicer cars, but I still avoid high monthly payments.

Conclusion

There is no magic way to reduce your DTI ratio. It usually takes raising your income or lowering your monthly debt payments. A few lenders exist that do not consider your DTI ratio, but they usually either lend high dollar amounts on large investment properties or on many investment properties at once. If you find yourself with a high DTI ratio, talk to your lender. Make sure they calculate it correctly. Meanwhile, concentrate on reducing your monthly debt payments.

CHAPTER 36

What Are Down Payment Assistance Programs?

For the cheapest loans, the down payment can range from 3 percent to 5 percent of the loan amount. Closing costs consist of lender fees, an appraisal, insurance, prepaid interest, title fees, closing company fess, and can be 2 to 5 percent of the price of the house. On a $200,000 owner-occupied house, a buyer may need $10,000 in cash to cover the down payment and closing costs using a low-down payment loan. Luckily, there are down payment assistance programs (and other methods) to reduce the cash needed to buy a house. In fact, many owner-occupant buyers can buy a house with as little as $1,000 in Colorado and some other states. In this chapter, Mike Bowen helps me explain how down payment assistance programs work. Mike is a lender with Guild Mortgage in Colorado.

What are down payment assistance programs?

Down Payment Assistance (DPA) programs are available in some shape or fashion in most states. In the past, these programs were reserved for first-time buyers, but today, most are open to any person or persons that meet the income limits and qualify based on income and credit. Colorado is fortunate to have many great programs that offer free money in the form of non-repayable grants. The grant is used to offset the buyer's down payment and/or closing costs and ranges from 3 to 4 percent of the total loan amount. Depending on which loan a potential buyer qualifies for (most commonly FHA or Conventional) the grant can pay for all or most of the minimum down payment required. The real value in these programs is that it allows a buyer to get into a house with a minimum of $1,000 total out of pocket. Since the grant is non-repayable, the only negative is the interest rates on these programs are about .25 to .50 percent higher than a loan without down payment assistance. A .25 percent interest rate increase means your monthly payment is about $30 higher on a $200,000 loan.

Do other states besides Colorado offer down payment assistance programs?

Colorado is not unique. Fortunately, down payment assistance programs are available across the country. For example, Arizona has a few key programs with grants similar to Colorado's but with some different guideline restrictions. Also, California offers CalHFA, which is very similar to Colorado's CHFA program. Many other states also offer down payment assistance programs.

How do you qualify for down payment assistance?

Qualifying for a loan with down payment assistance is fairly straightforward. Since these loans follow normal FHA and conventional guidelines, you typically need a minimum credit score of 620, a solid two-year work history, and a down payment of $1,000. You also must have a decent debt-to-income ratio.

How can you find a great lender who knows about down payment assistance programs?

Not every lender knows about grants and down payment assistance programs. In Colorado, you must be an approved lender for some of the programs, and lenders who are not approved may not tell consumers about all the options available. When looking for a lender with experience with these programs, I recommend going directly to the program's website and searching for "top lenders." From there, you will see a list of reputable lenders in your area. Then, you can conduct phone interviews to find a good personality fit as well as someone with the experience necessary to get your loan done smoothly and on time.

If you are working with a great real estate agent, they may be able to recommend a reputable lender. Once again, not every lender works with these programs, so make sure to ask about down payment assistance programs. Do some research on your own to find out what programs are available in your state, and make sure your lender is telling you the entire story!

Conclusion

Buying a house can be very expensive, even with low-down-payment loans. Thanks to down payment assistance programs and other strategies, the money a buyer must have can be greatly reduced. One thing is for sure: these programs offer the dream of homeownership to those that would not otherwise be able to buy a house. I want to thank Mike Bowen for providing much of the information in this section.

CHAPTER 37

What is Mortgage Insurance and How Does It Work?

Mortgage insurance is a fee lenders charge when buyers put down less than 20 percent of the price of the house. The reason lenders charge this fee is because the less money someone puts down, the riskier the loan is, and mortgage insurance helps mitigate that risk. There are many different types of mortgage insurance, and a few loans don't charge it. Some mortgage insurance can be removed after a certain amount of time, and some can't. The cost of mortgage insurance also varies greatly depending on the loan program you use.

Why do lenders require mortgage insurance?

In 1934, the Federal Housing Authority (FHA) was created to help the economy during the great depression. Prior to FHA, almost every buyer had to put down 20 percent. Most banks figured it was safe to loan to someone who could put down 20 percent. The practice of putting 20 percent down made the housing market more stable, but it also meant much fewer people could own a house.

The more houses that are bought and sold, the better our economy does. That is why owner-occupants and investors realize huge tax incentives for owning a house. The government stimulates sales by offering FHA-insured loans, which don't require 20 percent down. FHA was not created to finance homes but rather to create insurance for banks who loaned to those who couldn't provide a 20 percent down payment. There are also conventional loans that require less than 20 percent down.

To help mitigate the risk with low-money-down loans, lenders charge mortgage insurance, which may be about one percent of the loan amount per year. Mortgage insurance allows banks to lend to those who can't put down that 20 percent because the insurance will reduce the losses the banks incur in a default.

Does the bank keep the mortgage insurance?

Although banks require mortgage insurance, they don't keep the money. On conventional loans, private mortgage insurance companies keep the premiums. If a property defaults (goes through foreclosure), the mortgage insurance company will either take the property or pay off the bank for the amount insured.

With FHA loans, the mortgage insurance is paid to the federal government, and they insure the loans for the banks. FHA houses that go through foreclosure and are reclaimed by the government become HUD homes.

How much is mortgage insurance on residential properties?

FHA has set guidelines for how much they charge for mortgage insurance. The current cost is 1.75 percent up front, and the monthly fees vary based on the amount of the loan. The monthly rate FHA charges is around 0.85 percent. The amount FHA charges changes frequently since FHA must keep two percent of its total liability as cash. Due to the housing crisis, the fund dropped well below two percent, which caused FHA to increase mortgage insurance rates.

The upfront mortgage insurance is paid when the buyers close on their house, and the monthly payments are made as long as the loan exists. On a $100,000 loan, the payment would be $506 (without taxes and insurance) based on a 4.5 percent interest rate, and the payment increases to $574 after FHA mortgage insurance is added. The upfront mortgage insurance cost would be about $1,700, which can be financed into the loan.

Private mortgage insurance varies between banks and loan programs. Private mortgage insurance typically costs 0.5

percent to 1 percent of the entire loan amount every year. On a $100,000 loan, the homeowner would pay $83.33 per month, or $1,000 per year, with a 1 percent fee.

Can private mortgage insurance (PMI) be removed?

FHA mortgage insurance cannot be removed for the life of the loan (except in the case of some older FHA loans). However, some types of private mortgage insurance can be removed after a certain amount of time passes and once equity reaches a certain point. Some private mortgage insurance can be removed after two years if the amount owed on the loan is 75 or 80 percent or less than the value of the house. If your house goes up in value or you pay off much of your balance, you may be able to have the PMI removed. The lender may require an appraisal or a simple BPO to determine the value of the property. You must check with your lender when you get your loan to see if the PMI can be removed. Not all conventional loans allow the PMI to be removed.

Which loans don't require mortgage insurance?

VA loans do not have mortgage insurance. VA loans can only be used by military veterans, active duty personnel, or certain honorably discharged military.

Another option is getting two loans on your house. The first loan would be 80 percent of the value, and the second loan could be 10 or 15 percent of the value. These loans were more common before the housing crisis but are still available. The second loans that are available now are for owner-occupants only and tend to have much higher interest rates than first loans. The actual savings of getting a first and a second is not that great over getting a first with mortgage insurance.

Conclusion

PMI and FHA mortgage insurance push up the cost of buying a house. However, for many people it is well worth the extra cost to put less money down. At some point, you may be able to remove the mortgage insurance, but always check with the lender first because some private mortgage insurance cannot be removed.

CHAPTER 38

Which Is Better: a 15- or 30-Year Loan?

15-year loans appear to be more cost-effective than 30-year loans because they have a lower interest rate, but I would much rather have the flexibility of a 30-year loan. The problem with a 15-year loan is you are locked into a higher payment every month. As we have discussed, a higher payment raises your debt-to-income ratio. If you ever run into financial problems, you cannot pay less on the 15-year mortgage. If you get a 30-year mortgage, you can pay more every month to pay it off faster. You will also have a lower debt-to-income ratio, and if you run into financial problems, you can simply stop paying extra towards the loan.

What are the advantages of a 15-year loan?

The biggest advantage of a 15-year mortgage is the lower interest rate. The difference in rates changes daily and varies among banks, but the rates on a 15-year loan are usually about .5 percent less than on a 30-year fixed mortgage.

Some people think the biggest advantage of 15-year loans is the shorter term. But I don't agree because you can pay off a 30-year loan early if you choose by paying more each month.

What are the interest savings on a 15-year loan?

If you get a 15-year, $100,000 loan with a 4 percent interest rate, the payments will be $740 a month (check out Bankrate.com's mortgage calculator if you'd like an easy way to calculate these figures). Over those 15 years, you will pay $33,143 in interest. With a 30-year loan at 4.5 percent interest, you will pay $82,406.

On the surface, it looks like you are saving almost $50,000 by getting a 15-year loan. However, you are paying interest over 30 years on one loan and over 15 years on the other, which is deceiving. The payment on a 30-year loan is only $507 a month, which is $233 less per month than the 15-year loan. If you were to take that $233 and put it back into the 30-year loan each month, the interest paid on the 30-year loan drops to $39,754, and you could pay it off in less than 17 years. It costs a little more to have the higher interest rate, but over 15 years that only amounts to $550 annually.

Why would a 30-year loan be better than a 15-year loan?

While you'll pay less interest on a 15-year loan, assuming you pay only the minimum monthly payment, you end up having a higher monthly payment with the 15-year loan. If you dig into the numbers on the 30-year loan, you actually save $2,796 per year and $41,940 over the extra 15 years.

That extra money can be used for many things that will make you much more money than that $6,000 in interest you save. You can use the money to build an emergency fund. You could invest the money into your retirement. You could invest it for your children's college. You could also pay extra on the mortgage, and if you ever need the money later, you can stop paying extra.

Using a 30-year ARM (adjustable rate mortgage) versus a 15-year fixed loan.

When I finance my rental properties, I use 30-year ARMs. An ARM is an adjustable rate mortgage that has a fixed interest rate for a certain amount of time. The interest rate on an ARM can go up or down after a certain amount of time. My portfolio lender offers 5- and 7-year ARMs with a 30-year amortization. The rate will stay the same for 5 or 7 years, but may go up after those terms are up. There are limits on how much the rate can go up each year, and there is a ceiling that it can never go over. The great part about ARMs is they have a lower rate than a 30-year fixed-rate loan and even the 15-year fixed-rate loan. I will talk more about ARMs very soon.

Why is a 30-year loan safer than a 15-year loan?

Many people have a tough time saving money, and the higher your mortgage payment, the harder it will be to save. Having an emergency fund is very important for financial stability. If you do not have an emergency fund, do not get a 15-year mortgage. Get the 30-year mortgage, and save up for the emergency fund. Once the emergency fund is established, (6 months of living expenses) you can pay off your mortgage early if you would like.

Remember that you realize no real benefit by paying off your mortgage early unless you pay off the entire loan, refinance, or sell. Your house payment will stay the same until the loan is paid in full. If you need to access the equity in your house, you cannot ask the lender to return the extra amount you've paid. You will have to sell the house or get a new loan (refinance or home equity line of credit).

If you get a 15-year loan and have a medical emergency, lose your job, or cannot work, the bank will not lower the payment for you. You must keep paying that high mortgage payment every month. If you had a 30-year mortgage and were paying more to it every month, an emergency would not be nearly as devastating because you could stop paying extra.

Conclusion

On the surface, a 15-year fixed-rate mortgage may seem like the best way to go. The interest you pay over the life of the loan is lower, and the term is shorter. However, I believe the 15-year loan is the worst choice because you are tying up your money, making it harder to qualify for loans, and you could be investing that money in something that gives a higher return. If you get a 30-year ARM, the interest rate will actually be lower than the 15-year loan, and you might be able to pay that loan off faster than the 15-year loan.

CHAPTER 39

What Is an Adjustable Rate Mortgage (ARM)?

I use adjustable rate mortgages (ARM) on my rental and personal properties for many reasons. Many people feel that an ARM is very risky because the rate can rise over time. Many ARMs are, in fact, risky and are not the best option for all buyers. For some homeowners, an ARM can be a very good loan that saves money, lets you buy more properties, and is not very risky.

ARMs have gotten a bad rap the last few years because many people used them before the housing crisis to buy houses they could not afford. An ARM is a loan that starts with a low interest rate, but the interest rate can rise after a set period. A 5/30 year ARM is a 30-year loan with an initial rate that is fixed for the first five years but can increase on the sixth year. There is a cap for how much the interest rate can rise after the adjustment period, and a there is a minimum it can't fall under. ARM rates go up or down depending on nationwide interest rates. On my loans, the rate might start at 4.5 percent but could reach 8 percent. The rate cannot rise more than 1 percent in any given year.

Adjustable rate mortgages have lower interest rates than fixed mortgages

I like 5-year ARMs because they have a low interest rate that is guaranteed for 5 years. ARM rates can be up to 1 percent lower than a 30-year fixed rate loan. That 1 percent difference can save hundreds of dollars per month. Once, you could obtain ARMs that began with very low rates yet jumped very high within 6 months to 1 years. Often, buyers could not qualify with the normal 30-year fixed-rate loan, but they could qualify for the lower payment the ARM offered.

However, if you can't qualify for a 30-year fixed-rate mortgage, I don't recommend using an ARM.

An adjustable rate mortgage may be your only choice for financing multiple properties.

Another reason I use an adjustable rate mortgage is they are one of the few options available from my local lender. I use a portfolio lender, who lends their own money; they do not sell their loans to other companies or investors like most banks do. My portfolio lender offers a 5-year and 7-year ARM as well as a 15-year fixed loan. The 5/30 year ARM has the lowest payment, lowest interest rate, and works perfectly for my strategy. The reason I use a portfolio lender is many lenders will not loan to investors who have more than four mortgages. My portfolio lender will lend on as many loans as I can qualify for, but I must use their limited loan options. Portfolio lenders can also be a great option for getting a loan on a house that needs repairs.

Are ARMs riskier than fixed-rate loans?

ARMs are viewed unfavorably due to the high number of loans that were foreclosed on during the housing crisis. The reason so many people lost their houses with an ARM was they qualified for the low initial interest rate. When the rate on the adjustable rate mortgage went up after five, three, or even one year, the homeowner could no longer afford the payment. If you are thinking of getting an adjustable rate mortgage, make sure you can afford the payment increases, even if you think you will have the loan paid off by then. Do not depend on being able to refinance to get yourself out of the loan.

An adjustable rate mortgage may be cheaper than a fixed-rate loan

The interest rate on an ARM is lower in the beginning of the loan than the rate on a fixed-rate loan. The ARM may be cheaper than a fixed-rate loan even if you do not pay off the ARM right away and the rate increases. During the five years that the ARM is at its lowest rate, you are saving money every month over the fixed-rate loan. Even if you don't pay off that ARM and the rate increases, it would still take years for the total cost of the ARM to catch up to the fixed rate loan. If you reinvest the money you are saving from the ARM and make a higher return on that investment than the interest rate on the loans, you will make even more money. It usually takes 8 years for an ARM to reach its maximum amount before the fixed-rate loan saves you money.

Conclusion

ARMs are great loans, especially when you have few other options. Be smart when deciding to use an ARM, and it can be a great tool for any homeowner. The biggest mistake you can make is not being prepared for a payment increase if you are not able to pay off the loan or refinance. If you are prepared to hold the loan, you should be just fine.

CHAPTER 40

What Is an Appraisal and Why Do You Need One?

When you get a loan on a house, most lenders will require an appraisal. An appraisal is a report that values the house and tells the lender that the house is worth what you're paying. If the appraisal comes in lower than the contract price or the appraiser requires repairs, it can kill a deal and cause a lot of frustration. Appraisals and the guidelines appraisers must follow can also be very confusing to people who are not familiar with them.

This chapter goes into details on how an appraisal is completed. If you don't quite understand what I talk about, do not worry! Many real estate agents don't understand how appraisals are completed either.

Why do banks require appraisals?

Banks and mortgage companies love to lend money on houses because houses are a more secure debt than cars or businesses. If the borrower defaults on the loan, the bank can foreclose and take possession of the house. However, foreclosures are not cheap after you factor in attorney and selling costs, not to mention lost interest. To reduce the amount of money a bank loses from foreclosures, they make sure to lend to qualified buyers, and they ensure the house they're lending on is worth what the borrower pays.

If banks do not confirm the value, the borrower could buy a house for $50,000 more than it is worth. If the house is a foreclosure, the bank would not only lose money on lost interest, selling costs, and attorney's fees, but they would also have to sell the house for $50,000 less than they thought it was worth (assuming prices did not drop since the loan was made).

What is an appraisal?

An appraisal is a valuation of a house or property and is done by a licensed appraiser. I complete many broker price opinions (BPOs) as a real estate agent, but a BPO is not an appraisal and is not as detailed. BPOs are used to determine market value for banks who may be trying to complete a short sale or for banks who need to know the value of house that are going into foreclosure or have been foreclosed on. BPOs are not used to determine house values for new loans.

To complete an appraisal, the appraiser will view the entire home, take pictures, measure the house, inspect the condition, and complete a report that assigns value. The report consists of sold comparables, which are houses that have sold recently and are most like the house being appraised (subject house). The appraiser follows certain guidelines regarding the comparables used to value a house. Sold comps should:

- Have sold in the last six months.
- Have above-ground square feet within 20 percent of subject.
- Have similar basements (finished or unfinished if applicable).
- Have been built within a certain timeframe of the subject (usually ten years).
- Be in similar condition as the subject.
- Have similar bedroom and bath counts.
- Be in the same neighborhood or within a certain distance of subject (usually one mile).

If there are not enough sold comparables to meet these guidelines, the appraiser can expand his criteria and make adjustments. If a house is in a rural area, the appraiser may have to look within ten miles of the subject for comps or look for houses within 20 years of age because there are no other comps. When an appraiser makes adjustments, they will add or subtract value from the comparable properties for different characteristics. The adjusted values show what the subject property is worth.

How do appraisal adjustments work?

When an appraiser uses comparables that are different from the subject, the appraiser must subtract or add value to the comp. If a comparable sold for $150,000 but is superior to the subject by $10,000, the comparable value would be $160,000. On the report, the $160,000 adjusted value of the comparable would indicate the subject house is worth $160,000. To come up with adjustments, the appraiser will compare the important characteristics of the subject and comparable sales (usually at least three comp sales are used). If the subject has 3 bedrooms and the comparable has 4, the appraiser may deduct $4,000 from the comparable because it is superior to the subject. If the comparable characteristic was inferior to the subject, the adjustment would be positive.

Below is an example of some adjustments that might be used by an appraiser:

Subject	Comparable	Adjustment to Comp
1,500 SQFT	1,700 SQFT	-$6,000
3 bedrooms	4 bedrooms	-$3,000
2 baths	3 baths	-$2,500
2 car attached garage	1 car attached garage	$4,000
1,000 SQFT unfinished basement	no basement	$7,500
Built 1979	Built in 1988	– $5,000
Total adjustment		-$5,000

If this comparable house had sold for $150,000, the adjusted sales price used to value the subject would be $145,000. The appraiser would then do the same thing with at least two more sales comps and come up with a value for the subject using these values.

Do appraisers use active comps in appraisals?

One frustrating aspect of appraisals is appraisers will primarily use sold comps for valuation purposes. Sold comps must be used because you can list your house for whatever price you want, but you won't know what it is worth until it sells. If an appraiser used active comps, the value could vary greatly based on whether or not the asking price is close to what the house is really worth. An appraiser may occasionally use an active comp if there are very few sold comps available to help justify value. The active comp is used to supplement the sold comps...not to be the primary focus.

A lot of people try to figure out what their house is worth based on what other houses are selling for. This is a very inaccurate way to value houses because they could be overpriced by $50,000!

What happens if an appraisal comes in less than the contract price?

Banks want the appraisal to come in at or above the contract price to confirm the value of a house. Banks will lend on many different loan-to-value ratios. The bank will base the loan-to-value ratio on the lower of the contract price or the appraisal. If the contract price is $100,000 but the appraisal comes in at $90,000, the bank would base the loan amount on the $90,000, not the $100,000. In this scenario, with a 20 percent down payment, the loan amount would be $72,000 instead of $80,000. With no money down, the loan amount would be $90,000 instead of $100,000.

As you can see, the appraised value can greatly affect many buyers' ability to buy a house and affects the money they need for the purchase. Low appraisals have killed many deals when the buyer was not willing to bring more money to closing or the seller was not willing to lower the price.

How can you deal with a low appraisal?

If an appraisal comes in low, you can challenge it, but the appraiser may not change his value. I will talk more about challenging appraisals in the next chapter. The lender can help you challenge an appraisal, but there usually must be a gross miscalculation or mistake on the report for the appraiser to change the value. You can also do a few things to help appraisals come in at value before the appraisal is completed, which I will discuss later.

If you can't get the value changed, the buyer will have to bring more money to the closing or the seller will have to reduce the price. Sometimes a combination of the two or the real estate agents reducing their commission may make the deal work. If the two sides can't come together on price, a second appraisal may be done in some circumstances, but you would have to talk to your lender to see if that is a possibility.

Do FHA appraisals stick with a house?

When a buyer uses a conventional loan, the lender will order a conventional appraisal. If the conventional appraisal does not come in at value, a different lender can order a new conventional appraisal, which may come in at value. If the buyer is using an FHA loan, the appraisal sticks with the house. That means, for at least 4 months, any FHA loan will have to use that same appraisal. If an FHA appraisal comes in low and the sellers will not reduce the price, the sellers will most likely not be able to sell the house to any other FHA buyers for at least four months (unless they lower the price to the FHA appraisal amount).

In some cases, a lender will also require two appraisals. I flip many houses, and lenders get scared because the price I sell them for is much more than the price I buy them for. When the lender or underwriter sees a huge price difference, they usually want a list of the repairs I made and a second appraisal to confirm the value.

Why are appraisal guidelines so strict, and why do appraisals come in low?

Much of the recent housing crisis was caused by inflated values, and some of those values were high due to lender fraud. In my town of Greeley, Colorado we had a few instances of fraud. Here's an example of what happened:

- Builder builds a house.
- Realtor for builder finds unknowing buyer and promises low payments ($500 on a $250,000 purchase).
- Realtor, builder, and lender all convince buyer to use an ARM where payments will more than triple in one year (many times, the buyer does not know how much more the payment will be).
- They all sell the house for at least 20 percent more than it is worth (sometimes much more), and the buyer agrees because of the low payment.
- Appraiser is in on the fraud and inflates his appraisal to confirm the value.

This caused hundreds of houses to go through foreclosure, and many people went to jail. To stop this type of fraud, appraisers were scrutinized for any values that appeared high. To avoid scrutiny, appraisers learned what to avoid:

- Mentioning a rising market for prices, because this could justify higher values.
- Coming up with a value higher than any sold comps.
- Using active comps to value a house higher.

Basically, appraisers avoid anything that could be considered a judgement call because they don't want to be investigated for fraud. This makes it tough on buyers, especially in a rising housing market because the sold comps may not be as high as their contract price.

What if an appraisal requires repairs?

A low appraisal value can destroy a house sale, but an appraisal can also call out repairs. On most loans, the lender will require a house to be in livable condition. That means all the major systems must work, including the plumbing, heating, electrical, roof, and sewer. The appraiser will also make sure there is nothing dangerous like peeling paint (could be lead-based paint and poisonous), holes in the walls, floors, broken windows, or mold.

If you are trying to sell or buy a house that has any of these issues, the appraiser may require them to be repaired before closing. The seller could have the items repaired, or in some cases the buyer may be willing to make the repairs before the closing (on REO and HUD homes, it is usually not an option for the buyer to make repairs). If the seller can't or won't make repairs, the deal will usually die, and the house will have to be sold with a loan that does not require repairs or that requires buyers to pay cash.

Unlike an inspection, the seller cannot simply agree to lower the price in lieu of making the repairs. The lender and appraiser will require the repairs be made before closing, unless the repairs can be escrowed.

Conclusion

Appraisals that come in low or require repairs can be a huge pain for buyers and sellers. However, they are necessary for sellers who want to get the most money for their houses or for buyers who want to get a loan.

CHAPTER 41

How Can You Challenge or Prevent a Low Appraisal?

Often, appraisals come in low, especially in an appreciating market. Low appraisals can kill deals, but there are ways to challenge an appraisal or help the appraiser come in at value before completing the report. Some appraisals will also require repairs be made before closing, which can also kill a deal. There are many things you can do to help prevent an appraiser from calling out repairs.

I constantly deal with low appraisals, whether on my own sales or on houses I find for buyers. However, we have made many changes over the last couple of years that have helped reduce the number of low appraisals we see:

- **Give the appraiser comps to use**. I was skeptical about doing this because I did not know if giving the appraiser comparable or sold properties was ethical or legal. When I do broker price opinions for banks, I am not allowed to take comparable sold properties from the listing agent or anyone involved in the transaction. However, the real estate commission in Colorado recommends agents provide comps for the appraisers. When an appraisal is scheduled, we provide the appraiser with as many similar sold properties as we can. I tell the appraiser they are welcome to use these if they would like to, but I never pressure them into using my comps. I make sure the comps support the value in the contract, and I make sure there are no abnormalities (distance from property, SQFT etc). I tell the appraiser, in detail, why I chose those properties. Most appraisers are very grateful, and this has helped values come in much higher.
- **Inform the appraiser about completed repairs**. This lets the appraiser know the house may

be in better condition than similar sales in the area that may be used as comparables. It also helps to justify when the price I sell a fix-and-flip for is noticeably higher than what I bought it for.

- **Promptly return the appraisers calls or emails**. I try to be as professional as possible with all appraisers. I don't want to give them any reason to get annoyed at me or the property. If the appraiser calls me, I will call or email them back as soon as I can. If the utilities must be on, I make sure they are or explain why they can't be on so the appraiser does not have to make multiple trips to the house.
- **Make sure the house is clean and looks great.** First impressions mean a lot to anyone. If your house is completely remodeled but has junk all over, the appraiser may miss all the remodeling work. Present the house to the appraiser like you would a regular buyer.

If you treat the appraiser right and give them comps that help justify the value, you will have much more success with appraisals coming in at value. If you are not an agent, make sure your agent is doing these things for you.

Can you challenge a low appraisal?

Even after providing comps, some appraisals come in low. If you get a low appraisal, there are ways to challenge it.

If an appraisal comes in at less than the contract value, you can ask the lender to challenge the appraisal. Usually there must be something wrong with the appraisal, and you need some really good comps to prove the value should be higher. I ordered a VA appraisal on a house for some buyers. The house was newly constructed, and the appraisal came in $7,000 low. Luckily, there were some major flaws in the report, and we were able to get the appraised value raised.

- The appraiser used a house that was 16 years old and over 2 miles away from subject.

- The appraiser used a house that was 11 years old and over 1.5 miles away from subject.

The appraised house was brand new and in a suburban area with many new construction sold comparables available in the same neighborhood. I have no idea why the appraiser used these comps when so many other properties had sold in the same neighborhood in the last six months. I provided six comps that were very similar to the subject in price, age, and location. The lender challenged the appraisal using those comps, and the appraiser raised the value. On this deal, the appraisal was not brought up to the full contract price, but the value was raised $3,000 and the seller agreed to lower the price to make it work for the buyers.

There is no guarantee the appraiser or appraisal management company will change the value, even with gross errors in a report, but it is worth a try. I have seen other appraisals with worse values remain unchanged. On one occasion, an appraiser raised the value by $30,000 after we provided comps.

When you challenge an appraisal, you (or your real estate agent) must be able to provide comps that clearly support value and are superior to the comps used in the appraisal. Or, you must find errors in the appraisal. If the appraiser said the subject only had a one-car garage and it had a two-car garage, that error can be challenged. If an appraisal comes in low, don't rely on the lender to look it over and decide if they want to challenge it. Look it over yourself, or if you are not an agent, have your agent look it over closely. Look for any errors or anything wrong with the comps used. Were they too old, were they too far away, were they sold too long ago, was the square footage off, was a finished basement excluded? In some cases, the value is just low and there isn't much you can do about it.

Conclusion

If you have appraisal issues, don't give up hope! I know many lenders will not pursue these avenues unless they are asked. Many real estate agents will not pursue these options either because they don't know they exist. In some cases, there is nothing you can do about a low appraisal or one that requires repairs, but it doesn't hurt to try to get the value raised. Remember, appraisal requirements are not limited to owner-occupants. Many investor loans will have the same repair and value requirements as well.

CHAPTER 42

How to Get a Loan on a House That Needs Repairs

Houses needing repairs often can be bought below market value. I base my investing strategy on buying houses below market value and financing those properties, which is not always easy. When you buy a house that needs repairs, many lenders will not lend on that house if the repairs affect livability. Whether you are an investor or owner-occupied buyer, repairs can cause a deal to fall apart. This is why cash offers are so attractive to many sellers who have a house that needs work. If you are an investor or owner-occupied buyer, there are ways to get a loan on a property when it needs repairs, even if they're extensive.

Which repairs will prevent a lender from loaning on the house?

Most lenders will use FHA guidelines to decide what condition a house needs to be in. That means all major systems like the plumbing, electrical, and heating systems need to be in working order. The roof needs to be in good condition, and there cannot be any holes in the walls or floors. FHA historically required flooring to be in good condition, but that is no longer the case. All carpet can be missing and the house will still go FHA. The tricky part is not all lenders go with exactly what FHA requires.

An FHA loan is federally insured by the government and is a big reason owner-occupants can buy houses with little money down. Conventional loans are loans that are not federally insured or sponsored by any government agency. Many types of conventional loans and many different requirements on conventional loans exist depending on the lender. Some conventional loans will require everything FHA requires, some will require less, and some will require more.

My lender does not require any repairs on houses that are in horrible condition. If you have one conventional lender that will not loan on a house, that doesn't mean another conventional lender will adhere to the same guidelines.

The government sponsors other loans, like VA and USDA. Different states also have loan programs that will have varying requirements. Most government loan programs will have the same or stricter requirements than FHA.

How do you get a loan on a house that needs repairs?

There are many ways to work through lender-required repairs. Your choices will differ depending on if you are an owner-occupant or an investor. The first strategy is to ask the seller to make repairs so the house is in livable condition. Which situations allow the seller to make repairs?

- **Traditional seller:** If the house is selling at retail value, the seller usually expects to make repairs if the lender requires them. A house must be in livable condition to command top dollar. For those of us who want a great deal, we usually deal with sellers that want to sell quickly without doing any repairs. The better the deal, the lower the chance the seller will make any repairs.
- **REO properties:** REOs are bank-owned foreclosures. Some REO sellers will make repairs and some will not. The decision to repair or not is usually made on a case-by-case basis depending on how much work is needed. Many REO sellers will say a house is sold as-is, which indicates they will not make repairs. However, some REO sellers will still make repairs if the lender requires it.
- **HUD Homes:** HUD will not make any repairs under any circumstance for lender required items. HUD does have a program to allow FHA buyers that I will discuss later. If you are an investor and your lender requires repairs, you will have to cancel the contract or find a new lender.

- **Short sales:** Most short-sale sellers do not have a lot of money. If you know a short sale needs work and your lender will require repairs before closing, there is a great chance the work cannot be done. In most short sales, sellers don't receive any money, and they don't want to spend any more money on the house.
- **Auction sales:** Don't expect to successfully request repairs on auction properties. Properties at auction are almost always sold "as is."

Before you write a contract on a house, know who you are dealing with.

When you start shopping for a house, you should have already talked to a lender, and you should know what condition they will require a house to be in. If you are using a conventional loan on a HUD home and the water can't be turned on but your lender requires it, the contract will fail. If a short sale needs $10,000 in repairs to meet lending requirements, the deal will probably never go through. On an REO or a traditional sale, the seller may or may not make repairs. Don't expect HUD or an REO seller to make repairs just because your lender requires it.

How can an owner-occupant get a loan on houses that need repairs?

If an owner-occupant wants to get a loan on a house that needs repairs but the seller won't perform those repairs, the deal is not always over. HUD offers a program for FHA buyers that allows them to escrow for repairs and add the repairs to the buyer's loan. HUD's program is called the FHA 203b loan. It can only be used on HUD homes where repairs cost less than $5,000. This escrow cannot be used on any other type of loan like VA or conventional. For repairs costing over $5,000, HUD offers an FHA 203k loan that can be used on any house. This loan covers an unlimited amount of repairs but will take more time to close and have more fees. FHA loans are only available for owner-occupants.

How can an investor get a loan on a house that needs repairs?

Since FHA loans are only available to owner-occupants, it is more difficult for investors to obtain loans on houses that need repairs. That doesn't mean investors are out of luck. I buy houses that need work all the time, and I get loans on almost all of them.

I use a portfolio lender that does not have any repair requirements. I can buy houses with bad roofs or bad heating, and my lender does not even require the utilities to be on. Not all portfolio lenders have the same repair requirements, but many will work with investors much more than the big banks. My portfolio lender has saved many deals for investors and owner-occupants whose original lenders would not lend on a house because it needed too much work.

Investors may also be able to escrow repairs. In some cases, investors can escrow the repairs so they are done after closing. The terms and chances of this happening all depend on the lender. Usually, the lender will escrow for minor repairs but may be hesitant to escrow for major repairs.

Investors can use a Homestyle Fannie Mae Renovation loan to repair houses after they close. This loan is like the FHA 203k loan but is meant for investors.

If you are an investor and your lender will not loan on a house that needs repairs and the seller will not make those repairs, don't give up. Search for a local portfolio lender who might have different guidelines and will give you a loan. Hard-money lenders will also lend on houses needing work.

Hard-money lenders will be much more expensive than conventional lenders, and they offer short-term loans of (usually) less than one year. Hard money usually works better for fix and flips because the loan term is so short. Hard-money lenders may be a decent short-term solution, but you will have to refinance the loan very quickly.

Conclusion

If a house needs work, getting a loan is tough...but not impossible. Owner-occupants have many more options for buying houses in need of repairs, but an investor should be able to work around repair issues as well. Buying houses that need repairs is one of the best ways to get a great deal.

CHAPTER 43

How Does an FHA 203k Mortgage Work?

While traditional lenders with traditional loan programs may not be able to lend on houses that need a lot of work, there are loan programs that provide funding for repairs. FHA 203k loans are an awesome product that allow buyers to purchase a house in any condition and get an FHA loan.

How do FHA 203k loans work?

Normal, and most conventional, FHA loans will not work for houses that need significant work unless the seller is willing to make repairs before closing. If you are buying an REO, short sale, or another type of distressed sale, the owners most likely will not make any repairs before closing. This means the buyer must have cash or local bank financing lined up.

An FHA 203k loan is an FHA loan that includes the ability to finance and make repairs to a house after closing. A house can need $10,000 or $100,000 in work, and there are FHA 203k loans that will help in those situations. There are some drawbacks to FHA 203k's (like higher costs), and you must be an owner-occupant, but they can be a great loan for the right situation.

Here is how the loan works:

- Talk to a lender about the program, the extra costs, and how much you can qualify for.
- When you find a house that needs work, get a rough estimate of the needed repairs to make sure you can qualify for the purchase price plus repairs.
- Make an offer using the 203k loan, making sure the dates are in line with lender expectations.

- Get the house under contract, line up contractors to do the work, finalize budgets, and finalize the loan amount.
- Close on the property.
- Have an approved contractor make repairs on after closing, and the lender will pay that contractor directly from the loan proceeds.

What are the drawbacks of an FHA 203k loan?

When you get an FHA 203K loan, there are some definite drawbacks. For one thing, you must be an owner-occupant and live in the house at least one year. FHA 203k loans also can take 60 days or longer to close. They tend to fall out of contract more often than regular loans as well. Due to the longer closing time and the frequency that they fall apart, many sellers are hesitant to accept contracts with FHA 203k loans.

That does not mean you cannot find a seller who will accept a contract with a 203k loan, but it will be more difficult. One great option for buyers using 203k loans is HUD homes. HUD does not care if you use a 203k loan or cash. They look at both offers the same and give priority to owner-occupant buyers.

Here are some more challenges that come with 203k loans:

- Many lenders do not offer the loan and will convince buyers not to use it because it is more work and takes longer.
- The fees are higher because there must be two appraisals. Also, the interest rate is higher, and there are more fees depending on the 203k loan type.
- Contractors who perform 203k work must be approved to perform the repairs and can be more expensive than other contractors. The website for 203k contractors is http://203kcontractors.com/.
- You must be able to qualify for the end loan amount after the repairs are done. If you buy the house for

$100,000, but it needs $30,000 in repairs, you need to be able to qualify for $130,000.

What are the different types of FHA 203k loans?

There are two types of 203k loans: streamline and regular. The streamline option can be used on houses that need less than $35,000 in repairs (the minimum amount is $5,000). The streamline is faster and cheaper than the regular and works for the following scenarios (note that the streamline option cannot alter the building's structural integrity):

- Repair/Replacement of roofs, gutters, and downspouts.
- Repair/Replace/Upgrade of existing HVAC systems.
- Repair/Replace/Upgrade of plumbing and electrical systems.
- Repair/Replacement of existing flooring.
- Minor remodeling, such as kitchens and baths.
- Exterior and interior painting.
- Repairs called out by an FHA appraisal.

The regular option applies for almost any repair as long as the original foundation remains untouched. The regular option can also be used to add a second story, an addition, or to make any other repairs a buyer wants. However, with the regular loan, you must use a mortgage consultant, who will charge the following fees based on the repair amount:

- $400 fee for repairs of $5,000 to $7,500
- $500 for $7,501 to $15,000
- $600 for $15,001 to $30,000
- $700 for $30,001 to $50,000
- $800 for $50,001 to $75,000
- $900 for $75,001 to $100,000
- $1,000 for $100,000 or higher

CHAPTER 44

Should You Pay Your Mortgage Off Early?

A house payment is the biggest expense for most people, and many people dream of paying off their house. Homeowners need to know how paying off their mortgage will affect them financially. While it seems like a great way to reduce a huge payment, does it make sense? You should consider how much you're saving, your interest rate, how long it will take to pay off, and what would happen if you find yourself in a bind and need to access equity.

How long does it take to pay off a mortgage?

Different mortgages have different loan terms. The most common mortgage term is 30 years, but some mortgages can be 15 years, 10 years, or even 5 years. A 30-year mortgage will be paid off in 30 years if you make the minimum payments every month.

If your mortgage is 30 years with an original amount of $200,000 and an interest rate of 4 percent, the payment would be about $955 (which does not include taxes and insurance). What scares people is that over those 30 years, the borrower pays over $143,000 in interest. That is almost as much money in interest as the loan itself! If a borrower decides to pay off the loan early by increasing the monthly payments by $100, the interest paid drops to $116,000. The loan term also drops from 30 to 25 years. That seems like a smart financial move on the surface, but there are many other things to consider.

Are you able to save the extra money you'd pay toward your mortgage?

I have talked about this often, but it is a really important point, and I want to drive it home. I think the first thing a homeowner should look at before paying off their mortgage is the amount they currently save. Everyone should have an emergency fund. If you cannot save any money and live paycheck to paycheck, focus on saving money before you spend anything extra on your mortgage.

Accessing the equity in your house is not easy (equity is the difference between what you owe on your house and what it is worth). If you plan to save money by paying off your mortgage, you will have to refinance, sell, or get a line of credit against the house. The tricky part to getting a line of credit or to refinancing is qualifying for a new loan. If you lose your job or are in a bad spot financially, qualifying can be tough, even if you have a lot of equity. For many people who need to access their equity, the only option is to sell. However, when you sell, you must pay real estate agents and other costs, which could total as much as 10 percent of the sale price. You also must find a new place to rent and go through the hassle of moving. Your house should not be used as a savings account, and if you cannot save money now, don't pay extra toward your mortgage.

How much money do you save by paying your mortgage off early?

If you have an emergency fund and are saving money, you may want to consider paying off your mortgage early. You should consider your current investments and the return you're getting from them. The interest rate on most mortgages is less than 5 or even 4 percent.

The difference between paying off a loan and investing that money in something that earns interest is that you will not see any advantage from the payoff until the mortgage is gone. If you have an investment that earns 5 percent, you begin earning that as soon as you invest. However, your monthly payments don't go down if you pay your mortgage off early, that is unless you sell, refinance, or fully pay it off. If you have a $200,000 mortgage and your monthly payment is $954 you could pay until your owing balance is $5,000, but your monthly payment will still be $954. The payment will not drop or change until you completely pay off the loan. Even though you are earning equity and increasing your net worth on paper, paying extra each month doesn't benefit you until the loan is completely paid off.

However, making extra payments will reduce your total interest. If you pay $100 more every month, you will pay the loan off 5 years sooner and pay $27,000 less in interest. $27,000 is a lot of money, but that only amounts to $900 per year over 30 years. Paying $100 more every month means you're losing $1,200 per year that you could be saving or investing in something else. If you invest that $100 in something that earns 5 percent interest every year for 30 years, you would have $59,554 saved after 25 years (the same time it would have taken to pay off the loan).

Most people will make more money and be more secure by saving and investing instead of paying their loan off early. If you lose your job or get hurt, it is much easier to tap into a savings account than to tap into your equity.

Some loans will allow a loan recast. With a loan recast you may be able to lower your payment based on your owing balance. Not all loans offer loan recasts, and a loan recast does not shorten the length of the loan. Check with your lender to see if your mortgage is eligible. If you get an adjustable rate mortgage, the payment also changes based on the owing balance, so that is a case where it may make sense to pay down the loan.

What is mortgage insurance and how does it change if I pay the loan down early?

One advantage to paying off a mortgage early is the removal of mortgage insurance. FHA mortgage insurance stays with FHA loans, but some conventional loans have removable mortgage insurance. If the loan amount is less than 80 percent of the value of the house after a few years of payments, the mortgage insurance can be removed.

If a homeowner does not think they will have enough equity built up to remove their mortgage insurance through regular payments, it may make sense to pay extra towards the loan. Once the loan amount reaches 80 or 75 percent (the actual figure varies by number) of the value of the house and enough time has passed, the borrower can ask the lender to remove the insurance. At that point, the lender will order an appraisal to determine value and may remove the mortgage insurance. This is one of the few cases where the homeowner will realize a lower payment before the loan is paid off.

Should you pay off other debt first?

Most mortgages last for 30 years, which means the lender cannot call the loan due for 30 years. The payment most likely will not change much, unless taxes or insurance go up or you get an adjustable rate loan. Most student debt, car loans, credit cards, and other loans have shorter terms, higher rates, and higher payments. Concentrate on paying other debt off before you pay off your mortgage. Additionally, if you need money, it is a lot easier and cheaper to sell a car than it is to sell a house. With credit card debt, the more you pay off, the lower your payment will be, meaning you see an immediate benefit.

What are the benefits of paying a mortgage off early?

Some borrowers prefer the peace of mind being debt free brings. However, debt is not always a bad thing. I would rather have a large sum of money saved or invested and carry some debt than have no savings and no debt. When people get into financial trouble, it is not easy to access the equity in a house. It is much easier to access cash from other investments or a savings account. However, there are some cases where paying a mortgage off makes sense.

- Some people may not be disciplined enough to save money. If that is the case, it may make sense to pay off your mortgage early as a way of forcing yourself to save.
- When you pay off debt, your DTI ratio goes down, making it easier to qualify for a new house or car. However, DTI ratio is based on the monthly payments, not the total amount of debt. Paying down debt will not help your DTI ratio unless you are able to remove your mortgage insurance or recast the loan.
- Paying down loans can increase your net worth (assuming you are not saving that money).
- If you pay down your debt and the real estate market declines, you may be able to sell your house more easily. Again, if you would have saved that money, you could still sell your house and bring some of the saved money to closing.

Paying your mortgage off early offers some advantages, but most of them benefit those who cannot save money on their own. Many people will spend any money they save. If you can't make yourself save money, paying off your mortgage may be a good way to build a nest egg, but it will be hard to access your equity, and you won't realize many advantages until the loan is completely paid off.

CHAPTER 45

What Does Refinancing Mean, and What Is a HELOC?

A cash out refinance allows you to take cash out of your house using a long-term mortgage. A home equity line of credit (HELOC) allows you to take money out with a short-term loan. A HELOC is more flexible regarding the amount of money that can be withdrawn and when it can be withdrawn, but HELOC terms are shorter and carry higher interest rates. I have used both a cash-out refinance and a HELOC, and I will detail the advantages and disadvantages of each.

What does refinancing mean?

When you refinance your house, you get a new loan that replaces any current loans. Many people will refinance to get a lower interest rate, to decrease their payments, or to take cash out of the house. Refinancing is similar to getting a first mortgage on the house. You must qualify for the loan based on credit, income, time at your job, and more. The terms can be 30 years, 15 years, or less depending on the borrower's needs. Interest rates and loan costs will be very similar to those you pay when you first buy the house.

A cash out refinance involves taking out cash during the refinance. To complete a cash out refinance, you must have a certain amount of equity because you'll obtain a bigger loan than what you currently owe. Since the balance on the new loan is higher than your old loan, you receive cash at closing. You must still pay closing costs, which may include an appraisal, loan origination fees, recording fees and more. Those closing costs will reduce the amount of cash that you get from the refinance.

What is a Home Equity Line of Credit (HELOC)?

A HELOC is much different from a refinance because you may not have to pay off your current loan. If you have a $100,000 loan but your house is worth $200,000, you may be able to get an $80,000 line of credit and keep the $100,000 loan in place. When you take out a line of credit, you do not have to use the money right away (or ever). You can use as much of the money as you want and pay it back when you like. You can borrow the money again after you pay it off. With a refinance, once you pay off the loan or pay extra to it, you cannot borrow from it again.

A HELOC will have closing costs, but they will usually amount to less than those from a cash out refinance. Fees will differ depending on if the line is taken against an investment property over a personal residence. The term could be two years, five years, or longer, but it can never be 30 years. HELOC rates are also usually higher and can go up or down as interest rates go up or down.

When is a HELOC better than a cash out refinance?

A HELOC has many advantages over a cash out refinance. With a HELOC, you do not have to take out the full loan amount; with a refinance, you do. This gives you the option of taking out the money at some point in the future if you don't need it now. You can also pay back the money from a HELOC at any time and take it out again at any time. With a refinance, once you pay back part or all of the loan, you cannot take that money out again without completing another refinance.

If you have a loan on a house that you want to keep, you can get a line of credit without paying off the loan. The HELOC can be placed in second position and the first loan can stay in first position. When you refinance, you usually must refinance any loans on the house.

If you think you may need money in the future for your business or rental properties, but you won't need it for long-term reasons, a HELOC may be perfect. If you need long-term money for financing rental property down payments, a cash out refinance may be the better option.

When is a cash out refinance better than a HELOC?

A cash out refinance carries a much longer term than a HELOC. I use my cash out refinances to fund down payments for more rental properties. I knew I did not want to pay those funds back quickly, so a cash out refinance was perfect. If you need long-term money, a cash out refinance may be the better option than a HELOC. You pay interest on the money you withdraw in a cash out refinance, so it is smart to put it to use right away.

If you have a loan that carries a much higher rate than current rates, refinancing may make sense. Remember you will pay about 3 percent in closing costs, which will be rolled into the loan and increase the owing balances. Rates on the new loan should be significantly less than those on your current loan.

CHAPTER 46

How to Find a Great Lender

The lender you use can make the difference between an awesome experience or a horrible one that costs you a lot of money. The quality of lenders and banks varies greatly. I avoid banks in my area because they almost always mess up a deal. The lender may work with one bank, one mortgage company, or may be able to shop multiple banks and mortgage companies for you. I know of lenders who work with great banks, but they manage to botch deals on a regular basis. I have worked with banks that tend to mess up every deal they do unless you work with one of their great lenders. It is important to line up both a great lender and a great bank.

Many lenders and banks advertise online and on the radio. Most of these lenders are national and work throughout the country. In my experience, it is much better to work with a local lender. They know the title companies, the local traditions, which fees are charged and to whom, the appraisers, and more. When one of my clients wants to work with a national lender, I expect loan delays and problems.

How do you find a great local lender?

The best and easiest way to find a good lender is to ask your trusted real estate agent. Hopefully your agent has some experience selling houses and knows who the good lenders are. Your agent should recommend a couple of good lenders. Interview those lenders and pick the one you feel the most comfortable with. Most lenders will have similar rates and terms for owner-occupied loans. Rates and terms start to very if you are an investor, are looking for a line of credit, or need a different type of financing.

You should also check with the bank that holds your checking and savings accounts. Some of these banks have great lending programs, but not all of them. If you want to use your own bank, ask your agent if they have any experience working with that bank. Some large banks in my area are horrible at mortgages.

You may also find online mortgage companies that sound great but may not pull through when needed. I have had multiple experiences with online mortgage companies that offered lower rates online than what they actually gave consumers. These lenders greatly misrepresented the time it would take to close a loan or made other huge mistakes. Remember, a local lender must maintain their reputation in the community. The better job they do, the more people will use them, and the more money they will make. A national lender can screw up and not care because they get their business from advertising—not reputation.

How do lenders botch deals?

Here are just a few of the things lenders do to delay or kill deals:

- **Ordering the appraisal too late:** In Colorado, and some other areas of the country, appraisals are taking weeks to complete. If a lender does not order the appraisal right away, the closing can be delayed for weeks. If you need to sell a house before you can buy another, a late appraisal can kill the deal.
- **Improperly qualifying a borrower:** Not long ago, with just one week left before closing, a lender discovered that one of my buyers had a recent bankruptcy! This should have been discovered even before an offer was made. The buyer could not get the loan and lost money on the inspection and appraisal.
- **Lack of knowledge:** You would think a lender would know how their loans work, but that is not always the case. Some lenders grossly overestimate how fast they can complete a loan and even misquote the costs.
- **Thinking they know the seller better than the listing agent:** Many lenders assume HUD and REO sellers will act like normal sellers by making repairs,

etc. HUD and REO sellers are very different and often will not make any repairs even if they're required by an appraisal. Many buyers waste a lot of money because the lender did not know how HUD or REOs work.

- **Not knowing the buyer's best loan option:** We have discussed many loan options: VA, USDA, FHA, FHA 203k, conventional, and more. You can also use down payment assistance programs with many of these loans. Not every lender is approved to offer every loan product. Some lenders may steer a buyer towards the wrong loan because they do not offer the right loan for that buyer (like a 203k rehab loan). That lender may not be approved to offer state-funded down payment assistance, so they convince the buyer to use a much more expensive loan.

What should you ask a lender?

Not every lender is great, and just because your real estate agent refers them to you, it doesn't mean you should use them. Agents should give you some choices, but you can ask these questions to make sure you have the right lender:

- Are you approved for down payment assistance programs, and if so, which ones?
- How much do you charge for origination fees?
- What other fees do you charge?
- What is your current rate on a 30-year fixed-rate mortgage?
- How long will it take to close?
- What DTI ratio will I need to qualify?
- Do you have loan programs for houses that need repairs, such as FHA 203k, other rehab, or escrow loan programs?
- Do you lend on HUD homes and are you familiar with their repair escrow program?

- Do you offer loans with removable private mortgage insurance?
- Does your company/bank sell the loans they originate or keep them in-house?

Many of the answers will not mean much to you. That's why it is important to talk to a couple of different lenders and see how their answers differ. You will start to see which lender offers the best deal and has the most options.

One of the biggest advantages of buying a house is being able to get a great deal. One of the biggest challenges of getting a great deal is that many of those houses need repairs. The right lender should be able to work around repair issues using the right loan.

What if a traditional lender does not have the loan for you?

As a real estate investor, I ran into problems buying rental properties because traditional lenders stopped lending to me. They said I could not have more than four mortgages and I could not finance fix and flips. Those banks and mortgage companies made it sound like I had no options. The truth was their company or bank would not lend to me, not that no one would lend to me. The same goes for owner-occupants who want to buy a house that needs work. We have saved many deals because we convinced a buyer to change to a local bank after the national bank denied their loan.

What is a portfolio lender and why are they important?

Portfolio lenders are local banks that lend their own money and do not sell their loans. Most national banks sell their loans on Wall Street, and those loans must meet specific guidelines. A portfolio lender can be a great asset because they may be more willing to finance a real estate investor. A portfolio lender will often have less-stringent requirements than large national banks, which makes it easier for investors to get loans. Big banks may not finance an investor if they have more than four mortgages, but many local banks might. I have a great portfolio lender who allows me to finance as many properties as I want as long as I continue to qualify and have enough reserves. Having a good portfolio lender is extremely important to my strategy, which depends on buying many properties.

Many banks will not give you another mortgage if you already have four financed properties. Some banks will finance between four and ten properties, but they have many restrictions. Those restrictions include a 25 percent down payment, high credit scores, and no cash out refinance. Very few banks will give you a mortgage if you have ten or more financed properties. Most banks have restrictions on the number of mortgages they will give to one person because they sell their loans to institutional investors who only buy loans that conform to Fannie Mae guidelines.

A portfolio lender lends their own money, and they do not sell their loans to institutional investors. Because portfolio lenders do not have to conform to Fannie Mae guidelines, they will lend on more than four and even more than ten mortgages. They also may allow a cash out refinance and be flexible with many other financing options. My portfolio lender does not require a property to be in livable condition to give me a loan. Some portfolio lenders do not require an appraisal, may not require as high of a credit score, and might not be as concerned with debt-to-income ratios.

Which loan types does a portfolio lender offer?

Since a portfolio lender is a local bank that lends their own money, they do not have to meet Fannie Mae lending guidelines, which allows them more flexibility. However, they do not offer all the loan programs that large banks offer. My portfolio lender does not offer a 30-year fixed mortgage; they only offer a 15-year fixed, 5/30 ARM, or 7/30 ARM. To get the lowest interest rate, I use a 5/30 ARM on most of my rental properties. Each portfolio lender has different terms and loan programs. Some local banks require 25 percent down, some will only offer 25- or 20-year amortizations, and some carry higher interest rates. If you are looking for a portfolio lender, make sure you shop around to find the best terms.

A portfolio lender may also want you to have all your accounts and money in their bank. This is usually not a big issue for most people since a portfolio lender will have very competitive programs and products that align with the larger national banks. The better relationship you build with a portfolio lender, the better loans you will get.

How does my portfolio lender save deals for clients?

I have sold many houses that were owned by HUD or a bank. Very specific rules apply to these sales, and not all lenders know those rules. HUD very clearly states they will make no repairs and the buyer cannot turn on the water for inspections or an appraisal if the pipes do not hold air pressure. HUD discloses on their website whether pipes hold pressure or not on every house they sell. I constantly have issues with lenders and real estate agents who try to complete an inspection yet don't realize the water must be off prior to bid acceptance.

Most lenders will not lend on a house if they cannot verify that the utilities work. When we ran into this problem, we saved many deals because we told the buyer about a local lender who did not require the water to be on. The buyer switched lenders, switched loan programs, and was able to buy the house.

How did I find my lender?

I found my portfolio lender because I am a real estate agent, and I heard from other agents that my portfolio lender was the best bank for investors. After I ran into problems with my mortgage broker during the financing of my fifth rental property, I contacted a portfolio lender to see what they could offer. The portfolio lender had the perfect loans for my investment properties. It took me about a week to move all my accounts to the new bank so I could easily finance new rentals.

I have since purchased 16 rentals, and 15 of them were financed with the same local bank. This local bank has also financed my fix and flips and raw land.

How do you find a portfolio lender?

The first method is to ask everyone you know. Some people may not know what a portfolio lender is; ask them if they know a local bank. Who else can you ask?

- Real estate agents know many lenders and may be your best source.
- Other lenders may be able to refer you to a portfolio lender once they know they cannot give you a loan.
- Investors in the area will know portfolio lenders; the trick is meeting them. Real estate investor meetings are a great place to meet investors and get local information.
- Ask your local bank if they are a portfolio lender or what types of investor lending programs they offer.
- Ask title companies who local investors use to finance their rental properties.
- Call your chamber of commerce and ask if they know who the most investor-friendly banks in your town are.

Search the internet.

The internet is the easiest way to start your search for a portfolio lender. Simply search for a portfolio lender in your state using any search engine. I have used this method for people in different states, and I always get results. Once you find a bank that mentions portfolio lending in your state, call and ask what type of investor programs they offer.

Cold-calling portfolio lenders.

If none of the options above works, you may have to resort to calling local banks. Ask them what type of investor loans they offer. If they do not have what you are looking for, ask if they know which bank might. Keep trying until you have called all the local banks you can find.

What questions should you ask during your search?

Many banks do not advertise they are portfolio lenders, and many people working at the bank may not even know what a portfolio lender is. If you call a bank and they say they are not a portfolio lender, do not give up! Ask to talk to a loan officer and ask specific questions regarding the investor programs they offer. Here are some good questions to ask:

- Do you loan to investors who already have four mortgages?
- Do you have a commercial or business loan department?
- Do you sell your loans or keep them in-house?
- Do you allow investors with four or more mortgages to do a cash out refinance?
- What terms and loan programs do you offer investors? ARM, 15-year, 30-year fixed, balloon?
- What interest rates do you charge and what are the initial costs for your loans?
- What loan-to-value ratios do you offer investors for a new purchase and a refinance?
- What are your seasoning requirements for refinances?

Conclusion

Finding a great lender is not easy, but it makes the house-buying process a lot easier. Portfolio lenders are usually great for investors, but they can also help owner-occupants who need to buy a house that needs repairs. My portfolio lender has been awesome with financing both my rental properties and fix and flips. Most owner-occupant buyers will be fine using a traditional lender, but make sure they are the right lender for you.

Part IV: How to Sell and Maintain or Repair a House

At some point, you may need to sell a house. Even if you never buy a house yourself, you may inherit a house or need to help someone sell one. Many misconceptions and questions surround the process. Should you use an agent? Which repairs should you make? How do you value the house? In this section, I explain the best way to sell a house. I have sold my own houses and have sold houses for many others. Over the years, I have learned what works and what does not work. Selling a house on your own is not easy, and it usually does not save you any money. The better condition your house is in, the more money you will make on the sale, but some improvements cost more than they are worth. In the following chapters, I recommend the most lucrative improvements and explain how to maintain your house so you can sell it for the highest possible price.

CHAPTER 47

How to Sell Your House for the Most Money

Even if you never buy a house, you may have to sell one at some point in your life. Throughout this book, I mentioned that great deal on a house can greatly improve your financial situation, but if you don't sell your house correctly, you can lose that advantage. By following some basic principles, you'll get the most money for your house without pulling your hair out due to stress. If you use an agent, keep the house in good condition, and price it correctly, you will profit.

Which repairs should you perform?

The condition of your house is one of the most important factors for selling at the best price. Seasoned investors and those experienced in real estate can see the potential in fixer uppers. However, many first-time or move-up buyers have a hard time picturing a house if it needs work or does not show well. Many buyers let paint color or furniture persuade them.

The repairs you make are extremely important. The number and type of repairs will vary based on market conditions and the price of the house. Usually, the more expensive the house, the more repairs and updates it will need. When I flip houses, I typically buy and sell on the low side of the market price. Our median price is around $260,000, and our flips usually sell for less than that, even after they are fully repaired. I recently bought a high-end flip with a selling price above $800,000. I repaired the house and listed it, but it was not selling. The feedback I received from other agents was not good either. I realized I had repaired the house according to the low-end market I flip in. In the high-end market, I had to make the property perfect, but with less-expensive houses, they do not have to be nearly as nice. I took the house off the market, made more repairs, re-listed it, and it sold. You must make sure your house is comparable to other houses selling in your neighborhood.

Will staging help sell the house?

Staging can mean spending thousands of dollars to rent furniture for a vacant house, or it can mean picking up and organizing an occupied residence. When we sell a vacant house, we don't spend money putting furniture in it. We sell a lot of houses, and to be honest, one of the reasons we don't stage them is we don't have the time to do it. I know many investors who swear by staging and feel it brings them much more money than if they didn't stage. I think staging can create a very positive effect if done correctly. You can't throw a table and two chairs in the living room and call it staged. To properly stage a house, each room needs to have at least the bare minimum furniture that someone would want to live with. Staging shows potential buyers what the house would feel like if they lived there. Personally, I like how big a house feels when it is completely vacant and has new paint and carpet.

I think staging becomes very important when a house is occupied. Many people tend to collect furniture and personal items over the years that clutter a house. The key to staging an occupied house is to de-clutter and de-personalize as much as possible. When buyers view the house, you want them to look at the features, not your personal pictures. You want buyers to picture themselves living there, not someone else. When de-cluttering, remove all non-essential furniture and most decorations. You want the house to feel as large as possible, and the fewer the items in it, the larger it feels. When you sell a house, make sure your furniture is not too big for your rooms. Nothing makes a house feel small more than a king-size bed in a small bedroom.

Another factor to consider is what other sellers are doing in your market. Is every vacant house being staged? If all your competition is staging, you may have to stage your vacant house as well.

What else do you need to do before selling your house?

Even if you don't stage your house, or if you live in it, you must make it look appealing. Here are some tips. I will expand on many of these throughout this part of the book:

- Have it professionally deep cleaned. Many people clean houses themselves but do a lackluster job. Pay for it to be done before it is listed.
- Make sure the yard is mowed, weeds are pulled, and all trash is picked up.
- Remove extra, unneeded vehicles.
- Trim the trees.
- Remove signs of pets if possible.
- Have the carpets professionally cleaned.
- Make needed repairs or updates before it is listed; do not offer an allowance.
- If painting, use neutral colors.
- Be economical (but not cheap) when making repairs. Most $100,000 kitchens will not return that in value unless it's a multi-million-dollar house.
- Do not trust online value estimators; they can be way off.

What do you need to do for showings?

Showings are a key part of selling a house. Here are some tips for what to do during showings. A good real estate agent should help you prepaire your house to sell and handle showings.

- Open all blinds and curtains.
- Make sure heat or air conditioning is at a pleasant temperature.
- Bake cookies or something that smells good and leave them for buyers (this is great during open houses as well).
- Be flexible and ready to leave at any moment.

- If you have pets, take them with you during showings.

How important is the asking price?

The selling price will attract buyers more than anything else. Buyers and real estate agents use the price to sort out potential properties when they search MLS. Many buyers want to live in a certain neighborhood or a certain area for a certain price. If your house is priced higher than all the others in the neighborhood, selling it can be very difficult. Most buyers have expectations for what certain areas cost, and if a house costs significantly more than that expectation, many buyers may never consider or view it. You may also run into an appraisal issue if your house is priced too high but goes under contract. You cannot count on a low offer if the house is priced too high. Most buyers will move to the next house instead of taking the time to write an offer they don't think will be accepted.

Different types of markets will determine how you sell. In a seller's market, many buyers are looking but supply doesn't meet demand. In a seller's market, you can command a higher asking price and dictate which repairs you'll complete. I will actually price houses a little high in a seller's market because there is very little competition. Even if I price a house slightly high, buyers will still look at it and may offer me less than I am asking yet still make an offer. In a seller's market, I can sometimes make fewer repairs as well because I don't have five or ten other houses to compete with.

In a buyer's market, everything changes. I will price my houses slightly below what I think market value is. I do this because I don't want to get caught chasing a declining market. If you chase a declining market, you may try to lower your price to get buyers, but you may not be able to lower it enough to catch the decreasing prices. Your house may stay on the market 3 months or more and become stigmatized. Whenever a house is on the market for an extended period, buyers automatically think something is wrong with it. Even if the price is great and the house is perfect, buyers will think there must be some reason no one else has bought it.

One of the biggest mistakes flippers make is pricing their houses too high. They overspend on repairs, and it takes them longer to sell than they thought. To make up for the added expenses, they raise the price. Buyers do not care how much money you spent on repairs or how long it took you. They care about the price compared to other houses they can buy. Make sure you price based on what the market says the house will sell rather for how much money you've sunk into it.

How quickly do you need to sell a house?

If you want to sell a house you occupy, the time it takes to make repairs or get it perfect for marketing may not matter as much. You'll live in it while it is being repaired. If you are an investor or have already moved, you pay carrying costs while the house sits vacant. Most likely, you have a loan and you are paying interest, not to mention utilities, insurance, and opportunity cost. Opportunity costs are those that prevent you from making a new deal because your money is tied up and you can't buy anything else. It can cost $50, $100, or more every day to carry a vacant house with a loan on it. By trying to squeak out a few thousand dollars with a high price, you may be costing yourself thousands.

Not only does pricing a house too high cost you added carrying costs, but repairs will also delay the sale. When considering whether to make minor or major repairs, make sure you figure the extra time it will take to make those major repairs.

If you need to sell your house fast, the best way to get rid of it is to price it low. The best way to motivate buyers is to give them an awesome deal. When I flip houses, I look for houses that are priced well below market value. As a flipper, I can pay cash for houses and close very quickly. There are many other flippers in almost every real estate market, but to flip houses, you must get great deals. When you see ads about buying ugly houses, paying cash for houses, or get a letter from an investor wanting to buy your house, they probably want to flip it. If you need to sell fast, selling to a flipper will get the job done, but you will sell it for much less than you would by listing it with an agent.

Should you use a real estate agent?

Real estate agents are expensive, but they are worth it. As an agent myself, I may be biased, but there are only a few specific instances where I would try to sell a house without an agent. I am interested in buying some commercial properties, which I am not an expert in. Even though I am an agent, I am hiring another agent to represent me because of the experience they have with commercial properties. I also pay another agent who represents the buyers on most of the houses I sell. Here are some of the main reasons you should use an agent:

- Real estate agents have access to the MLS, which you should use to sell your house for the most money. Most buyers depend on an agent to find them a house, and if yours is not in the MLS, there is little chance an agent will find it. You can use a cheap, limited-service company to list your house in the MLS, and you will save some money in some states (in Colorado limited-service listings are illegal). However, you will still have to pay the real estate agent representing the buyer, and you will not have any representation, while the buyer will. Going into a deal without professional representation when the other party does is never good.
- Selling a house is very tricky. In Colorado, the contract is 17 pages (longer in other states). Then, you have the state addendum and disclosures, which add up to another 15 pages. The contract is that long to cover all the possible cases where someone may get sued.
- A good agent will know exactly how to market your house. There is more to marketing than putting a sign in the yard. You need great pictures, virtual tours, color fliers, open houses, agent tours, and an

internet presence. Good agents will put listings on multiple websites, including Craigslist, Facebook, and Twitter.
- Agents can recommend the most important repairs you should make. A great agent knows exactly how to sell a house and how to get it into showing condition.
- An agent can set your selling price. Determining market value without access to the MLS and sold listings is very difficult. As I mentioned before, the asking price is extremely important.

What is the best time of year to sell?

Time of year affects how you sell. If you have a choice, it's best to sell during the spring or summer. The part of the country you live in can affect this. If you live anywhere with a cold winter, the tips below apply. If you live in a resort area or a place where people move in the winter, the opposite may apply.

- **Spring**: Spring may be the best time of the year to sell. In spring, people are outside enjoying the nice weather and the longer days. Many people work until 5 and can't view houses until after work. During the winter, it is dark after work, which makes viewing houses more difficult.
- **Fall**: Fall is a decent time to sell, but it is also a risky time. People start to get very busy, with kids starting school, activities, and sports. Halloween and Thanksgiving also preoccupy families and take their focus off buying a house
- **Winter**: Winter is the toughest time of year to sell. The holidays and cold weather tend to slow the housing market. I happen to find many of my great deals in winter because other buyers are preoccupied with the holidays. The days are very short and don't allow much viewable time.

- **Summer:** Summer is a great time to sell. The weather is warm, the days are long, and many people have more free time. Many buyers also want to get settled into a house before school, and the activities that go with it, start.

I am not saying you should never sell in the winter or fall, but selling in the spring and summer is usually easier. We sell houses all year, and if you do everything else right, you can sell any time of the year. If you need to sell right away, the time of year should not deter you. There are times that are best to sell, but it may not make a huge difference in the selling price.

Can appraisals affect the selling price?

Appraisers must use sold comps when they determine value. Finding enough sold comps to justify rising prices in an appreciating market can be tough. When you are deciding which repairs to make, look at the sold comps in the neighborhood and make sure the sold comps support a higher value. If your house is nicer and more expensive than everything else in the neighborhood, you may run into an appraisal issue.

If a house does not appraise for the contract price, the buyers must base their loan value on the appraisal value. Often, buyers don't have a lot of extra cash, and the only solution to a low appraisal is to find a new buyer or lower the price. If an FHA appraisal was done, that appraisal stays with the house for four months, and any new FHA buyers will have to use that same appraisal. A low appraisal will almost certainly cost the seller money.

How does the 90-day flip rule affect the selling process?

FHA loans once contained a 90-day flip rule. The rule prevented lenders from loaning on properties that had sold within the last 90 days. Even though that rule was suspended, many lenders still abide by it. Some lenders, to verify value, will allow a second appraisal within 90 days of a sale; some will make everyone wait 90 days before they can sign the contract; and others don't pay attention to the rule at all. Bank-foreclosed houses are exempt from this rule. If you are going to flip a house and plan to sell it within 90 days of when you purchased it, the 90-day flip rule may cause you problems.

Conclusion

When you sell a house, there is a lot to think about. I am still learning myself! If you want to make the process easy, hire a great real estate agent. Otherwise pay attention to your house's appearance, the repairs you make, your asking price, and the time of year.

When we sell a house in a normal market, we get an offer around the third week on the market, assuming it's priced correctly. I have no idea why it ends up being three weeks, but that seems to be the sweet spot. If we price a house too low, we will get multiple offers in the first week, and if we price too high, we won't receive any offers in the first month. If we don't receive offers in the first month, we will lower the price about 5 percent. We don't want our houses sitting stagnant on the market. If the market is extremely hot, we might sell perfectly priced houses within a day or so.

CHAPTER 48

Why You Should Always Use a Real Estate Agent

Using a real estate agent can be expensive, and many sellers think selling a house themselves is a great way to save money. A seller may save a commission by selling a house themselves, but trying to sell a house without an agent may actually cost them more money than the commission they saved. People will claim they saved thousands by selling without an agent, and they may even claim they sold within one day! There is a reason they sold it in one day: they left a lot of money on the table! A great agent could have more than made up for the commission they charged by pricing a house correctly and working for the seller's best interest. While commissions may seem high to some, it is important to know they are negotiable. Real estate agents can charge so much because they provide great value and usually get you much more money than you could on your own.

Agents are marketing experts, know the sales process, and know how to value a house. Many think agents make too much money for the time they spend, but they are paid for more than just the time it takes to sell a house. They are paid for all the licensing courses and continuing education they must take plus their experience with marketing and selling houses. They can charge a lot for these services because good they make their clients much more money.

When you sell a house yourself, tou may not save as much as you think.

When you try to sell a house yourself, it may appear you can save 5, 6, or even 7 percent of the sales price by avoiding a commission (all commissions are negotiable). However, most buyers work with agents because it is usually free for buyers. If you don't pay the real estate agent representing the buyer a commission, you eliminate most of the buyers in your market. Eliminating most buyers will definitely lower your selling price and cost you money. If you agree to pay a cooperating broker, you only save half of the commission. On top of this, the buyer is represented by an agent and you are not. Who will have the upper hand during negotiations and the selling process? The buyer's agent will have the buyer's best interest in mind, not yours.

Why is it so important to value a house correctly?

If you price a house too low, or if you overprice it, you could lose thousands of dollars. The best time to sell is when your house first goes to market. Buyers wait for the perfect house to come up for sale, and it is vital that a house is priced correctly from the beginning. Here is a great statistic for people who try to sell a house themselves versus using a real estate agent:

- FSBOs (for-sale-by-owner) accounted for 8% of house sales in 2015. The typical FSBO house sold for $185,000 compared to $240,000 for agent-assisted sales.

From http://www.realtor.org/field-guides/field-guide-to-quick-real-estate-statistics

Why will overpricing cost a seller money?

If an overpriced house comes up for sale, a buyer may not even look at it. An overpriced house will sit on the market for weeks or maybe even months. When buyers learn a house has been on the market for an extended period, they start to wonder what is wrong with it. Even if the price is lowered to the right value after a few weeks, the house still may not sell for what it would have sold for had it been priced correctly to begin with. Houses become stigmatized when they sit on the market for extended timeframes. For an investor or a homeowner that no longer occupies the house, a stigmatized listing is very bad. Every month a house sits vacant, it costs the seller money, and if there is a loan on the house, it can cost the seller thousands of dollars per month. If the seller had priced the house correctly to begin with, they would have sold quickly and saved thousands of dollars.

Why will underpricing cost a seller money?

Underpricing can cost just as much as overpricing. When you underprice, you may sell quickly, but there is a good chance you will sell the house for less than it is worth. Underpricing can stir up a lot of activity and produce many offers, but it does so at the cost of lost profit. In a multiple-offer situation, it is possible to get a contract for over asking price. The problem with underpricing is it attracts buyers (like myself) who want a great deal. Often, a multiple-offer situation will actually scare away some buyers who do not want to get into a bidding war and will not bid on a house that has multiple offers.

If you underprice and receive an offer over your asking price, remember you could have received an even higher offer had you priced correctly. Most buyers will base their offer off the list price and not what the house is actually worth. Buyers tell me all the time, "I offered $10,000 over asking price and still did not get the house!" Those buyers base their offer on the list price, assuming the seller is asking fair-market value. Those buyers are not basing their offer on what the house may actually be worth. Another downside to an offer that comes in well above asking price is it may give an appraiser a reason to come in at a low value. If an appraisal comes in low, it could cost the seller even more money! By pricing the house correctly to begin with, you will almost always sell for the most money.

Why is valuing a house difficult without a real estate agent?

Valuing a property is the most important aspect of selling a house. Without a lot of experience and MLS access, it is very difficult to do. Without MLS access, it is tough to get information on recently sold properties. Recently sold properties are the most important piece of information needed to value a house. People have access to active listings through websites like Zillow, but only licensed agents have access to the MLS, which lists sold houses. Active listings can give an idea of house values, but you have no idea if houses are overpriced or at what price they will actually sell. Every house is different because every house has different features. Location also drives value. Real estate agents are experts at determining value based off these characteristics. It can take years to understand local markets, and local markets can change extremely fast. Determining the correct value is very difficult and takes a lot of time, especially if you are not an agent.

How accurate is Zillow?

Zillow also provides a "Zestimate" for house values. Many people think this value is accurate, but it can be very inaccurate. Zillow was off by as much as 40 percent on one of my properties! You should never value a house based solely on a Zestimate. I talk more about how far off they are later in the book.

A real estate agent knows how to deal with a low appraisal.

If you end up with a buyer who is getting a loan, they will most likely need an appraisal. The bank will lend the buyer money based on that appraisal, and if the appraisal comes in low, there is a good chance the buyer will need the house price to be lowered. With rising home prices, we see low appraisals every day, and there is a way to deal with appraisers. Agents know how to proactively work with the appraiser and know how to challenge an appraisal if it comes in low.

Agents know how to market.

There is a definite art to marketing a house correctly. You can't just stick a house in the MLS and wait for offers to come in (unless you price it too low). An agent knows how to take the best pictures, do virtual tours, create the best brochures, the best websites to use, which magazines and newspapers to advertise in, and much more. Agents also know people and have their own marketing list of potential buyers. Often, an agent will know buyers who are waiting for a house just like yours.

Why can't a seller use a low-fee service to enter a house in the MLS?

Many companies now offer a low-fee MLS service. You pay a couple hundred dollars and get your house entered on the MLS. There are many problems with using this type of service:

- The service may never see your house and may enter incorrect information with no pictures.
- The seller still must take calls and set up showings with many of these services.
- You will have to pay the buyer's agent if you enter the house in the MLS. Once you have paid the MLS listing company and buyer's agent, are you really saving much money?
- You still have all the disadvantages of not having an agent represent you while the buyer will have representation. You'll receive no help with contracts, negotiations, inspections, appraisals, etc.
- Limited-service listings are not available in all states.

Agents know how to handle state contracts.

I've already mentioned how lengthy contracts are. Agents know exactly what to look for in a state contract, what is customary for the seller to pay, and what is customary for the buyer to pay. In Colorado, the seller customarily pays for title insurance and many other costs that are split between the buyer and the seller. The buyer also pays many costs. If you do not have an agent to help you understand what you and the buyer should pay, you could easily pay many more costs than you should.

Agents know title companies, lenders, and other agents.

Agents know the market, and they also know people in the business. They can help a seller find the lowest-fee title company that offers the best service. They can help the seller find the best contractor if repairs are needed before the listing or after an inspection. Here are a few more things an agent will help a seller with.

- Price negotiation
- Inspection negotiation
- Appraisal negotiation
- Title-resolution negotiation
- Multiple-offer negotiation
- Seller concession negotiation
- Earnest money negotiation
- Inclusion and exclusion negotiation
- Conditional-sale-contingency negotiation
- Survey resolutions negotiation
- Due diligence resolutions negotiation
- Obtaining and reviewing buyer's qualification letter
- Closing and possession date negotiation

You should also exercise caution when using an agent

Earlier, I covered the best ways to find an agent. However, you must make sure your agent knows what they are doing. If your agent prices your house incorrectly, it can be just as harmful as an owner pricing their house incorrectly. Obtaining a couple of opinions regarding value doesn't hurt. Remember, the higher value is not always the best! Some agents will give a higher value than they really think the house is worth to get the listing. Therefore, it is important to get sold comparables from the agent and really look at them to make sure the value they give is correct.

Another problem I see is agents trying to double end listings. Double ending means they represent the buyer and seller, which may earn the agent two commissions. There is nothing wrong with the agent representing both sides of the transaction in most states, but you must make sure your house is being marketed to everyone. In some cases, the agent may list the house as "coming soon" by putting a sign in the yard and telling their buyers about the listing. The agent does not put the house in the MLS system because they do not want other agents to know about it. This gives the listing agent the chance to get the house under contract with their own buyer before the house is marketed to everyone.

The problem with the house going under contract before it is in the MLS system is the seller may not get as much money. Often, the agent will convince the seller to take less than list price or to list below market value so they have a better chance of getting the house under contract with their buyer. I suggest declining any offers, especially from your listing agent, until the house is active on the MLS for at least one day...if not longer.

Conclusion

Using an agent to sell your house is almost always better than doing it yourself. An agent will make you more money on due to their knowledge and experience. I know many investors who have their real estate license yet still use another agent to sell their house for them. Those investors know that another agent has the time and expertise needed to sell the house. Before you try to sell a house on your own, consider whether it is worth the time it will take to understand the process and whether you will actually save any money.

CHAPTER 49

Why Do Real Estate Agents Charge So Much?

Selling a house is expensive, and much of the cost goes to agent commissions. The seller usually pays the commissions, and they can be significant. Agents do not charge so much because of the time it takes to actually sell a house. They charge that much because it takes work and money to market. It is also hard to get licensed and become an agent, and they must pay for dues and insurance. Plus, agents usually must split their commissions with their broker.

The biggest reason an agent gets paid so much is they are worth it! An agent will usually sell your house for much more money than if you sold it yourself.

How do agents make money?

In most situations, an agent represents the buyer and seller, and the seller pays both commissions. This may not seem fair, but there is a very good reason the system works this way. Making the seller pay both agents' commissions allows the buyer pool to be larger and house prices to be higher.

Most buyers need all the cash they have to pay for the closing costs and down payments. If a buyer had to pay for their agent too, there would be much fewer buyers who could afford a house. With a bigger buyer pool, more houses sell, and sellers can charge more for their houses. Even though the seller pays for the buyer's agent, the seller makes more money in our current real estate system due to the higher prices caused by more buyers.

How much is the commission?

This is a tricky question for me to answer because I am an agent. There are no typical or set commissions; they are all negotiable. As an agent, I can't legally disclose what commissions total. Instead I can tell you HUD pays a 6 percent commission to sell houses: 3 percent to the buyer's agent and 3 percent to the seller's agent. I have seen higher and lower commissions than this, but remember there is no typical or set commission rate. Using HUD's structure, the seller pays the agents $12,000 if the house sells for $200,000.

Why does a real estate agent make so much money on one sale?

On the surface, it may look like an agent makes a killing, especially if they earn $6,000 on each side of the sale. An agent may work 10 hours or less on the listing side, which equals a rate of $600 per hour. That is a lot of money, but an agent does much more than work directly on the listing. The listing agent most likely must pay the broker part of that commission, which may mean a 50% reduction in their commission. As you can see, an agent may only make $3,000 on each side of the sale.

There are many more reasons why that $6,000 is not as much as it may seem. An agent must get licensed, must take continuing education, must pay for MLS, must pay for board dues, must pay for insurance, and must market themselves. Being an agent involves a lot of overhead, and an agent doesn't just charge for the time it takes to list a house. They charge for their experience and market knowledge, both of which allow the seller to make the most money.

Most agents do not sell many houses.

The average income for a real estate agent is only $39,000 per year. This is so low because most agents must pay a broker, and many work part-time and do not sell a lot of houses. The average agent sold 12 houses in 2012, which equals only $36,000 per year if the agent only nets the $6,000 mentioned in the example above.

CHAPTER 50

How Accurate are Zestimates?

Many people use Zillow to value their house, but how accurate is Zillow? Zillow uses what they call a Zestimate to provide values for almost every house in the United States. The problem with the Zestimate is it uses a computer algorithm to come up with a value. When valuing real estate, you need to have real people valuing houses in order to be accurate. When I look at my rental properties, Zillow comes pretty close to values on some, and on others they are way off. The problem is how do you know if their value is correct or not?

How does Zillow determine house values?

Zillow says they get their price from a proprietary formula using public and user-entered data. If you want to get a more accurate value from Zillow, you can actually set up an account with them and change the details about your own house. Zillow clearly states that their price estimate is a starting point for homeowners and buyers and should not be the only data used when determining value.

Zillow also provides rent values.

Zillow provides rent rates. Rent values are much harder to compare than house values because you cannot tell if a property is rented out or occupied by the owner. I use sold comparable properties to determine house values in most cases, but rental rates are much more difficult to determine because rents are not published in most cases. The best way to determine market rents is to see what people are currently asking for their rental properties, but you never know if properties will actually rent out for those amounts.

Why can't a computer accurately determine house values?

Computer programs can determine the value on things like cars pretty accurately. Most cars are very similar, and it is fairly easy determine values using mileage, condition and options. However, houses, unlike cars, are not produced on assembly lines. Every house is different and located in a different market area, which changes the value. Because no two houses are the same, it is almost impossible for a computer program to accurately determine value. To accurately value a house, you need to have a local market expert who knows how to value houses and knows how much the location, condition, and design features will affect the value.

What are my actual property values compared to Zillow's values?

I reviewed each of my rental properties, including what I bought them for, what I think they are worth, and what Zillow says they are worth. I am holding these properties for the long run and have no plans to sell them. In this section, I'll provide an accurate value for what I know these houses would sell for in our market right now. Since I don't plan to sell them, I have no reason to stretch their value as it does not benefit me.

I made my initial comparison a few years ago but just compared my values again in 2017. You can see that Zillow has improved some but can still be pretty far off. Here is the comparison I did a few years ago. In each case, I'll provide the Zillow Zestimate, their rent estimation (if available), and what I actually earn in rent and could sell the properties for.

Rental property number one

I bought my first rental property in December 2010 for $96,900. It was my first rental, and I got a great deal. It is now rented for $1,100 per month. Zillow says the house is worth $145,797 and should rent for $1,200 per month.

The rent is very accurate, but my estimated value is about $170,000. If I listed it for $145,000, I would have five offers in the first two days and could sell it for well over asking price. The current renters are at the end of their lease, and rents have been rising. I bet I could get $1,200 or more per month now if I was to rent it out again.

Rental property number two

I bought rental property number two in October of 2011 for $94,000. I put $15,000 of work into it before it was rented out, and it earned me $1,100 per month since. I know this rent is low: I rent it to my brother-in-law. I could rent it out for at least $1,300 per month in today's market.

Zillow's Zestimate says this house is worth $151,000 and does not provide a rent amount. If I were to sell it, I could command at least $170,000.

Rental property number three

I bought this property in November of 2011 for $92,000. I put about $18,000 of work into it before it was rented, and it is now rented for $1,250 per month.

Zillow says this house is worth $165,000 and the rental amount is not listed (I am not sure why they list rent values on some but not others). This value is much more accurate, and I would estimate this house is also worth right around $170,000.

Rental property number four

I bought rental property number four in January of 2013 for $109,000. This house needed $15,000 in work and earns me rent of $1,300 per month.

Zillow estimates this house is worth $166,000, which is not too far off. I think this house is worth closer to $180,000 or maybe $185,000. It is larger than my other houses and has more features.

Rental property number five

I bought rental property number five for $88,249 in December of 2012. This house needed a lot of work, and I spent about $20,000 on repairs before it was rented. This one earns me $1,200 per month.

Zillow says this house is worth $90,000, and I think they value it so low because I bought it recently. My estimate for the value is at least $155,000. This is a case where the Zillow value is way off.

Rental property number six

I bought rental property number six for $115,000 in March of 2013. I put about $17,000 into it, and it is rented out for $1,300 per month.

Zillow says this property is worth $132,000 and again does not list a rent value. I feel it is worth $160,000, which outlines another big difference in house values, possibly due to being a recent purchase.

Rental property number seven

Rental property number seven was purchased for $113,000 in April of 2012. I put about $7,500 in repairs into it, and I earn rent of $1,400 per month.

Zillow says this house is worth $148,000 and does not list rent. This house is in a very hot neighborhood and is now worth about $170,000. This was an awesome deal, and I wish I could find ten more like it!

Rental property number eight

I purchased rental property number 8 in November of 2013 for $97,500. I haven't rented it out yet, and I have not started any of the work on it either. I estimate it will take about $15,000 to get it ready to rent.

Zillow lists it as being worth $130,000! I thought this value was very interesting since I just purchased the house for $30,000 less than the Zillow estimate. Zillow does list the recent sale prices, so they know how much it just sold for. Once this house is fixed up, I estimate it will be worth around $150,000 and it should rent for $1,200 to $1,300 per month. It is not fixed up yet, so I will leave my purchase price as the actual value since I just purchased it. I do like to buy properties below market value though, so it is worth a little more than the $97,500.

Should you trust Zillow values?

As you can see, Zillow values can vary widely. Zillow lists values on some of my houses very low and, on one, pretty high. Here is a list of all Zillow values along with my estimates:

Properties	My estimate	Zillow estimate	Difference	% difference
Rental 1	$170,000	$145,000	$25,000	15%
Rental 2	$170,000	$151,000	$19,000	11%
Rental 3	$170,000	$165,000	$5,000	3%
Rental 4	$180,000	$166,000	$14,000	8%
Rental 5	$155,000	$90,000	$65,000	42%
Rental 6	$160,000	$132,000	$28,000	17%
Rental 7	$170,000	$148,000	$22,000	13%
Rental 8	$97,500	$130,000	-$32,500	-25%

Overall, I think Zillow does a good job of giving ballpark values, but do not depend on Zillow if you plan to buy or sell a house. The easiest way to get an accurate value is to ask a local real estate agent to complete a CMA for you, which should cost you nothing. As you can see from the above values, many Zillow estimates are pretty close, but some are off by over 40 percent! I would hate to be the person that sells their house for 40 percent less than market value or pays 25 percent more than market value on a house. The tricky part is there is no way for someone to know which values are accurate and which are not.

Updated Zillow values in 2017

I've bought more rental properties since doing my first analysis. Zillow's values appear to have improved. The price differences on my houses vary from 0 to 14 percent. 14 percent is still a lot of money to leave on the table if you price your house wrong. If you look at my recent flips, there are even bigger discrepancies.

I sold all these flips within the last year. Zillow was right on target with one, but with the others, their prices were all over the place. I am sure it is tough for Zillow to value flips because I buy them cheap, fix them up, and resell them for much more. This is a good lesson for homeowners. Condition, type of sale, and updates make a huge difference in house values. You must obtain your value from an expert who can evaluate all of these things.

What can Zillow tell us?

As I mentioned, it is hard to get accurate values from Zillow. They show recent sold comps, but Zillow has no idea what condition these houses are in or what kind of sale occurred. It is almost impossible for a computer to give an accurate value.

Zillow also shows pricing trends, which tend to be fairly accurate in my opinion. That can tell you if prices are going up or down in certain areas. Zillow also lists houses that are for sale, and they provide local real estate agents. Overall, I think Zillow has a lot of great information, but don't count solely on their values.

CHAPTER 51

How Long Does It Take to Sell a House?

The time it takes to sell a house can vary greatly depending on how you sell it and who you sell it to. A quick cash closing can take as little as 10 days, but when a loan is involved, the selling process can take 45 days or longer. That is just the time it takes to sell the house after a contract has been accepted. A homeowner must also get the house ready to market, list it as for sale, and find a buyer willing to pay the right price. The selling timeline can also vary depending on what the real estate market is like in your area and how expensive the house is. Houses will sell faster in a seller's marker (a seller's market occurs when demand exceeds supply, giving the seller the advantage) than they will in a buyer's market (a buyer's market occurs when supply exceeds demand, giving the buyer the advantage). Depending on the market, the house, the type of sale, and the asking price, selling it can take from 10 days to 6 months or longer. Homeowners can do many things to reduce the time it takes to sell and to increase the selling price.

What do sellers do before they put their house up for sale?

The better condition a house is in, the faster it will sell and the more it will sell for. If a homeowner wants to make the most money they can on the sale, they need to make sure it is in great condition. A lot of sellers think they can lower the price or offer an allowance for needed repairs. However, this strategy costs the seller money because buyers want a discount if they must make repairs. If a house needs $10,000 in repairs, buyers don't want to pay $10,000 less than what the house is worth after repairs. Buyers will want to pay $20,000 less than what the house is worth after repairs because it takes time to make those repairs, and it is not easy to finance them. If you want to make the most money, it is almost always better to make any repairs before you sell. It can take a couple of days to make minor repairs or a couple of months to make major repairs.

How long does it take to get a house under contract once it is listed for sale?

Once your house is ready to sell, you should list it with a real estate agent. An agent will put the house in the MLS, where other real estate agents will see it. Many sellers try to save money by listing a house themselves, but this usually backfires.

The amount of time it will take to receive an offer will depend greatly on your local market. In some markets, offers will come in within a week or even on the same day the house is listed. In other markets, it may take weeks or months to get an offer. I have found that if you price your house right, it takes about three weeks to get it under contract. When a house is under contract, the buyer and seller have signed a contract. Houses sell quickly in a seller's market, and they sell more slowly in a buyer's market.

How long does it take to sell a house once it is under contract?

Once the buyer and seller sign the contract, the closing (when the actual sale happens) can take much more time. In almost all transactions, the buyer will want title insurance, which can take a week for the title company or attorney to prepare. The shortest closings happen over 7 to 10 days. The buyer may also want an inspection, which can take 7 to 14 days. The buyer may need to get a loan, which can take from 30 to 60 days. Most loans will require an appraisal, which can take from 7 to 45 days depending on your market. Luckily, most of these things can be done at the same time, and you do not have to wait for one to be completed before another can start. The time it takes to close with a loan usually depends on how fast the lender is and how fast the appraisal can be done.

What can delay the sale?

If things go smoothly, it normally takes 2 to 3 months to sell a house once it is listed. You cannot count on your house selling that fast; there are many things that can delay the process:

- **Pricing your house too high:** We talked about this already, but when you price your house too high, it can add months to the selling timeframe.
- **Neglecting to make repairs:** A house that needs work will take much longer to sell unless it is priced very low to attract cash buyers.
- **Contracts falling apart:** It is not rare to see the first contract fall apart. The inspection could scare the buyers or uncover major problems. The buyer's loan may be declined, or there could be problems with the appraisal. This situation could add a month or two to the timeline.
- **Contractor delays:** Repairing your house prior to the sale smart, but contractors can be tough to deal with. Often, they take much longer than they say they will.

How can you sell a house fast?

I have a lot of experience both helping others sell houses and selling my own houses. There are ways to sell your house fast, but they will not earn you the most money. Investors like myself will be happy to buy a house within 10 days if it is a good enough deal. Investors do not want to pay 10 percent or even 15 percent less than what a house is worth. They often want to pay 30 percent less to make it a good deal for them. Most people would rather take their time when selling their house to command the most money, but if you need to sell right away, there are investors who would be happy to help you.

Conclusion

You can sell a house in 10 days, but you will lose a lot of money. If you want to make the most money possible, count on the sale taking a few months. If you have time to spare and want to try to make even more money by pricing your house higher, it probably won't work. Houses tend to sell for the most money when they are priced right, not when priced too high or too low. If you want to buy another house after selling your house, you need to make sure you price it right so you can sell quickly.

CHAPTER 52

How Can You Both Buy and Sell a House at the Same Time?

Houses are huge investments, and often, buyers will purchase the most expensive house they can afford. When you buy the most expensive house you can qualify for, buying another house without selling the house you own first becomes very tough. It is possible yet tricky to sell the house you currently own and buy another house the same day. This allows you to avoid temporarily moving your possessions while you wait to buy a new house. When you plan to sell and buy on the same day, you must make sure you have awesome real estate agents and lenders who can help everything work as it should. One complication or oversight can cause delays, which can cause huge problems for both the seller and buyer.

Why can't many buyers buy a house before they sell their current one?

Most buyers will get a mortgage. The amount they can qualify for will be based on many factors, like credit, down payment, work history and debt-to-income ratio.

As a buyer, you do not have to figure out these complicated equations yourself. A lender can look at everything and tell you what you can qualify for and how much your payments will be. Most buyers see these figures and buy a house that nearly maxes out the amount they qualified for. When buyers do this, they'll find it difficult to qualify for another house while they still own their first.

If you want to move up, move to a different area, or even downsize, you will most likely have to sell your current house before you can buy the new one. Most lenders will not give you a loan based on the assumption that your current house will sell. Instead, lenders prefer your house be sold and your loan paid off. Some of you may think that you can satisfy lenders by renting out your current house. However, most lenders will not count rent income until it shows up on your taxes, and many will not count all of your rent as income because renting out a house comes with many expenses. If you want to rent out your house instead of selling it, it will need to be rented out for a certain period of time before you can qualify for another house.

How can you both buy and sell a house at the same time?

There are various short-term housing options for those who find them in between houses, but it is possible to both sell your old house and buy a new one without needing to move somewhere temporary. Here's how this works:

- Either find a house you want to buy or list your house for sale and find a house you want to buy.
- Write a contract on the house you want to buy, and make the sale of your current house a contingency.
- If you price your house correctly, you should get an offer right away.
- Try to time the closing on the house you are selling to be just before you close on the house you are buying.
- Close on the house you are selling. Move all your belongings into a moving van. Close on the house you are buying and move into it.

This scenario pans out quite often. Usually, it works out great, but in some cases, one delay on any side of the transaction can cause serious problems. Chains of contingent sales also happen, which can make everyone involved very nervous. For example:

- You have a contract to buy a house that includes a contingency that your current house must sell.
- The contract for the house you are selling is contingent on those buyers selling their house.

- The sellers of the house you are buying are buying a new house and their contract is contingent on their house being sold to you.

I have seen even longer chains than this, and if one thing goes wrong, everyone's deal can fall apart. If the buyer of your house loses the buyer on the house they are selling, they can no longer buy your house. As a result, you don't have a buyer for the house you want, and the sellers of that house have lost their buyer too!

What are contingencies and how do they work?

Contingencies are conditions that can kill a contract if the contingency is not satisfied. A contract can be contingent on a satisfactory inspection, an appraisal, the loan approval, surveys, and many other things. When someone both buys and sells a house at the same time, the contract is often contingent on the seller finding a buyer for their house by a certain date.

This is what a contingency looks like:

- This contract is contingent on the buyer's house at 123 main street going under contract by October 20th, 2015. If the buyer's house is not under contract by this date, this contract will terminate.

If the date in this example passes and the buyer's house is not under contract, you can try to extend this date if the seller agrees. If the seller does not agree, they can terminate the contract and look for a new buyer. You may also see first-right-of-refusal clauses in contracts, which apply to buyers who must sell their house first. Some sellers may not want to tie up their house under a contract that is contingent on a house that is not under contract yet. This is an example of a first-right-of-refusal clause:

- This contract is contingent upon the buyer's house going under contract by October 20th, 2015. If the seller receives another acceptable offer, the buyers have 36 hours to remove the contingency on their house or this contract will terminate.

This contingency allows the sellers to continue to market their house to new buyers until the buyers with the contingency can get their house under contract.

How to make your contingent offer more likely to be accepted?

If you must sell your house before you can buy another, you are at a disadvantage. Buyers who don't need to sell their house are in a better position. A contingent contract is less likely to perform, and sellers and real estate agents know this. If I am a seller, and I receive two identical contracts with the exception that one buyer must sell a house and the other does not, I will accept the offer from the buyer who doesn't have to sell every time. In this case, if you are a buyer who must include the sale of your current house as a contingency, there are certain things you can do to make your offer more likely to be accepted.

- Put your house on the market before you make offers on another. If I receive a contingent offer, but the buyers have not even listed their house, it tells me they aren't that serious.
- Get your house under contract before you make an offer on another. This is risky because there is a chance that you will not find a house, but sellers will find your offer to be much more attractive.
- Price your house so that it sells quickly! Any houses involved in a contingent offer should be priced to sell. If they are overpriced, the chances of the deal going through are very slim.
- If you have a contingency, you might have to offer a bit more than you want on the new house. If you are competing against other offers that have no

contingency, raising your offering price may convince the seller to take your offer.

- Make sure you are pre-qualified! If you are making an offer contingent upon your house selling, you should have a pre-qualification letter showing you can get a new loan once your house sells.

What happens if you have everything lined up to sell on the same day and something goes wrong?

Real estate transactions frequently go bad. The buyer may get turned down for their loan because they bought a new car or lost their job. The appraisal can come in too low on one of the houses, or lending troubles can cause delays. If you are selling a house and cannot buy a new house because you are turned down for the loan, you may still be obligated to sell your house depending on how far along in the process you are.

If you are buying a house and there is a contingency that yours must sell yet the potential sale of your house falls through, you will most likely be able to cancel the contract on the house you are buying and get your earnest money back. In the case of delays on the house you are selling, the closing on the house you are buying will be delayed because you can't buy that house without selling yours first. In the case of delays with the house you are buying, you may be homeless for a couple of days or weeks while you wait for the new house to close. It is best to have some sort of short-term housing lined up in case you need it. You could stay with friends, family, or move to a hotel.

The seller might let you rent their house before you close, or the buyer of your current house may let you temporarily rent from them until you can move into the new house, but do not count on this!

How can you avoid a contingency for selling your house altogether?

If you want to buy a new house, the best way to do it is to avoid a contingency for selling yours. This is not possible for everyone, but many people may be able to avoid contingencies if they think outside the box:

- You can make an offer than is not contingent upon your house selling. If anything happens and you cannot follow through on your contract because your house does not sell, you might lose your earnest money. If your earnest money totals $1,000 or $2,000, the risk might be worth it to get a better deal on the house you are buying or have a better chance at getting a house you love.
- Use a co-signer to make an offer without having to sell your house first. If a parent, sibling, or friend will co-sign the new loan with you, you may not have to sell your house first to buy the new house. The co-signer will be on that loan until the loan is paid off or refinanced. Make sure they know what they are getting into and that this loan could affect their debt-to-income ratio.
- Borrow money on a short-term basis from family or a hard-money lender. This is risky as well because the interest rates will most likely be very high. If you borrow money for the new house, you can take your time selling your old house. When the old house is sold, you can refinance the new house and pay back the hard money-lender or your friends and family. I used this technique when I had to pay cash for a house I bought at a foreclosure sale.
- Be willing to sell your house first and plan to live somewhere in the short term. You can sell your house before you look for another. You will not have to stress about selling quickly and finding another house fast. You can sell your house, move out, and take your time looking for a new house.

Conclusion

Buying and selling houses when you must sell your current house first is tricky. There are ways to pull it off, and smooth transactions happen all the time. I've also encountered sellers who don't want to list their house until they find the perfect house to buy. Their offers are rarely accepted because they can't tell if their house is priced correctly. Plus, their house has had no exposure to open it to offers. Try to make your contingencies as attractive to the seller as possible, and if you can remove your contingency, it will make the process much easier.

CHAPTER 53

What Happens If You Cannot Make Your Mortgage Payments?

Things happen that cause people to miss or become unable to make their mortgage payments. Many people panic and ignore the problem, but the bank will not ignore the issue. The best thing you can do when you get into trouble is talk to your bank, a real estate agent, an attorney, and an accountant. Missed mortgage payments hurt your credit and make it very tough to get new loans for anything. If you miss too many payments, the bank can foreclose on your house. If you lose your house or hurt your credit, you may not even be able to rent because potential landlords will see your financial problems and won't want to rent to you. The sooner you figure out a plan to save your house, sell it, or restructure your loan, the better off you will be.

What happens when you miss your mortgage payments?

Most mortgage payments are due on the 1st of every month, but they are not considered late until the 15th. If you get your money to the bank by the 15th, you should be fine. If you pay after the 15th, the bank can charge late fees. If you are more than 30 days late, it will start to affect your credit. In fact, one late mortgage payment can drop your credit score 100 points! Multiple late payments can drop your credit score even more. Late fees can add up to be hundreds of dollars per month, making it even harder for you to catch up.

If you miss enough payments or fall far enough behind, the bank can start the foreclosure process. A foreclosure means the bank takes possession of your house. Foreclosure laws vary in every state, but it can take as little as a few months to lose your house in some states or as long as 3 years in other states. This is one reason to talk to your bank, real estate agent, or an attorney as soon as possible. Some states even offer free legal advice for people who are in foreclosure. Also, many companies exist that charge a lot of money to help people in foreclosure. Most of these companies will not help you, and most information should be free.

Why is it best to talk to your bank as soon as you miss a payment?

When you make a late payment, the bank will call you to see what is going on. Many people ignore these calls and hope the problem will go away, but that never happens. The bank does not want to foreclose because it costs them a lot of money. They must pay lawyers to complete the foreclosure, and they often lose money because the house sells for less than the loan amount. The government pressures banks to avoid foreclosures. They encourage banks to offer loan modifications and short sales before foreclosing.

If you miss payments due to financial hardship, the bank may be willing to modify your loan. The loan modification could reduce your payment, roll late fees into the loan, or even reduce the balance you owe so that you can make your payments. There is no guarantee the bank will offer a loan modification, but it's possible. The bank may also offer the borrower a short sale, which means the homeowner sells the house but pays the bank less than they are owed. A short sale is much better for your credit than a foreclosure but still hurts it. Some banks will even pay homeowners to complete a short sale! When you complete a short sale, you may face tax consequences because the bank is forgiving debt. Forgiven debt can count as income, which can be taxed. Therefore, you need to talk to an accountant or attorney when you start missing payments.

Why should you talk to a real estate agent when you fall behind?

When you want to sell your house, you need to talk to a real estate agent to figure out what it is worth. You should do the same thing if you fall behind on your payments. The agent can tell you how much your house is worth and what all the selling costs would be. Even if you do not plan to sell, it is good to have a backup plan in place. If you have enough equity in your house, you should be able to pay the real estate agents, sell your house, and move on. If you do not have enough equity, you may want to consider a short sale.

A short sale is a lot of work. The bank will want financial records for the last couple of years to prove that you are facing financial hardship. They will not allow a short sale just because you are behind on payments and the house is not worth enough money to sell. A short sale is a much better option than a foreclosure in most cases.

What happens if your house goes through foreclosure?

In Colorado, the foreclosure process takes about 6 months, but in New York, it can take 3 years.

Once the house is sold at the foreclosure auction, the bank owns the house (unless a real estate investor bought the house at the foreclosure sale). If you are foreclosed on, you do not have to move out right away. Legally, you can stay there until you are evicted or come to an agreement with the new owner. Often, the bank will even pay people cash for keys to vacate the house. Banks do not want to evict people, and they may pay the occupants a thousand dollars or more to move out within 30 days. I list foreclosures for banks, so I am very familiar with how the system works.

When the house sells at the foreclosure auction, the previous homeowner may even get some money back! The bank is paid the loan balance, late fees, and attorney fees. If the homeowner owed $50,000, they might also owe an additional $10,000 in late fees and attorney fees. If the house sells for $100,000 at the foreclosure sale, the previous owners would get $40,000 back.

There are also times when the bank will make a deficiency bid on a house. That means they bid less than the amount they are owed. If the house sells for less than what the bank is owed, the deficiency amount may be considered forgiven debt. Therefore, letting your house go through foreclosure is risky. Talking to an accountant or attorney to learn how the forgiven debt could affect you is very important. This can affect real estate investors more than owner-occupants.

Conclusion

If you fall behind on your payments, do not shut yourself off from the world. Talk to your lender, talk to a real estate agent, and talk to an attorney or accountant. The sooner you figure out a plan, the better off you will be financially. If you end up going through foreclosure, buying a house again could take three or more years. A short sale is a better option, but it can still make it very hard to buy in the future. If you buy a house you know you can afford, have an emergency fund, and buy below market value, you'll greater reduce your risk of foreclosure.

CHAPTER 54

How Much Does It cost to Repair a House?

Whether they are my personal house, my rental properties, or my fix and flips, I fix up a lot of houses, but I don't do the work myself—I have a contractor do it for me. The most difficult part about this process is finding a contractor. Estimating repair costs isn't easy, but you must know the basics so the contractor doesn't rip you off. Repair costs will vary based on the quality of products used, the cost of labor in your area, and the age of the house.

What does it cost to paint a house?

Unless the paint and floor coverings are brand new, I always have the house repainted and the floor coverings replaced before I sell the house. The cost to paint a house has increased a lot the last few years because the cost of paint and labor have increased. Painting the interior costs me about $1.50 to $2.00 per square foot. For a 1,500-square-foot house, repainting the entire interior costs roughly $2,200. That includes painting the trim white and the walls a different color like beige or gray.

Painting the exterior costs more because the paint is more expensive, more prep work is needed, and the weather must be nice. Exterior paint jobs run $3.00 per square foot or more depending on the complexity and condition of the house. If the existing paint is peeling, it will cost much more to scrape and prepare the surface for new paint. If the old paint is lead based, the preparation and cleanup work needed to dispose of the old paint will cost even more. Your contractor or painter must be certified to remove lead-based paint or they can face huge fines from the government.

How much does it cost to replace flooring?

We use a variety of flooring. Depending on the age of the house, we might put in carpet or laminate. Laminate flooring looks like hardwood but is much cheaper. We usually use tile in the bathroom and possibly the kitchen if the floors are mostly level. In older houses, an uneven floor will cause the tile and grout to crack. If a house has hardwood, I will refinish the hardwood, but I don't add to it or replace it because of the cost. Hardwood floors cost three times as much as carpet. Replacing the carpet in a 1,500-square-foot house costs me $3,000 to $3,500. Vinyl or tile for the kitchen and baths costs another $500 to $1,000. These costs assume middle-of-the road materials that don't cost a fortune but look nice and will last. Refinishing hardwood floors in a 1,500-square-foot house costs about $2,000 (assuming it is mostly hardwood).

How much does fixture replacement cost?

Replacing light and plumbing fixtures is a great way to update a house. New lights, door handles, and matching faucets can transform a house. I like to use antique bronze, but we have also used brushed nickel. Light fixtures are as cheap as 2 for $20 for basic bedroom and bathroom lights. You can find good chandeliers and ceiling fans for under $150. Door handles are $20 or less depending on the style. Faucets run from $35 to $150. You can replace all these items for roughly $1,200, including installation.

How much does appliance replacement cost?

Adding new appliances is another way to refresh a house. We install stainless steel appliances in almost all our houses. I can get a stove for $500 to $600, a dishwasher for $300, and a microwave for $250. I usually do not buy a fridge for my flips, but I do for my rentals. Appliances make a huge difference in the look of a kitchen, even if the cabinets are dated.

How much do cosmetic updates cost?

If you do all the work mentioned above and the rest of your house is in decent shape, it will make a huge difference in the look and feel. I almost always do these repairs on every fix and flip. With my rentals, I usually do most of those repairs, but if a house is in decent condition I can get away with less. Here are the total costs for a cosmetic upgrade on a 1,500-square-foot house:

New interior paint: $2,200
New floor coverings: $4,500
New fixtures: $1,200
New appliances: $1,300
Total cost: $9,200

Fixing up a house almost always costs more than you think, so be prepared to spend more than what you calculate. I rarely spend less than $10,000 on any house that I fix up because there are usually many little things that need to be repaired as well. Drywall holes, outlet covers, landscaping, and many more things will increase the costs. I usually have more major repairs than expected as well.

What do major repairs cost?

The repairs on my flips and rentals vary from basic cosmetics to a massive remodel. Here are other common repairs and their cost:

- **Kitchens**: Replacing a kitchen is not as expensive as you might think. I can replace a basic kitchen, including cabinets, counter tops, and sink for $2,500 in materials. After labor, the entire replacement usually costs less than $10,000.
- **Baths**: Bath repairs can involve full gut jobs or a simple vanity replacement. For a full gut job, I can usually get the job done for less than $3,000. Replacing a vanity, toilet, and bath surround can usually be accomplished for less than $1,000.

- **Roof**: I have a great roofer who will replace the roof on a 1,500-square-foot house for around $6,000.
- **Electrical:** Electric repairs can vary a great deal based on what needs to be done. Minor repairs can cost a couple hundred dollars, and major rewiring jobs can cost $5,000. It is important to get any electrical concerns checked out to see how serious they are.
- **Plumbing:** Plumbing is like electrical. A minor job can be very cheap, but re-plumbing a house can cost $5,000 or more. A minor repair may only cost $200.
- **Sewer:** Sewer-line repairs or replacements can be very expensive, usually costing anywhere from $3,000 to $15,000.
- **Foundation**: Most foundation repairs are not fun to deal with. Settling, water leakage, grading issues or structural problems can all cause issues. If you have water problems in the basement or crawl space, there may be a major foundation issue which will cost $10,000 or a simple grading issue that some dirt work will fix. It is best to have an engineer look at any possible foundation problems.
- **Windows:** I replace a lot of windows because I constantly buy older houses. My contractor usually charges me $300 for each basic vinyl window, which includes materials and labor. Many window companies try to sell people on windows that cost $1,000 or more for each. Unless you have a million-dollar house, there is no reason to spend that much. It will not save you that much money on utility bills. Buyers don't care if you have $300 or $2,000 windows as long as they are newer.
- **Doors:** We also replace many interior doors. Six-panel white doors really spruce up a house. Doors are usually $100 to $150 each, including installation.
- **Stucco and siding:** I rarely replace the siding, but sometimes I do. On one of my flips, I installed new stucco, and it cost $8,500 (the house was 1,250 square feet). Replacing wood siding is cheaper, but

you must paint it. You can still re-side and paint a house for less than stucco in most cases.

- **Drywall/Sheetrock:** In old houses, I see a lot of plaster and bad drywall. New drywall makes an old house look so much better than uneven, crumbling plaster. I recently replaced the drywall on the walls and ceilings in three rooms of a fix and flip, and I paid $3,000 for 500 square feet.
- **Furnace/hot water heater:** I recently installed a new forced-air furnace for about $5,000. Furnace replacement alone costs $2,500, and the hot water heater alone costs $800.

How much do I spend on remodels?

On my most recent fix and flip, I spent about $18,000 on the remodel. That included interior and exterior paint, new carpet, new doors, new trim, some electrical work, some new drywall, trash-out, landscaping, and many little fixes. On another flip, I will spend over $50,000 on the repairs. That house needs new plumbing, new electric, new paint everywhere, siding work, new windows, new doors, new drywall, new baths, new kitchen, new floors, new fixtures, new trim, and more.

Many contractors love to charge homeowners a lot of money because they know they don't know any better. Contractor rates can vary from $30 to $100 per hour based on their skill level and marketing. It is best to pick a contractor who may not be the cheapest but who is also not the most expensive.

Where do I buy materials?

I use Home Depot for almost all of our supplies. Because I repair so many houses, we get an awesome deal. We have a managed pro account, which means we save tens of thousands of dollars per year by purchasing in bulk. Home Depot works well for a regular homeowner as well. You do not have to buy materials at trendy bath and kitchen stores, which will cost three times as much.

Conclusion

It doesn’t cost $50,000-$100,000 to make basic cosmetic repairs. Television shows often highlight $50,000 kitchen remodels, and I can't believe my eyes and ears! Even if you use high-end materials like granite counters and custom cabinets, you should not spend $50,000 on a kitchen unless it is in a million-dollar house. Repairs can add up quickly, and I always plan to pay about 20 percent more than expected due to unknowns. Find a great contractor, make sure that contractor does their work, and shop around for the best prices to keep your costs down. Remember, these costs are what I pay to fix up houses in my area. If you live in an expensive town, your costs may be significantly higher.

CHAPTER 55

Should You Do the Repair and Rehab Work Yourself?

I always use a contractor to rehab my fix and flips and rentals. I also use a contractor to remodel my personal residence. A few years ago, I decided to rehab a fix and flip myself. I thought I would save money on the labor by doing it myself. While I may have saved on labor, I lost money in the end due to the time it took and the opportunities I lost while focusing on the work. Now, I always use contractors.

What kind of flip did I decide to rehab?

I am not a professional contractor, and I had to learn how to do much of the work. This particular house was about 60 years old, needed paint, carpet, new floors, new doors, new windows, a new kitchen, wall demolition, and many more minor repairs. I may have been qualified to paint the house, and that was about it. It was a long process!

Although I had done minor repairs before, I had never done anything to this extent. I was sure that doing the work myself would save me thousands of dollars. The problem was...it took me six months! I had to learn how to do all the work while on the job, and that took me at least three times as long as it would have taken a professional. It may have saved me a little money but not much because it took me so long.

When I flip a house, I use financing for most of the purchase price. I also get insurance, pay utilities, taxes, and many other costs. Those costs add up very quickly. Therefore, it is important to sell a fix and flip quickly. The longer it takes to make repairs, the less money you will make.

If you live in the house, you may be able to afford to fix it up slowly. There is no rush to sell and you can repair things at your leisure, but you still must avoid biting off more than you can chew. Remodeling is not easy, and you should hire a contractor for major jobs. Often, remodels do not add much value due to poor-quality work.

How much money did it cost me to do the work myself?

The work took me at least four months longer than it would have taken a contractor. The carrying costs totaled $2,832, which is less than a contractor would have charged me for labor. That actually isn't too bad, but the truth is it cost me much more than that.

I've mentioned you must sell flips quickly. Not only does this save on costs, but it also allows you to use your money to buy more houses and complete more flips. If all your money is tied up in one house for eight months, you may miss an incredible deal because you don't have the ability to buy another flip.

The longer you hold a house, the better the chance the market will change. The housing market is currently appreciating, but that could change quickly. I like to sell my flips quickly because I never know what the future holds.

I did not save on labor because my time is worth something.

I may have saved money by doing the work myself, but how much time did it cost me? My time is worth something, and since I still had my real estate business, the business suffered greatly because I spent so much time working on this house. I had the worst sales year of my life because I had no time to go after business.

Not only did my real estate career suffer, but my fix and flips suffered as well. This was the only flip work we were doing at the time because I was not looking for new projects. Focusing on this house cost me tens of thousands of dollars because I couldn't look for other houses.

I also hate to think about the quality of my work. I was doing jobs a pro should do without professional training. I learned as I went, and the quality probably suffered. I did have some contractor help on some large jobs because they involved structural integrity

Conclusion

It may be wise, in a few cases, to complete rehab work yourself. It makes sense to do so if you're a contractor. It also may make sense if you don't have a job and have plenty of time to do the work. Otherwise, you are probably costing yourself a lot of money by trying to do repairs yourself. You may be able to save some money if you have someone who knows what they are doing and can help you out. You also must remember your family may not be very happy if you spend all your free time working on the house, especially if they expect the jobs to be completed quickly.

CHAPTER 56

How to Find a Great Contractor

One of the most important and difficult parts of homeownership or real estate investing is finding a great contractor. Contractors can be hard to find, very expensive, may take a long time to finish, or may even quit on you. If you can find someone with clear and detailed bids, great communication skills, and a great work ethic, you're in luck. If you don't have a great contractor, costs can skyrocket due to long timelines and increased repair costs.

Even if I buy houses that need no work at all, things will break at some point. I remodel my rentals before renting them out, but they still need occasional work.

What is the easiest way to find a great contractor?

Finding a great contractor is not always easy and can take a lot of trial and error. My advice is to ask your friends, family, and co-workers for references before you try any other resource. When you get a recommendation, it's no guarantee you've found a great contractor, but it gives you a place to start. Recommendations are usually a better sign of how good a contractor is than any advertising they can do. Real estate agents, property managers, and builders are just a few people you can talk to who may know a great contractor.

Anyone who owns a house may have used a great contractor at some point, so don't be afraid to ask your friends or family. You will still have to oversee that contractor to make sure they are doing what they promised. One of the easiest ways to let a rehab project get out of control is neglecting to watch over the contractor's work.

A good recommendation doesn't make a good contractor.

I used a new contractor two years ago when my current contractors could not keep up. My broker and a couple other agents in my office gave me a recommendation. The contractor was a builder who seemed to know what he was talking about and gave great, detailed bids. I put him to work on two projects at once. He told me he had a great crew and could handle as much work as I could give him. He ended up finishing one project on budget, but he didn't start the second project for two months!

He told me everything was going well, so I took his word for it, but the property was 40 minutes away, and I had not physically seen the work start yet (not properly overseeing the job and visiting the site was completely my fault). I was shocked when I visited the property and saw nothing had been done. I called the contractor, and he gave me a story about having too many jobs and his workers getting sick. He had been telling me everything was going great and the work was almost done. Either he hadn't been monitoring his workers properly or he had lied to me. He completed the job three months after it started and three months after it was supposed to be completed. I never used that contractor again, not because it took so long to finish the job, but because he lied to me.

How to keep an eye on a contractor.

Whether it is the first time you have used the contractor or the 20th, it is always best to keep an eye on their work and schedule. In my experience, the more communication and oversight you provide, the better job the contractor will do. Even if I've worked with a contractor 20 times, they'll slow down if I don't push them. If a contractor does a great job once, they may not do a great job again. Never trust a contractor to do unsupervised work.

This year, I fired a contractor who always did great work on many of my properties. He stopped visiting his work sites and started telling me jobs were done when they were not. His prices went up, and the time he took to finish increased because he was never at the site and did not keep track of his workers.

Here are a few tips on how to make sure your contractor is doing a great job:

- Constantly communicate with them
- Visit the property often
- Always get a written bid first
- Get a written estimate for the completion date
- Don't prepay for any work (This is not always possible. Some contractors require a deposit up front for material cost, but you should not pay for the entire job).
- Help pick out materials and paint colors

How do you meet and vet a contractor?

I always talk to contractors on the phone before I meet them in person. I want to make sure they know what they are talking about, and I want to get an idea of what they charge. A contractor should tell you their hourly rate, the size of their crew, and how long it takes them to do an average job. I also want to know how busy they are and how many other jobs they are working on.

If I like what I hear on the phone, I will set up a meeting at one of my houses. I will go over what I want done and have them write up a bid. If you are new to real estate and finding contractors, always get multiple bids so you know you are not getting ripped off. Try to talk to the contractor as much as possible and learn about their family and the kind of jobs they normally do. In my experience, contractors like to talk a lot, and if you get them talking, they may tell you some things that will help you decide. One contractor told me he had two recent DUIs, including one while he was on the job!

After I meet with the contractor, I ask them to write up a bid and email it to me or call me when it is done. This is another test and shows how quickly they provide a bid and how responsive they are. I recently talked to two contractors who never sent me a bid, never emailed, and never called me.

If they can't send me a bid, they probably can't do the job, so it was easy to eliminate them.

How can you find a great contractor through large box stores?

Home Depot offers a rehab program that will actually handle every repair you might need. However, they're more expensive than contractors. I asked Home Depot about their contractor program pricing, and they were very honest and said it would be cheaper for me to use my own contractors. They did mention a few contractors who frequent the store often and have been around for years. This was not a recommendation from them in any way, but it gave me a lead on a great contractor who I am going to start using.

Another way to meet great contractors at large stores is to visit the store early in the morning and see who is buying large amounts of supplies. The people buying materials are probably contractors, and they may be looking for more work. You know they have at least one job going since they are buying materials.

How to find a great contractor online.

I have hired many contractors through Craigslist, but you must be careful. Contractors can post on Craigslist for free, so you can get a wide range of people to interview. We often find affordable contractors on Craigslist because it is free. They cannot afford to advertise on the more expensive sites like Angie's List, Thumbtack, or HomeAdvisor. With Craigslist, you must take your time. Talk to them and make sure they are legit before you hire them or give them any money.

One nice thing about pay sites is they have reviews. Also, check the Better Business Bureau for reviews. You can also check Yelp reviews. If a contractor has a bad review, you may still hire them, but you should be able to see how they responded and judge how serious the problem is.

How do contractors vary between investors and homeowners?

Contractor charges can vary greatly. Some contractors will charge $40 per hour and others will charge $100 per hour. More-expensive contractors may do amazing work, but most homeowners and investors will not need someone that expensive. Most investors who are flipping or buying rentals will not be able to afford a contractor who charges that much. Many contractors do not like working with investors because they know investors won't pay as much as homeowners.

Many homeowners have no idea how much repairs should cost, so they hire a contractor and pay whatever the bill is. Most investors have a good idea of repair costs and have experience dealing with contractors. If you are remodeling a kitchen in a $200,000 house, it should not cost $50,000! It should cost less than $20,000 or even $10,000 depending on how fancy it is.

Conclusion

Finding a great contractor can be tough, but it is extremely important. Many contractors will perform poor-quality work, will quit on a job, will take three times as long as they quote, or won't even show up. It is vitally important that you take your time and interview multiple contractors to ensure you find the best one for you.

CHAPTER 57

How to Make Sure Your Contractor Will Do a Good Job

Once you find a contractor, you must make sure they do their job well. You can do many things to ensure they're doing their job correctly and in a timely manner. No matter how good their references are or how great the contractor tells you they are, you must follow these steps to make sure the contractor follows through.

The problem that many people run into is it may be hard to tell the difference between a good and a bad contractor until they start the job. Contractors can get too busy, take too big of a job, or fail to manage their workers. Any of these circumstances can cause a job to take too long or be done incorrectly. Keys to ensuring good contractor work are constant communication, written agreements, and oversight.

Always walk through a job site with your contractor.

It is always a good idea to walk a job with your contractor so they know what needs to be done, even if you have worked with the contractor before. Make sure the contractor writes everything down. I have had a few contractors write nothing down when I discussed exactly what I wanted, and when I visited the worksite, they were doing things I had not asked for and not doing things I had asked for. If a contractor doesn't write anything down, it is a bad sign.

Always get a written bid for any job.

You always need to have a written bid when you have any work done. A written bid serves multiple purposes that will save you time and money.

- A written bid makes sure both the contractor and the homeowner know exactly what services and repairs are being done. You don't want any confusion about what was and what was not supposed to be repaired.
- A written bid lists the price that the contractor charges for specific work. You don't want to be surprised by a massive bill after work is completed that you never agreed to. A written bid helps keep the contractor honest.
- A written bid may also include a timeframe for the work. Some investors will add incentives for getting a job done quickly. The faster they finish, the more the contractor gets paid.

Most contractors require bids to be signed by both parties. The written bid not only keeps both parties honest, but it also reminds everyone of the scope of work to be done. I have many jobs going at one time, and I tend to forget what we talked about. A written bid avoids any confusion regarding repairs and costs.

Keep in constant contact.

If you never hear from your contractor, that doesn't mean things are going great. On one job, I never heard a thing from the contractor, and I assumed it was going well. I assumed he would tell me if there were any problems or delays. It turns out he had never started the job! Call your contractor to get updates on the job, and stop by the job site to see how things are progressing.

Don't be afraid to ask your contractor if they are on schedule and budget. Ask your contractor if there are any changes to the bid or if there is any more work that needs done. If there are any changes, make sure the contractor requests your approval. Some contractors take it upon themselves to change a job or add work without asking the homeowner.

If the contractor is working on a house you don't occupy, you must check up on them. Some of my biggest failures with contractors happened because I was not visiting job sites. I think you should always visit the job site at least once a week to make sure work is being done. Do not tell the contractor you are coming, either! I have a contractor who had 6 guys working on a job whenever he knew I was coming. When I showed up to that job unannounced, no one was there.

Don't pay a contractor for work they have not completed.

Some contractors want partial payment before any work is started. If you have worked with a contractor before and this is their policy, it may work to pay them some money to get started. You never want to pay more than 25 percent of the job upfront. Before you pay anything, you need to vet them by checking reviews and references (if possible). One way to get around paying a contractor upfront is by offering to buy the materials. We pay for all the materials on our jobs using mostly Home Depot.

A contractor can place a lien on a house if they don't receive payment for completed work. It is much harder to track down a contractor who skips town after taking money for work that hasn't been done. However, the contractor has a much easier time collecting for unpaid work and should have no problem getting paid after a job is done.

Do a final walk through with the contractor to make sure the work was done right.

A contractor should take pride in their work and be happy to show you what was repaired. I always do a final walk through to make sure everything was done correctly. Often, I must request additional repairs for minor things or things we didn't notice the first time. Don't be afraid to point out work that you do not think is done correctly. If the contractor is hesitant about fixing it correctly, stand your ground. Most contractors will be happy to fix things that should have been but were missed. If you use a contractor over and over, you do not want to give them the idea that it is okay to leave work incomplete. Even great contractors will overlook things they were supposed to do, especially on big jobs.

CHAPTER 58

Which Improvements Will Give You the Most Bang for Your Buck?

You should spend your money on items that will add the most value. As an investor, I do not want to make repairs that will cost me more than the value they add. If a new kitchen will add $5,000 to the selling price but will cost $10,000 to put in, I don't do it. Owner-occupants may employ a different strategy because they really want a new kitchen and know they will be living in the house for another 20 years. Even if you occupy a house, make smart decisions about how much you spend and which items you repair or update. I have seen people spend a lot of money on things that added no value, like installing an outdoor pool in Colorado. If you must have a pool and do not care about the return on investment, great! But you should understand that, if you want to increase value, you must spend money on things that actually increase that value.

How do you know how much value a repair or update will add?

Some flipping TV shows provide value figures for every repair or rehab.

- $2,000 spent on the bathroom, value added $5,000
- $10,000 spent on the kitchen, value added $15,000

If I could tell you how much each repair or update would add to the value, it would be awesome, but I can't. You must look at the house as a whole and not the individual repairs. In some cases, you may be able to tell how much value something adds, like a garage or an added bedroom, but updates are tough.

A nicely updated house will sell for more money than a house that has bathrooms from the 1970s. A house with new carpet will sell for more money than one without. A house with new paint will sell for more money. Quantifying what those individual items add is difficult because every house is different and will have different levels of updates and repairs. You rarely find two houses that are exactly the same, let alone two houses that are exactly the same, sold recently, and had the same update. If I only perform a couple of updates on a house and try to sell it, it may not come close to competing with other houses in the area. I usually try to make as many updates as I need to compete with other houses without going overboard.

How do the repairs you make vary based on the area?

More expensive houses require more expensive materials and fancier designs. It is easy to overspend on repairs and get too crazy! When you sell a house, most buyers will not care about the materials used are as long as they look nice. You can often buy materials at Home Depot that look similar to materials from a fancy designer store yet cost five times less. The best way to choose which updates to make is to view other competing houses. You must look at several houses. Look at the kitchen, bathrooms, flooring, etc. The fanciest houses in a neighborhood usually won't sell for much more than nicely updated ones where the owner didn't overspend on material and repairs. You don't want to be the fanciest house because there could be appraisal restrictions that won't let your house sell for much more even if the buyers are willing to pay more.

Extra, unnecessary items—like a pool in a cold climate—usually do not add much value. In fact, a pool in a cold climate may reduce value because most people see it as a hassle. A hot tub does not add much value either, except for very specific buyers (unless you live in an area where you expect every house to have a hot tub). If the hot tub is in bad shape, getting rid of it could be a huge hassle. If you turn a garage into a bedroom, it may hurt the value of the house depending on your market. Therefore, it is important to study trends in your area to see what adds value and what does not. A real estate agent can often help homeowners determine the best options.

What are the first repairs you should make?

Repairs that will help the house qualify for a loan will add much more value than cosmetic repairs because most buyers who can't qualify for a loan will be eliminated. If your house needs a roof, a furnace, has holes in the walls, or has other major problems, fix those first. When major repairs are involved, homeowners sometimes run out of money or get tired of the house. Fix major issues first so the new buyer can get a loan if you must sell before you planned.

What are the best items to update in your house?

Kitchens and baths are always a good place to spend money, but you want to make sure you do not over-improve for your neighborhood. You also do not need to spend $50,000 or $100,000 on a kitchen like they do on some of the remodel shows on TV (unless you have a million-dollar house). I recently saw someone spend $80,000 on their kitchen before selling the house. The house was worth less than $400,000, and there was no way they would ever get close to that investment back. The house would have sold for just as much with a $15,000 kitchen remodel. Shop stores for the best prices on counters, cabinets, and appliances. Prices vary, and most of the time, you will not need the most expensive materials. On the houses I flip, we can have a kitchen installed for less than $7,000, which includes new cabinets, counters, and appliances.

You can also add value by updating bathrooms, but again, you should think about how much you spend. If you spend $20,000 on a bath in a $200,000 house, you are never going to get that money back. We can remodel bathrooms for less than $3,000 when we completely gut them. Usually, kitchens and bathrooms add the most value if they need to be updated. If a contractor tells you remodeling your kitchen will cost $50,000, get a second opinion!

What are some of the worst improvements you can make to a house?

Additions rarely pay off unless you live in an area, like San Francisco, with an incredibly high price per square foot. If you add an addition, make sure you do it right, and do not simply stick a room on the back of your house. Often, poorly done additions will not add any value at all or may detract from the value. I've seen bedrooms added to another bedroom. In those cases, you had to walk through one bedroom to get to the other, which makes it a non-conforming room. You cannot count that room as a bedroom when you sell the house!

If you make major repairs, make sure you get a building permit. Most buyers will ask for permits on any work that requires it. Each town and county has different requirements for when permits are needed.

Painting, changing the flooring, and adding new fixtures, often add value as well. But you must make sure they are done so they appeal to most people. If you paint your house black, it is not going to add to the value. If you paint your house a bunch of crazy colors, it will deter many buyers. The more eccentric your improvements are, the smaller your buyer pool will be, and the less value they will add.

What items should you always update before selling?

Basics add the most value and make the house more enjoyable to live in. Paint, flooring, and fixtures can transform a house and add much more value than they cost. All these items should be newer or new when you sell. Doing these updates can make the biggest difference in the feel of a house and be the most affordable. You don't have to wait until you sell to make those improvements either! Many people wait to paint or replace the carpet until they get ready to sell. Then, they realize how nice it would have been to enjoy the updated house while they lived there.

Landscaping can make a huge difference in value, but going overboard will usually not provide a return on investment. Most buyers look at the house and not the yard. If the yard looks good, the buyers can concentrate on the house and tell if it works for them. But if the yard looks absolutely amazing, it may not add value. You definitely do not want an ugly yard, as that will deter many buyers from even looking. Some key items that buyers look for in a yard are:

- A fence.
- A patio or deck (does not have to be huge).
- Green grass (may vary based on location).
- A sprinkler system (may vary in location).

These items add the most value. If you go crazy with trees, gardens, walkways, and paved driveways, it may look nice, but it might not add any value. Crazy yards can detract from the value because buyers think about how much work it will take to maintain it.

Conclusion

Determining what to repair or update can be tough, but remember to get help from others. You also may want to make repairs that you know won't add value but will be important to you. Talk to a real estate agent about which repairs are necessary and which are not. Talk to contractors about cost, and shop around for the best deals.

CHAPTER 59

How to Maintain Your House to Ensure It Lasts as Long as Possible

You should always maintain your house and keep it in great shape. One of the best ways to get a great deal is to find houses that have been neglected. You don't want your house to become one that turns into a great deal for someone else. Maintaining a house isn't difficult, but you need to make sure it is done to prevent serious damage. I will go through many of the major items you should consider.

How does the age of a house determine how it will be maintained?

The older the house is, the more maintenance and care it will need. Even if an older house has been updated or remodeled, it will take more work. In the past, there were different building codes and building materials, and there wasn't as much knowledge on building houses to last. You may hear that houses were built better in the past, and some may have been. But I have seen many old houses that shouldn't be standing because they were built so poorly. Today, we have building codes and inspectors that ensure new builds are done correctly, but that was not always the case. You may find an old house that is very solid, or you may find one pieced together with no insulation that is about to fall down. Expect to spend more money maintaining an older house because things were probably not built as well.

Which major exterior items should be maintained?

Weather can destroy a house very quickly. Rain, ice, snow, and wind all do a lot of damage, especially to a house that is not maintained well. Here are some of the most common problems I see:

- **Grading:** The ground around the house should slope away from the foundation. The most common cause of foundation problems is bad grading where water sits along the concrete.
- **Gutters:** Most houses should have gutters and down spouts that direct water away from the house. This keeps walkways free of water and ice as well as protects the foundation.
- **Roof:** Roofs have a lifespan of about 30 years unless they are damaged by wind or hail. Not only can a roof leak cause damage to the interior, but it can also cause mold and damage to the attic, which the homeowners will not see. The longer you wait to replace a bad roof, the more expensive it will be to fix.
- **Paint:** Exterior paint lasts from 3 to 8 years depending on the quality of the paint and the climate. When paint starts to fade, it is a good time to paint again. When you wait too long to paint a house, the paint will start to peel. Peeling paint is much more difficult to take care of, and if the house was built before 1978, it's much more expensive to remove. When your paint peels, it also lets in moisture and can lead to wood rot.
- **Trees:** Trees can be a great addition to a yard, but they can also do a lot of damage. Trees brushing up against the house can cause siding or roof damage. Tree roots can cause foundation problems and your sidewalk or driveway to buckle. Small trees should be planted at least 5 feet away from the house or concrete, and maybe even further away if they are large.
- **Yard:** In Colorado, most houses have grass which must be watered daily. Other parts of the country have grass that is naturally occurring or desert landscaping that needs no watering. Whatever yard you have, you need to keep it free of weeds and

debris. The town or HOA can fine homeowners for poorly maintained grass, excessive weeds, overgrown trees, and trash in your yard.

All this may seem like a lot of work, but hiring people to help is really cheap. I happily pay a company to mow, fertilize, and weed my yard because I would rather spend my time on other activities. A roofing company can inspect your roof and gutters to make sure they are in good shape. When you buy a house, your inspector should let you know if there are grading problems that should be addressed.

Which interior items should be maintained?

The exterior of the house is what most people see, but you need to maintain the interior as well. I talked about the dangers you could encounter in a house earlier in the book, and there are ways to keep your house safe and last longer as well:

- **Furnace:** The furnace should be checked and cleaned every year. This will make it last longer and could possibly uncover potential hazards.
- **Hot water heater:** The hot water heater lasts about 10 years and can cause a lot of damage if improperly maintained. Usually, a hot water heater will simply stop working, but in some cases, they will rust and leak, flooding the area.
- **Sewer lines:** It is a good idea to have your sewer line scoped if you buy an older house. Many older lines are made of clay and decay over time. Replacing a sewer line is extremely expensive, and if a sewer line clogs, it can back up into the house. If you know your line is older or had blockages in the past, get it cleaned every year to keep it clear.
- **Carpet:** Carpets should be steam cleaned once a year to keep them durable and looking nice. Vacuuming helps but is not enough unless you like replacing carpet often.

- **Paint:** The inside needs to be painted just like the outside. The longer you wait to paint, the more expensive it will be.
- **Cleaning:** When a house is dirty, it can cause all types of problems. Mice, bugs, mold, sickness, and odors cause all the systems in your house to degrade more quickly. Make sure you deep-clean your house at least once a year.
- **Dryer vent and chimney:** If you have a wood-burning fireplace, the chimney needs to be cleaned every year or two if you use it. You also need to clean out your dryer vent every year! A clogged dryer vent can cause a fire very easily.

Taking care of these things may seem overwhelming, but you don't need to paint your house very often, and keeping the house clean will ensure it stays in better shape. You can have an HVAC company check out your hot water heater and furnace, a carpet cleaning company clean your carpets, and cleaners deep clean your house.

Is it a lot of work to maintain a house?

Maintaining a house, especially an older one, can take a lot of work. It's also expensive, especially if the house is older. If you are renting, you may not have these expenses, but you will still have to keep it clean. The cost of maintaining a house is another reason it pays to get a great deal as well as doing your homework before you buy.

Bonus Section: Investing in Real Estate

This concludes the book. I hope it provided you with information on the best way to buy, finance, maintain, and sell a house. There is a lot of information included in the book, so do not worry if you don't understand it all. Many real estate agents do not understand the entire process! If you picked up just a few ideas on how to better buy or sell a house, it will save you time, aggravation, and hopefully money. If you want more information on buying houses, you can check out my blog: https://Investfourmore.com, which has over 450 free articles that I have written to help homeowners, investors, and real estate agents. If you are interested in making a career out of real estate my blog was originally started to help people buy rentals, flip houses, or become a real estate agent. You can get much more information on these subjects in my other books:

- **Build a Rental Property Empire**: the no-nonsense book on finding deals, financing the right way, and managing wisely.
- **Fix and Flip Your Way to Financial Freedom**: Finding, Financing, Repairing and Selling Investment Properties
- **How to Make It Big as a Real Estate Agent**: The right systems and approaches to cut years off your learning curve and become successful in real estate.
- **How to Change Your Mindset to Achieve Huge Success**: Why your attitude and daily habits have more to do with making more money and having more freedom than anything else.

These books are available as paperbacks or eBooks on Amazon, and Build a Rental Property Empire is available as an audio book as well.

How Can I Help You?

I hope this book helped you understand the house buying and selling process. However, if you have more questions or need more help, let me know. I am still an active real estate agent and help buyers and sellers all the time.

One way I can help is by finding a great deal for you in Colorado or by referring you to a great real estate agent. I have connections across the country through my blog and professional real estate groups.

Send me an email, and let me know what you need!

Mark@investfourmore.com

Definition and Glossary of Real Estate Terms

1-Percent Rule: A rule of thumb used to determine if the monthly rent earned from a piece of investment property will exceed that property's monthly mortgage payment.

2-Percent Rule: A general guideline many investors use to determine if a rental property is a good deal. The basics of the 2-percent rule say the monthly rent from a rental property should be 2 percent or more of the cost of a rental property.

50-Percent Rule: The 50-percent rule is one way to estimate what the expenses will be on rental properties. The 50-percent rule states that the expenses on a rental property will be 50 percent of the rent. This rule does not account for any mortgage expenses.

70-Percent Rule: This is a common term used among many real estate investors when flipping houses. The 70-percent rule is a way to determine what price to pay for a fix and flip. To make money, the rule states that an investor should pay 70 percent of the ARV (after repair value) of a property minus the repairs needed.

1031 Exchange: A section of the U.S. Internal Revenue Service Code that allows investors to defer capital gains taxes on any exchange of like-kind properties for business or investment purposes.

Active Status: Most MLS systems use a specific status to show if a house is available. Active status means the house is available and has no accepted offers on it. Active/backup means the house has an accepted offer, but the seller is accepting backup offers. Pending means the house has an accepted offer and the seller is not accepting backup offers. The status meaning can vary by MLS.

Active/backup status: See above

Acre: a unit of land area used in the imperial and US customary systems. It is defined as the area of 1 chain by 1 furlong (66 by 660 feet), which is exactly equal to 43,560 square feet.

Adjustable Rate Mortgage: A type of mortgage in which the interest rate applied on the outstanding balance varies throughout the life of the loan.

Amortization: A method of equalizing the monthly mortgage payment over the life of the loan by adjusting the proportion of principal to interest over time. At first, the interest payment is high and the principal payment is low.

Appraisal: Most lenders require an appraisal to confirm the house is worth what the buyer is paying. The appraisal is conducted by a licensed appraiser.

ARV: After repaired value. This is the value of a property once it has been remodeled and marketed.

Asbestos: A natural material made up of tiny fibers that is used as thermal insulation. Inhalation of asbestos fibers can lead to asbestosis and mesothelioma.

Assignment: A term used with similar meanings in the law of contracts and in the law of real estate. In both instances, it encompasses the transfer of rights held by one party—the assignor—to another party—the assignee.

Attached home: Any property that is attached to another property. This could be half of a duplex, a condo or town home, which is attached to another unit.

Backup Offer: A backup offer can be accepted by the seller but will not go into effect unless the current offer terminates.

Bird Dog: A real estate investing term that refers to someone who spends their time trying to locate properties with substantial investment potential. Usually, the intent is to find properties that are distressed and selling at a discount that can be repaired or remodeled and sold for a sizable profit.

Broker: A real estate broker means different things in different states. Usually, a broker has more experience and education than an agent, which allows them to work independently or manage an office of agents. In most states, real estate agents who are not brokers must work under a broker.

BRRRR: A real estate investment strategy: Buy, Rehab, Rent, Refinance, Repeat.

Building Codes: See Code violations

Buyer's Agent: A real estate agent who is contractually obligated to help a buyer find a house. Agents also work with buyers without a contract but do not have as much responsibility helping that buyer find a house.

Carport: A shelter for a car consisting of a roof supported on posts.

Crawl Space: An area of limited height under a floor, giving access to wiring and plumbing.

Central Air Conditioning: Circulates cool air through a system of supply and return ducts.

Cistern: A reservoir, tank, or container for storing or holding water or other liquid.

Close in Escrow: This means essentially that a real estate transaction has been completed and that the sale is final. An 'escrow' is a common feature of standard real estate transactions. They function as an independent third party that holds all monetary funds and documents until the close of the sale.

Closing: When a house is considered officially sold. This usually occurs at a title company or attorney's office.

Closing Costs: Expenses over and above the price of the property in a real estate transaction. Costs incurred include loan origination fees, discount points, appraisal fees, title searches, title insurance, surveys, taxes, deed-recording fees, and credit report charges.

Closing Fee: A fee charged by the Title Company to close a real estate transaction.

Code Violations: Each city, county, or state creates or adopts municipal codes. There are codes for building, landscaping, and more. If a property violates these codes, it could be in violation, which allows the city to fine the property owner until the violation is fixed. If the property was once in adherence to the codes, but the codes changed, a property may be grandfathered in. When a property is grandfathered in, they may not be in violation of codes as long as the use of the property does not change.

Commercial Real Estate: Properties that are used for commercial purposes (stores, offices, etc.).

Commissions: A fee paid to a broker/salesperson in exchange for services in facilitating or completing a sale transaction.

Condo: A condo is like an apartment, but you own the space. A condo may have neighbors above, below, or beside it. The space in the building is owned, but in most cases, the land isn't. Condos will have association dues that cover exterior maintenance, landscaping, and common amenities.

Contingency: A clause in the contract that allows the buyer or seller to back out based on certain conditions (inspection, appraisal, etc.).

Consignor: If a buyer cannot qualify for a loan, they may be able to use a consignor. If a consignor signs for a loan, they are responsible for that loan and it can count against their debt-to-income ratio.

Conventional: Refers to a loan that is not insured or guaranteed by the federal government. A conventional, or conforming, mortgage adheres to the guidelines set by Fannie Mae and Freddie Mac. It may have either a fixed or adjustable rate.

Counter Offer: The seller can accept, reject, or counter an offer. When they counter an offer, the seller can change the price, dates, contingencies, or many other terms. Any changes the seller wants must be listed in the counter.

Covenants: Most HOAs have covenants which are rules the properties within the HOAs must follow. Covenants cover parking, size of the house, outbuildings and much more.

Credit: Credit is how lenders, banks, and other financiers judge a person's ability to pay back a loan. The higher your credit, the better chance you have of getting a loan. Late payments, judgments, foreclosures, and short sales all hurt credit scores. If you never have loan payments, it can also hurt your credit score.

Debt-to-Income Ratio: This is the ratio a lender looks at when qualifying a buyer. The lender looks at the buyers' monthly income versus their monthly debts. The ratio allowed varies based on the type of loan the buyers apply for.

Deed in Lieu: A potential option taken by a mortgagor (a borrower) to avoid foreclosure under which the mortgagor deeds the collateral property (the house) back to the mortgagee (the lender) in exchange for the release of all obligations under the mortgage.

Disclosure: What a seller must tell the buyer. They must disclose any material facts that are known.

Double Closing: The simultaneous purchase and sale of a real estate property involving three parties: the original seller, an investor (middleman), and the final buyer.

Due on Sale Clause: A clause in most mortgages that states when the owner of the house sells the property, the mortgage must be paid off.

Earnest Money Deposit: The money needed for a deposit to buy a property. This can be refundable under certain circumstances based on inspection, loan approvals, appraisal, and other contingencies.

Easement: A right to cross or otherwise use someone else's land for a specified purpose.

Eminent domain: The right of a government or its agent to expropriate private property for public use, with payment of compensation.

Escrow (held in escrow): Funds pertaining to a real estate transaction can be held in escrow. That means the title company, a real estate office, or another party can collect funds and hold them until they are ready to be released. Earnest money, money to repair a house after closing, and much more can be held in escrow.

Escrow (house in escrow): Some states call a house "in escrow" when someone has a contract to buy and the price is accepted by the seller. This is similar to a house going "under contract." Once the buyer and seller have signed a contract, the seller cannot accept another contract from a new buyer (except a backup offer) unless the current contract terminates.

Fee simple: A way that real estate may be owned in common law countries and is the highest possible ownership interest that can be held in real property.

FHA: The Federal Housing Administration (FHA) is a U.S. agency that offers mortgage insurance to lenders that are FHA-approved and meet specified qualifications... If a borrower defaults on a loan, the FHA pays the lender a specified claim amount.

FHA Loan: An FHA loan is a mortgage issued by federally qualified lenders and insured by the Federal Housing Administration (FHA). FHA loans are designed for low- to moderate-income borrowers who are unable to make a large down payment.

Fix and Flip: A type of real estate investment strategy in which an investor purchases properties with the goal of reselling them for a profit. Profit is generated either through the price appreciation that occurs as a result of a hot housing market and/or from renovations and capital improvements.

Fixed-Rate Loan: A loan with an interest rate that remains the same for the entire term of the loan.

Flood Zone: Geographic areas that FEMA has defined according to varying levels of flood risk. These zones are depicted on a community's Flood Insurance Rate Map (FIRM) or Flood Hazard Boundary Map. Each zone reflects the severity or type of flooding in the area.

Forced-Air Heat: System that uses air as its heat transfer medium. These systems rely on ductwork, vents, and plenums as means of air distribution, separate from the actual heating and air conditioning systems.

Foreclosure: If a homeowner stops making payments on their loan, the bank can take the house back. The foreclosure process is different in every state regarding how the bank takes possession of the house.

Habitable: Suitable or good enough to live in.

Hard Money: A short loan typically used for fix and flips (usually 6 months to 18 months). Hard-money loans normally have interest rates ranging from 10 to 16 percent.

HOA: Home Owners Association. HOAs are present in most newer subdivisions and regulate neighborhood ordinances or covenants. They may also take care of yard maintenance, common utilities, trash service, and other services for a monthly, quarterly, or yearly fee.

Hold Harmless Agreement: An agreement or contract in which one party agrees to hold the other free from the responsibility for any liability or damage that might arise out of the transaction involved.

Homeowner's Insurance: This protects against damage to a house. Lenders require that homeowners have homeowner's insurance to protect their investment. If your house burns down, homeowner's insurance will rebuild your house. It also protects against roof damage from storms, water damage from plumbing leaks, wind damage, and vandalism. However, it may not protect against actual floods unless you have separate flood insurance.

Hot-Water Heat: Central heating by means of hot water circulated through pipes or radiators.

House Hacking: This is when you use one of the multiple units of your investment property as your primary residence and have renters from the other units pay your mortgage and expenses.

HUD Home: This occurs when a government-insured loan (FHA) gets foreclosed and the Federal Housing and Urban Development pays off the defaulted loan and puts the house on the market.

ILC: Improvement Location Certificate (ILC) An ILC is not a survey but a certificate. Used so mortgage and/or title companies have some assurance that the improvements to a property are not encroaching into an easement or beyond the deed lines.

Industrial Real Estate: Properties that are used for storage, manufacturing, and possibly commercial purposes.

Inspection: Most contracts allow a buyer to conduct a house inspection, which allows the buyers to look for problems or code violations.

Interest Rate: A rate which is charged or paid for the use of money. An interest rate is often expressed as an annual percentage of the principal.

Leach Field: Subsurface wastewater disposal facilities used to remove contaminants and impurities from the liquid that emerges after anaerobic digestion in a septic tank.

Lead-Based Paint: The U.S. government defines "lead-based paint" as any "paint, surface coating that contains lead equal to or exceeding one milligram per square centimeter (1.0 mg/cm2) or 0.5% by weight."

Lease: A contract outlining the terms under which one party agrees to rent property owned by another party. It guarantees the lessee (the tenant) the use of an asset and guarantees the lessor (the property owner or landlord) regular payments from the lessee for a specified number of months or years.

Leasehold: The holding of property by lease.

Landlord: Someone who owns a property that they rent out to a tenant.

Legal Description: The geographical description of a real estate property for the purpose of identifying the property for legal transactions. A legal description of the property unambiguously identifies the location, boundaries, and any existing easements on the property.

Lender: Someone who works for a bank or mortgage company and is the direct contact for the buyer of a house.

Listing: A house that is up for sale.

Loan Payoff: A statement prepared by a lender showing the remaining terms on a mortgage or other loan. The payoff statement shows the remaining loan balance and number of payments and the rate of interest.

Loan Term: Period over which a loan agreement is in force and before or at the end of which the loan should either be repaid or renegotiated for another term.

Lot: A parcel of land that a house, duplex, or multi-unit property sits on.

Material Fact: A fact that, if known, might have caused a buyer or seller to make a different decision with regard to remaining in a contract or to the price paid or received.

Mixed-Use Real Estate: Properties that are used for a variety of uses, usually residential and commercial.

MLS: The Multiple Listing Service (MLS) is a marketing database set up by a group of cooperating real estate brokers. It also is a mechanism for listing brokers to offer compensation to buyer-brokers who bring a buyer for their listed property.

Mortgage: A type of loan used to buy houses with a portion of the payment going towards interest and principal each month. Money may also be collected every month for property taxes and homeowner's insurance.

Mortgage Broker: A mortgage broker is a lender who can shop loans from multiple banks. Sometimes, a mortgage broker can get a better deal for buyers by checking with different banks. In other cases, a lender can get a better deal because they work directly for the bank and there is no middle man.

Multifamily: A multifamily or multi-unit property has more than one unit on the same property. An apartment complex or a duplex could be multifamily if they are on the same lot.

New Construction: Refers to site preparation for, and construction of, entirely new structures, whether or not the site was previously occupied.

Offer to buy: A buyer makes an offer to buy a house using a contract. The contract lists all the terms, financing, and contingencies. The offer means nothing unless the seller accepts it by signing the contract.

Origination Fee: A fee charged by a lender upon entering into a loan agreement to cover the cost of processing the loan.

Owner-Occupant: A resident of a property who also holds the title to that property.

Patio Home: A patio home is usually a free-standing home, but the landscaping and exterior is maintained by an association.

Pending status: The status when a house goes under contract and the seller does not want to accept a backup offer.

Pre-qualification: Most sellers require a buyer be pre-qualified before they will accept an offer. A buyer must get pre-qualified with a lender who checks credit income and other financial information.

Prepayment Penalty: A clause in a mortgage contract stating that a penalty will be assessed if the mortgage is prepaid within a certain timeframe. The penalty is based on a percentage of the remaining mortgage balance or a certain number of months' worth of interest.

Principal: The portion of a mortgage payment that goes toward paying off the balance of a loan. Part of your payment will also go toward interest.

Private Money: Money borrowed from private individuals. Example: a loan from a parent to buy a house.

Pro-rated: To divide or distribute a sum of money proportionately.

Property Disclosure: A disclosure the seller fills out describing all material facts they know about a house.

Property Management: When a landlord uses a company to manage their rental property instead of doing it themselves.

Property Taxes: A levy on the value of a property. The tax is levied by the governing authority of the jurisdiction in which the property is located.

PUD: A planned unit development (PUD), is a type of building development and a regulatory process. As a building development, it is a designed grouping of both varied and compatible land uses, such as housing, recreation, commercial centers, and industrial parks, all within one contained development or subdivision.

Radon: A colorless, odorless, radioactive element in the noble gas group. It is produced by the radioactive decay of radium and occurs in minute amounts in soil, rocks, and the air near the ground.

Realtor: A Realtor belongs to the National Association of Realtors (NAR) and is also a licensed real estate agent. NAR is a trade association for agents.

Recording Fees: The fee charged by a government agency for registering or recording a real estate purchase or sale, so that it becomes a matter of public record. Recording fees are generally charged by the county.

REIT: Real Estate Investment Trust (REIT) is a company that owns, and in most cases operates, income-producing real estate. REITs own many types of commercial real estate, ranging from office and apartment buildings to warehouses, hospitals, shopping centers, hotels, and timberlands.

Rent-to-Own: An alternative way to buy a house: a rent-to-own agreement, also called a lease option. When buyers sign this kind of contract, they agree to rent the house for a set amount of time before exercising an option to purchase the property when or before the lease expires.

REO: Real Estate Owned, or REO, is a term used in the United States to describe a class of property owned by a lender.

Residential Real Estate: Properties that are zoned for residential use. You may not be able to legally run a business out of them.

REI: Real Estate Investors.

Senior Living: Some subdivisions are designated for seniors only, usually 65 or older. Only seniors can buy or rent properties in those areas.

Septic System: A septic system is a type of OWTS (onsite wastewater treatment system).

Settlement Statement: An itemized document of services and charges relating to the closing of a property.

SFR: Single Family Residence. This is a house that is zoned for one family to occupy (it is possible that zoning may allow more unrelated people to live in the property). The house can be detached (standalone) or attached (a neighbor connected), but the property comes with land ownership rights.

Short Sale: A short sale is when the mortgage company allows a homeowner to sell a house but pay less to the mortgage company than what they are owed. Mortgage companies allow this in some cases when the homeowners are behind on payments because it is faster and cheaper than a foreclosure.

Space Heater: A self-contained appliance, usually electric, for heating an enclosed room.

Staging: The act of preparing a private residence for sale in the real estate marketplace. The goal of staging is to make a house appealing to the highest number of potential buyers.

Survey: A process carried out to determine property lines and define true property corners of a parcel of land described in a deed. It also indicates the extent of any easements or encroachments and may show the limitations imposed on the property by state or local regulations.

Tax exempt: Some organizations, like churches and non-profits, are exempt from paying property taxes. In some areas, seniors pay fewer property taxes. In some areas locals pay less taxes than those who live out-of-state.

Tax Lien: When homeowners stop paying property taxes, the state can place a tax lien against the house or even sell it at a tax sale. If you have a mortgage, the mortgage company will usually pay the taxes if the homeowner does not.

Tenant: Anyone who leases a property instead of purchasing it.

Title Company: A company that provides title insurance and many times provides closing services for real estate transactions as well.

Title Insurance: Insurance that guarantees a property has no debts or liens against it when sold.

Townhouse: A townhouse is like a condo, but there aren't any neighbors above or below the unit.

Transactional Funding: A form of short-term, hard-money lending which allows a wholesaler the opportunity to purchase a property with none of his/her funds, provided that there is already an end buyer in place to purchase the property from the wholesaler within a short time frame, usually 2-5 days.

Turn-key Rental Property: A fully renovated house or apartment building that an investor can purchase and immediately rent out.

Under Contract: A house goes under contract when a buyer and seller accept a contract. A new buyer cannot buy a house that is under contract unless the accepted offer terminates.

USDA: USDA home loans from the USDA loan program, also known as the USDA Rural Development Guaranteed Housing Loan Program, are a mortgage loan offered to rural property owners by the United States Department of Agriculture.

VA: A mortgage loan in the United States guaranteed by the U.S. Department of Veterans Affairs (VA). The loan may be issued by qualified lenders. The VA loan was designed to offer long-term financing to eligible American veterans or their surviving spouses (provided they do not remarry).

Water Rights: The right to make use of the water from a stream, lake, or irrigation canal.

Well Water: An excavation or structure created in the ground by digging, driving, boring, or drilling to access groundwater in underground aquifers.

Wholesaling: A real estate wholesaler contracts with a seller, markets the house to his potential buyers, and then assigns the contract to the buyer.

Zoning: How the city, state, or county classifies the use of land.

About Mark Ferguson

Mark Ferguson is a real estate investor and real estate agent. Mark began his real estate career straight out of college after graduating from the University of Colorado at Boulder with a Finance degree. Mark joined his father's real estate team as an agent and fixed and flipped houses. Eventually, Mark found his niche as an REO and HUD listing broker, selling over 200 houses per year in late 2009 and 2010.

Mark started buying rental properties in 2010 and ramped up his flipping business in 2013. Mark currently owns 16 rental properties and flips 10 to 30 houses per year. As of 2017, Mark routinely has 15 to 20 flips going at any one time. Mark also runs a real estate team with 6 licensed agents and multiple assistants. He is a strong believer in building a team, which gives him more time for family and building the business.

Mark also started one of the most popular real estate blogs currently online. InvestFourMore was started in 2013 and currently receives over 200,000 visits per month. Mark created the blog to chronicle his rentals, flips, agent career, and success. Along with the blog, Mark has published multiple best-selling books on real estate and investing. Mark has a weekly podcast where you can hear him interview successful real estate investors or catch up on his investments.

Mark is married to his beautiful wife Jeni and has twins, Brecken and Kaiya, who will be 6 in the summer of 2017. Mark loves to golf and look for great deals on houses, and cars.

Made in the USA
Coppell, TX
14 May 2022